DIVE BOMBER
An Illustrated History

The 'Top Hatters' in formation. The famous dive bomber unit Bombing 3, in perfect formation with their Vindicators against the beautiful backdrop of North America in 1939.

(US Navy)

DIVE BOMBER!

AN ILLUSTRATED HISTORY

PETER C. SMITH

MOORLAND PUBLISHING Co Ltd
Ashbourne, Derbyshire

NAVAL INSTITUTE PRESS
Annapolis, Maryland

British Library Cataloguing in
Publication Data

Smith, Peter C.
    Dive bomber!
    1. Bombers — History
    I. Title
    623.74′63   UG700

    ISBN 0 86190 062 6

Picture sources. Photographs have been provided
by: U.S. Navy: p 21, 23, 29, 43 (upper and lower),
212; RAF Museum, Hendon: p 01, 52 (upper);
Commander Sadao Seno: p 36 (upper and lower),
188; Museé de L'Air, Paris: p 37, 119 (lower), 205;
U.S. National Archives: p 39, 41, 85, 159, 179, 190,
191, 197; Imperial War Museum: p 51, 52 (lower),
144, 161, 173, 214; Fleet Air Arm Museum,
Yeovilton: p 65 (upper and lower), 201, 213; Archiv
Franz Selinger: p 74, 75, 76, 78, 83; The Koku-Fan:
p 86, 158; ECP Armeés via Pierre Hervieux: p 90,
111 (upper); Nicola Malizia: p 93, 94, 95; Flygstaben,
Stockholm: p 99, 146 (upper and lower); ECP
Armeés via Dr P.F. Riviere: p 111 (lower), 128, 129;
Archiv Hanfried Schliephake: p 113; AMI via
Nicola Malizia: p 133 (upper), 174; A. Coppola via
Nicola Malizia: p 133 (lower); G. Di Giorgio via
Nicola Malizia: p 136; Rottmann via Nicola
Malizia: p 148; Passingham Collection: p 152, 168;
U.S. Marine Corps: p 165, 187, 215; Australian
War Memorial; p 178, 184, 209; Dennis Young: p
198; Fotokhronika TASS, Moscow: p 206, 208. All
line drawings are by the author other than p 204
which is©H.M.S.O.
Front cover: U.S. National Archives
Rear Cover: (Upper left) Commander Sadao Seno
            (Upper right) Archiv Hanfried
                Schliephake
            (Lower) U.S. Navy

Title page: Homeward bound! A pair of Junkers
               Ju87B-2 dive bombers of the Italian
               102^0 Gruppo of 5^0 Stormo Tuffatori
               return from another raid on Malta
               (Nicola Malizia)

Published and distributed in the United
Kingdom by Moorland Publishing Co
Ltd, PO Box 2, Ashbourne, Derbys DE6
1DZ

ISBN 0 86190 062 6

Published and distributed in the United
States of America by Naval Institute
Press, Annapolis, Maryland 21402

ISBN 0-87021-930-8

© Peter C. Smith 1982

Printed in the U.K. by Butler and Tanner
Ltd, Frome, Somerset

CONTENTS

GLOSSARY

AA	Anti Aircraft	NCO	Non-Commissioned Officer
ACTS	Assistant Chief Technical Services	ONI	Office of Naval Intelligence
AD/RDA	Assistant Director/ Research Directorate Armament	OR	Operational Requirement
AP	Armour Piercing	PS	Private Secretary
ATC	Air Training Corps	PM	Prime Minister
BAC	British Aircraft Commission	RAE	Royal Aircraft Establishment
BDU	Bombing Development Unit	RAF	Royal Air Force
BuAer	Bureau of Aeronautics	RAAF	Royal Australian Air Force
BuArm	Bureau of Armaments	RD(Arm)	Research and Development (Armaments)
BuOrd	Bureau of Ordnance		
BuSupp	Bureau of Supply	RFC	Royal Flying Corps
CAS	Chief of the Air Staff	RM	Royal Marines
C-in-C	Commander-in-Chief	RN	Royal Navy
DAF	Desert Air Force	RNAS	Royal Naval Air Service
DCAS	Deputy Chief of the Air Staff	SAC	Senior Aircraftsman
		SAP	Semi Armour Piercing
DDRD/Arm	Deputy Director Research and Development, Armament	SASO	Senior Armaments Staff Officer
		S-of-S	Secretary-of-State
DDTD	Deputy Director Technical Development	SESO	Senior Equipment Staff Officer
		SEAC	South-East Asia Command
DMC	Director Military Construction	TSR	Torpedo Spotter Reconnaissance aircraft
DNAD	Director of Naval Air Division		
DTD	Director of Technical Development	TV	Terminal Velocity
		USAAF	United States Army Air Force
DTS	Director Technical Services	USAS	United States Air Services
FAA	Fleet Air Arm		
FF	Fleet Fighter or Fighter Fleet	USMC	United States Marine Corps
GR	General Reconnaissance	USN	United States Navy
HE	High Explosive	USNI	United States Naval Institute
MAG	Marine Air Group		
MAP	Ministry of Aircraft Production	VB	Bombing Squadron
		VF	Fighter Squadron
NBC	National Broadcasting Company	VS	Scouting Squadron
		VCAS	Vice Chief of the Air Staff

1 EARLY EXPERIMENTS
The Genesis and Practice of low-level attack, 1910-18

In trying to trace the origins of dive bombing one is immediately faced with a mass of conflicting evidence. Just as it is almost impossible to find anyone who agrees on the diving angle at which dive bombing begins, so no two historians agree on who invented this method of attacking surface targets. The majority of published sources conclude that the United States Marine Corps should be given the credit. My own research suggests that this widely held belief is false, and my case is set out in the following chapters.

No study of dive bombing can exclude the concept of low-level attack in general. The two are so intertwined, especially in the formative years, that a basic outline of the former is essential for a complete understanding of dive bombing. I do not however intend to look closely at ground attack aircraft and methods, but only to record those initial operations and experiments from which dive bombing evolved. For those seeking further information on ground attack there are several excellent books on the subject. Nor can dive bombing be separated entirely from other forms of bombing.

What angle of dive is required for true dive bombing? This is perhaps the most vexing question of all and that which provokes most discord. The British Air Ministry produced three definitions, all of which were accepted by other nations at some stage. Shallow Glide Bombing: the bombs were released while the aircraft was descending at an angle not greater than 20^0. Steep Glide Bombing: bombs released while the aircraft was descending at an angle of between 20^0 and 60^0. Dive Bombing: bombs released while the aircraft was in a dive at an angle of between 60^0 and 90^0.

But to confine these studies to operations meeting only the last set of conditions would be to exclude a number of significant developments. For example, perhaps the most famous dive-bombing attack by a British force was the sinking of the German light cruiser *Königsberg*. Under the RAF rules we would have to ignore this watershed completely, since the Fleet Air Arm Skuas which carried out this daring and successful assault went in at angles between 70^0 and 40^0. Again, can one ignore the operations by aircraft designed solely as dive bombers, but which were in fact carried out in the traditional ground-attack manner, as with the US Marine Corps SBD missions in the Philippines in 1945? Overlap is unavoidable. The Spitfire, hardly best known as a dive bomber, carried out important sorties in this role, diving at angles over the 60^0 mark. The pre-war RAF tested the Fairey Battle and even the Handley Page Hampden at angles of $30-40^0$ to see how they would perform as dive bombers.

Who invented dive bombing? The most accurate statement is probably that of historian Lee M. Pearson, who said: 'No one knows who first turned his plane nose down and dove nearly into the ground to hit a pinpoint target with bombs'.

Although an earlier reference to a 'dive-bombing patent' being issued on 9 December 1911, in Great Britain to Alexander von Willisch of Wilmersdorf, near Berlin, was followed up, examination revealed this to be a red herring. More significant was the subsequent issue of Patent No 15,871 on 9 July 1914, to Henri Coanda. This French engineer filed a patent for what was in fact an automatic bomb or projectile-discharging tube designed particularly for air attacks on ground targets. This 'Complete Means for Discharging Projectiles from Aerial Machines', although not obviously a specific dive bombing method, is of great interest as a pioneering ground-attack system. It was probably far too heavy and cumbersome for application to aircraft of that period, but it was a far-sighted effort at a time when bombs were dropped, if at all, by hand.

A rather more primitive means of enabling the missile to reach its target from aloft was meanwhile being practised in the Mexican Civil War (1913-15). An American aviator, Leonard W. Bonney, was scouting around Mexico City, Yucatan and Tampico using a Moisant aircraft. But he by no means restricted himself to scouting, and has one of the best claims to be the sire of the dive-bombing technique. He carried out bombing missions with spherical dynamite bombs designed by Mexican engineers. The explosive was fired by a pin which exploded a rifle cartridge.

His usual method of attack was to fly at between 1,600 and 1,200ft to avoid clouds. He thus learned the major lesson of aircraft vulnerability, for his machine was frequently shot up by rifle fire. He returned from one trip with eleven bullet holes in his aircraft and a severed sparkplug wire. But it is the eyewitness descriptions of his bomb-dropping methods that is of the greatest interest, for they state quite clearly that Bonney dropped his bombs himself at the end of a dive, before he levelled out and that he employed no sighting or other device to assist in this.

Early in the war the French War Office reconnoitred the German airship hangars at Metz in preparation for their destruction. When the attacking aircraft arrived over the target, its engine failed at 8,000ft. Some quick thinking followed, and, according to a contemporary account, the pilot, not wishing to fall before executing his mission, volplaned,* and while doing so dropped his bombs. Smoke from anti-aircraft fire obscured the results, but it was believed at the time that the French pilot had hit his mark.

One of the most daring and successful of these early attacks was carried out by Flt Lt R.L.G. Marix of the RNAS against the Zeppelin shed at Düsseldorf on 8 October 1914. Piloting a Sopwith Tabloid, one of the most advance aircraft of the period, Marix took off from Antwerp armed with 20lb bombs and arrived over the sheds in misty conditions. Once in position he dived to an altitude of only 600ft and released his Cooper bombs. Direct hits were scored, the shed collapsed and flames rose to a height of 500ft. Despite a barrage of defensive fire, Marix managed to withdraw safely from the target, although his aircraft was hit. This brilliant attack was later found to have resulted in the destruction of the new Zeppelin *Z IX*, which had only just been completed and moved into the shed.

A contemporary assessment of the raid contained the information that after he had attacked in a dive he was justified in the results achieved and that this bore out the view that, for accuracy, the aircraft had to descend to a very perilous altitude.

The same methods were used as successfully in an attack the following month, again by the RNAS. The aircraft used were Avro 504s belonging to a special unit formed at Manchester. Carrying four 20lb Cooper bombs in improvised racks mounted under their lower mainplanes, the four aircraft flew 120 miles from Belfort to the Zeppelin sheds at Friedrichshafen, Lake Constance, on 21 November. Although one aircraft had to turn back, the remaining three, piloted by Sqdrn Cdr E.F. Briggs (873), Flt Lt S.V. Sippe (874) and Flt Cdr J.T. Babington (875), continued to the target. After a low-level approach across the lake, at 5 miles from the target they climbed to 1,200ft to deploy for the bombing run. Once in position the three aircraft dived down to about 700ft and released their bombs. All

8   * *Volplane.* To descend by gliding without use of engine.

these bombs except one, which failed to release, fell within an area of 700yd around the works and sheds. Two fell on the sheds themselves, one greatly damaging a Zeppelin under construction, the others destroying a gas works, which exploded.

As early as December 1914, a writer in a British magazine was discussing the merits of diving attacks as a means of achieving accuracy, arguing that when gliding from a height, with the aircraft under power, the tangent to the trajectory and the axis of the machine would gradually become parallel and therefore accuracy of aim would be increased when flying low and at high speed. He concluded that for the best results the bomb should be released at the end of a dive of 500ft when the axis of the aircraft was pointing at the target.

That diving attacks were far from rare is illustrated by the following journalistic reports describing sorties of this kind:

> French and British pilots did some very daring bomb dropping in the first year of the war. Arriving over their objectives, they dive to a height counted by a few hundreds of feet with engines full on, reaching almost incredible speeds as speeds were then regarded, and releasing their bombs at what they thought the crucial moment before making the best of their way out of the danger zone.

> An English warplane hovered over Zeebrugge and, defying the concentrated fire, made a sudden dive to within 300ft of the ground . . . the airman coolly dropped his bombs at short range on a submarine moored alongside the mole.

Despite the above examples it was not dive-bombing as such which developed as the principal aerial weapon during World War I as much as 'strafing', low-level ground-support missions by fighters and light bombers. Although it was again the British who first developed this form of warfare and later perfected it with great effect, both Germany, France, and later America, all experimented with the method and made extensive and effective use of it during 1916-18.

Perhaps the first indication of this use was contained in a memo originated at RFC HQ in October 1914 and sent to Maj Musgrave: 'Several instances have occured lately in which targets suitable for attack have been passed over without any action being taken. In future all aeroplanes carrying out reconnaissances will carry bombs and whenever suitable targets . . . present themselves they should be attacked by dropping bombs'.

The momentum soon increased. A directive from the same source in February 1915 stated: 'Accuracy to within 50yd is essential. If it cannot be obtained from heights of 5,000 to 6,000ft, the target must be attacked at low level — 500ft'.

From the time of the Somme offensive onward (1916) the mass use of fighters for strafing missions had become firmly established. The results were often spectacular, as with No 43 Squadron during the Third Battle of the Scarpe on 3 May 1917.

One historian noted how at the battles of Ypres and Cambrai in 1917 strafing had become a significant factor in the fighting. This was emphasised by the part the fighter-bombers played in breaking up the German offensive that began in March 1918, when the RFC's attacks often prevented the British retreat from becoming a rout.

Nor were the Germans slow in adopting such measures, and at Verdun in March 1916 their own scouts were employed in a similar manner. Formed into special *Schlachtstaffeln,* the German scouts were used *en masse* during the 1918 breakthrough. The Germans also developed special aircraft with armour protection for low-level attacks, an idea which the British copied after the war with the Salamander.

When the fledgling US Air Corps arrived at the Western Front, Gen Mitchell was profoundly impressed by these methods and formed strafing units which made their debut at the St Mihiel salient in the summer of 1918.

Further afield, the British gave striking demonstrations of the potency of this form of attack against unprepared troops, and three of the most notable incidents took place at the end of the war. The Turkish troops trapped in the defile north-east of Nablus on 21 September 1918, were subjected to five hours of concentrated strafing, at the end of which they had become '. . . a dispersed horde of trembling individuals, hiding for their lives . . . .'

The armies of Austro-Hungary broke and fled after the battle of Vittorio Veneto, and a similar retribution overtook them on 29-30 October 1918, when their fleeing columns were caught on the Conegliano-Pordonone road. Finally, again on 21 September 1918, the ill-fated Bulgarian Army met the same fate in Macedonia's Kosturino Pass.

Effective as this form of attack proved to be, it was also extremely expensive to the attacker in men and machines. Wg Cdr Slessor made this very point between the wars when explaining in a series of lectures just why the RAF was at that time no longer interested in following such a policy in future wars. He said that at Cambrai casualties in the British strafing squadrons averaged about 30 per cent per day, and similar ghastly figures during the low-flying attacks carried out during the March retreat and the Amiens offensive of 1918. He cited the example of No 80 Squadron in 1918, which he said, was almost continuously in action from the beginning of the March retreat until the Armistice. Their average strength was twenty-two officers and during those final ten months of combat no less than 168 officers were struck off the strength from all causes, an average of about 75 per cent per month.

It is therefore obvious why the policy lost its appeal after the war. Its fall from favour was accelerated by the embracing of the Trenchard conception of future warfare, which he saw as being won by the heavy bomber unaided by armies or navies. This doctrine, the cornerstone of inter-war RAF policy, saw little need for any kind of ground-attack capability. The dive-bomber, although not strictly a ground-attacker, suffered for the same reasons.

Nonetheless, the RFC and the infant RAF had done much to test the dive-bombing concept in the latter stages of World War I, even if they subsequently turned away from it.

2 BIRTH OF THE DIVE BOMBER
British pioneering work, 1915-18

The number of individuals claiming to have originated the dive-bombing form of attack is probably only exceeded by the number of nations and air services claiming that honour. Some of the British pilots who flew on the Western Front have described in their memoirs how they used diving techniques for bombing attacks, and they have as good a case as anyone.

One of these was Lt Duncan Grinnell-Milne, who was flying BE2Cs with No 16 Squadron from Lys in France in the early winter of 1915. The BE2C was to gain an uneviable distinction in the months ahead, when heavy losses earned it a reputation as the main course of 'Fokker fodder'. A single 70hp Renault engine pulled this two-seat biplane through the air at a stately 72mph. Though these were still early days for bombers, the aircraft was fitted to carry two 112lb or ten 20lb bombs under the wings. Aiming these weapons was a hit-or-miss affair, and No 16 Squadron was given the task of trying out a newly developed bomb sight in the hope of improving matters. Grinnell-Milne took off on his bombing mission on 27 November 1915, after a mere two days' instruction on this 'rather complicated apparatus'. The target was known to be well defended by AA guns. The new sight demanded a straight and level run in, but on arriving over the target he found a throng of aircraft jostling for position and being heavily fired on. Grinnell-Milne therefore decided to adopt his own method.

Putting his aircraft into a dive with the engine at half throttle, he lined up on the target, a rail junction. He dived from 10,000ft to 2,000ft and released the bombs, missing the target but hitting motor transport instead. He returned that afternoon, when the sky over the target proved to be less crowded. Nonetheless he

BE2c aircraft of No 13 Squadron lined up on their airfield in France. This improbable mount saw some of the first experimental dive bombing experiments in combat during World War I.

attacked in the same way as before, this time pressing in much closer. The first bomb hit a building, and he circled the area before diving to drop the second. 'I watched the bomb go down, diminishing rapidly to a pinpoint, then suddenly expanding again as it struck a building in the goods yard. A flash, bricks and dust, and lots of slow-spreading smoke . . . I flew home humming a tune.'

The results of these attacks, in which the RFC dropped four tons of bombs on one small railway station in the course of its biggest raid yet, were in fact very disappointing. But the raid showed the advantages of dive-bombing over level bombing. Only if a specific target could be located and pinpointed were the results worth the effort, and the destruction of an ammunition dump, ship or Zeppelin required a degree of accuracy which only dive-bombing could provide.

Another attack deserves mention. Lt Arthur Gould Lee, flying with No 46 Squadron from Izel-le-Hameau, west of Arras gave a graphic description of an attack he carried out on 30 November. He had to attack one particular house in the village of Bourlon with four 20lb Cooper bombs. The original plan called for four separate attacks dropping one bomb each time, but the flak proved too heavy for that to be attempted. Instead Lee went into an attack down to 200ft in a steep dive into the concentration of fire. His first attempt resulted in a near-miss by himself and his wingman and Lee had to return for a second attempt alone.

This time his steep dive was carried down to 100ft and the remaining three bombs were released at this height. He made his escape at the suicidal height of 20ft and, despite the opposition, escaped with but one bullet which shattered the handle of his throttle control, while another almost ignited his Verey pistol cartridges.

These then are typical examples of unofficial dive-bombing attacks. But in my opinion the strongest claim is held by 2nd Lt William Henry Brown, RFC, who staked his claim with No 84 Squadron in France in March 1918. The attack is well-documented and was, significantly in the light of what was to come, directed against a ship target of sorts.

No 84 was operating standard Offensive Patrols (OPs) with the SE5a fighter from Flez near St Quentin. The SE5a was a unlikely contender at first sight for a dive bomber, but as one historian later recalled it was a very versatile fighter, both strong and capable of being dived steeply.

Experiments were conducted early in March to ascertain the most accurate methods of utilising this machine as a bomber and Brown, being the smallest pilot in his unit, was the 'volunteer'. No bombsight was utilised and the target was a 100ft circle. He used wooden bombs and found that with a diving attack he could hit the circle every time. One 14 March 1918, he was allocated a live target, four ammunition barges located on a canal near Bernot.

The mission was described as 'Special Mission (Low Bombing Attack)' in No 84 Squadron's combat reports and his SE5a (No 5384) was equipped with four Cooper bombs to perform the task. Early morning mist delayed the sortie until midday and it was still foggy when he finally got airborne. Nonetheless only twenty minutes flying time sufficed to bring him to his target from his base. At Bois de Savy he climbed to 5,000ft and soon reached Bernot and the barges. He made two dives and scored near-misses each time. The third attempt was different, 'I dived straight for the barge'. His bombs struck it amidships from a release height of 500ft and it exploded very satisfactorily indeed. Within a week all his squadron had been similarly equipped and, added one magazine, '. . . a new word was added to the vocabulary of aerial warfare . . . dive-bombing'.

The arguments about which pilot, squadron or nation invented dive-bombing will undoubtedly continue into the future. But it can be claimed with complete confidence that it was the RAF (formed in April 1918 from a merger of the Royal

Flying Corps and the Royal Naval Air Service) that carried out the first air tests of the new method under carefully controlled conditions, at the RAF Armament Experimental Station early in 1918. The RAF's subsequent vigorous opposition to the dive-bomber tends to obscure the fact that it was Britain which first conducted controlled tests of the method. For example one historian states clearly that:

> Another interesting manifestation of the Camel was as the world's first dive-bomber. The Camel had been so widely used for land attack that dive-bombing seemed a logical development. Not many modifications were made to the Camel 2.F.1 which was tested in action. Some armour plating was added to protect the pilot from ground-fire. A mechanical airspeed indicator was fitted to the interplane struts to assist him in his attack.

But the Sopwith Camel was not the only aircraft to be used in the trails which took place at Orfordness. Lt Brown's exploit with his SE5a in March, 1918 may or may not have been the first real combat dive bombing, but the type was actually used in dive bombing tests several significant weeks before his action.

The work was carried out by Section 6, under Capt C.E. Fairburn, with Maj B.M. Jones as Chief Experimental Officer. Five different pilots were employed on this series, one of them being Oliver Stewart who subsequently explained why the Sopwith fighter, with its reputation as a killer of inexperienced pilots, should have been chosen as a testbed for such experiments: 'The Camel set a new standard in powers of manoeuvre, and even today it probably remains the most highly manoeuvrable aeroplane that has ever been seen'. Fine praise from a veteran pilot for a plane that almost killed him on the lonely Suffolk shoreline during these tests.

For the first tests the SE5a was employed. A small yellow flag was planted in the shingle acting as the target. A bomb rack was fitted under the left-hand wing of the aircraft and four dummy bombs were carried on each flight. The placing of the bomb load off-centre now appears strange, but it was done to avoid interference with the flying gear and this position was simplest. Further tests were carried out later to find out whether the SE5a could more usefully accommodate such a bomb load centrally under the fuselage.

Once in position over the target marker, the pilots were to dive their aircraft from about 1,500ft at 110-130mph with the engine throttled back. The bomb was to be released at 800-1,000ft. This seems quite high for the period and size of the bombs, but was no doubt determined by safety factors.

It was found that the pilots adopted the following method. After a few preliminary dives to get the feel of it, they would look along the left side of the engine cowling while diving at the target, the bomb being released when the target just passed out of sight under the cowling. This method was used generally after the first few attempts and worked quite well.

In all the tests the SE5a was dived upwind 'very approximately'. The trials were run in varying weather and, particularly, wind conditions, again to give an average result. The tests produced no startling results, though fully 26 per cent of the bombs fell within 10yd of the target. No sight of any kind was used, and it was found that, as expected, the pilots' shooting rapidly improved with practice.

According to the report, these tables gave a good indication of the amount of practice needed to become 'moderately proficient' in this form of bombing. The final verdict was that the lower the release the more accurate the bombing with the SE5a.

Because the tests with the SE5a had been based on 'eye shooting' only, it was suggested that the degree of accuracy, already impressive, would be much increased if the normal machine-gun sights were used in the dive to locate the   13

Pilot	Date	Height at start of dive (ft)	Bomb release ht (ft)	Speed (mph)	Wind Speed (mph)	Distance off target (ft)
1	27/2	1,500	500	120	10	108, 88, 104, 150, 33, 35, 44, 45, 52, 31, 45, 26, 17, 21, 20
1	28/2	1,500	300	120	20	28, 8, 6, 6, 19, 0*, 16, 11
1	21/3	1,500	300	120	10	14, 7, 13, 25, 2½, 10, 7, 13
1	21/3	1,500	3/500	120	10	14, 9, 23, 7, 7, 10, 13, 13
1	25/4	1,000	1/200	130/40	15	8, 17, 20, 22, 15, 9, 12, 18, 8, 9
2	24/2	1,500	500	110/30	20	6, 22, 30, 33, 25, 12, 26
2	26/2	1,500	3/600	110/30	20	13, 14, 14, 14, 15, 22
3	2/4	1,500	5/600	110/30	10	31, 20½, 4
3	6/4	1,500	500 400 200 100	110/30	9	49 16½ 30 1½
3	7/4	1,500	500 500 150 150	120	10	36 8 17½ 5½
4	22/4	1,500 2,000 1,800	500 700 700	120 115/25 115/25	10	55 52 50
5	23/4	800 800 900 600 1,000 1,000 1,000 1,000	300 300 200 200 500 500 500 500	105 105 100 100 110 100 110 120	10	44 10 87 10 17½ 21 39 6
5	26/4	1,000 1,000 1,000 700 800 1,000 1,000 500	200 200 100 300 250 100 100 200	120 120 100 110 115 130 130 105	12	21½ 18 2½ 14 32 5½ 5 10

Table 1: The SE5a Dive Bombing Trials at Orfordness 1918

* Direct hit on minute target from 300ft on second day of tests

target. Using the same target specified for the first tests it was proposed that '... if a bomb be released from a Camel dived at about 160mph when the Aldis gun sight bears on the target a good aim will be obtained'. It was specified that bomb-

14

Pilot	Height at start of dive (ft)	Bomb release ht (ft)	Speed (mph)	Wind Speed (mph)	Distance off target (ft)
	Table 2: The Sopwith Camel Dive Bombing Trials at Ordfordness 1918				
1	1,800 1,500	400 200	160 140	17 20	70½, 18 143, 55, 91, 24, 21, 188
2	1,200	150/50	120	20	92, 13, 28, 33, 43, 10, 16, 32, 34, 7, 7, 11, 7, 17
3	2,000 2,000 2,000 2,000 2,000 1,500	1,000 600 500 400 400 100	140	9	328 180 175 89 140 13

release height should not be more than 1,000ft. The 130hp Clerget-engined Camel was the version used by all the pilots in these second tests.

Bomb racks were fitted, one under each wing of the Camel and carrying one 20lb bomb each for the trial. It was decided not to place the racks under the front fuselage lest the bombs foul the undercarriage bracing wires. Placing the racks under the fuselage further aft would have upset the trim too much.

Three different pilots worked on these trials, dropping a total of twenty-eight bombs on the flag marker used for the SE5a tests. Once again, the pilots were chosen for their wide range of flying experience. The most experienced, Capt Stewart, had logged about 1,000 hours, his colleagues 600 and 250 respectively.

The Aldis sight was used exclusively in the first tests, by Capt Stewart. On runs two, four, six and eight the Aldis was aimed well ahead of the target to compensate for the shortfall found to be common when using the sight thus.

On the second of these runs, after the bomb had been released at 400ft, the Camel suffered engine failure, crashing into the shingle and rolling over. Stewart survived the impact, but was left upside down in his straps for more than two hours, jammed in the cockpit, with petrol dripping on him before the rescue party could reach him.

The most inexperienced pilot, No 3, aimed at the target with the sight for every shot except for the last one which proved to be the most accurate of all. This last bomb was dropped by eye in the manner of the SE5a tests.

Pilot No 2, seeing that the bombs would always fall short of the target when aimed with the Aldis sight, deliberately aimed well over, gradually increasing the distance of the 'aim-over' all the time. The difference in bombing accuracy was immediately apparent.

The three pilots reached the same conclusions:

1 Dive bombing with the Aldis sight was very unsafe as a result of the high speed called for at a low height while carrying bombs, '... more especially if the air is at all bumpy'. The use of the Aldis sight made the technique even more hazardous, preventing the pilot from getting a true impression of his closeness to the ground.

2 It was far easier to drop the bombs in a vertical dive with no sight at all. It could be put to limited use, not by looking through it, but by sighting along the top of it. This method indicated the target quite well if the aircraft was directed straight at the target.

3   At speeds of 120-130mph the sighted and unsighted methods were equally accurate, though the former required more practice. The sight was also found to require lower bomb-release heights and the safety factor was nowhere near as high.

They concluded that use of the Camel with the Aldis sight was 'quite unsafe' for an average pilot and that the results expected would not be worth the expenditure in machines and trained pilots. Thus RAF opposition to dive bombing was to be deep-set early on. They also stated that there was no advantage to be gained from using the Aldis sight at slower speeds than those specified, except in improving line errors by the pilot looking along the sight when approaching the target.

These trials, although proving the greater accuracy of dive bombing, had the ultimate effect of turning the RAF against it. The service was convinced that use of the method in combat would lead to casualties for little return. In much the same way, wartime experience had turned the RAF against 'strafing', as the Slessor lectures of the 1930s were to confirm.

By 1919 there was little RAF enthusiasm for any form of ground attack. Despite continued testing, and calls for specific aircraft to fulfill this role, dive bombing was relished last of all. This naturally affected Army co-operation, and in the twenty years between the wars the rift was to open into a chasm. One very distinguished general noted: 'Between the wars the former co-operation between the Army and the Air Force, close, intimate and effective in the Great War, ceased when the Air Force became a separate service.'

This indifference to dive bombing was also to have a crippling effect on the Royal Navy. Control of all RN aircraft had passed to the RAF in 1918 and the allocation of funds to that part of the service meant that the Fleet Air Arm was very much a Cinderella in both aircraft and designs.

Strangely enough, despite his experience during the trials, Stewart himself remained a dive bombing enthusiast. Over the years he was to become the major critic of the RAF's neglect of the method, conducting a campaign which culminated in a series of pointed articles during 1942. He remained convinced that dive bombing was a valid and valuable method of attack at a time when the official line was very different.

3 THE MOMENTUM FALTERS
Immediate post-war developments, 1919-22

We have seen how by the end of World War I the air forces of the major powers were using aircraft to support their armies, mainly by means of ground-attack operations. This was true of Britain, Germany, France and the United States, though the UK was unique in studying dive bombing as such. But the end of a highly destructive war was followed by a strong reaction against all forms of warfare, armaments and military experiments, leading to a heavy cutback in manpower, equipment, funds and research.

This applied to those powers which were allowed the rest of peace. But other nations were not so fortunate: in particular, Poland and the Soviet Union fought a murderous war in 1919-20 before Polish independence was secured. As this was more or less a continuation of World War I in that troubled area of Central Europe, the lessons were similar to those learned in 1918 elsewhere. Both nations soon recognised the value and the appalling dangers of ground-support operations.

Italy, influenced by the RAF's example at Vittorio Veneto in 1918, made similar advances and followed the same road. In Germany the ban on all armaments, especially aircraft, simply acted as a spur, and the re-creation of an effective air force was soon underway. Dominated, as the new force was, by ex-army flyers, it is not surprising that close support found high favour. Ironically, it was at this low point in German fortunes that the first tentative moves were made, in Sweden and the Soviet Union, towards the Stuka of a decade later, the means by which a resurgent Germany turned the tables on the victors of 1918 in a campaign of only a few weeks duration.

In America the situation was more complex. As in Britain, two strands of thought began to emerge: the naval, which favoured dive bombing for accuracy, and the air force, which saw the heavy bomber as the decisive factor in any war. But this polarisation did not take effect immediately, and it was the Army Air Force that was to provide the spark which rekindled the whole dive bomber fire.

Immediately after the war France led the world in the development of some dive bombing techniques for use against warships. But this proved a flash in the pan, and although the French Navy maintained an interest in this method of attack, it was so short of funds and had so many obsolete warships to replace that little could be done to follow through her early post-war advances.

Japan was in a similar state. Still nominally an ally of Britain, her growing designs on the Chinese mainland were rapidly drawing her into conflict with China and the Western powers. A British naval mission was however sent to Japan soon after the war to assist in the building up of Japanese naval air power, which was then almost non-existent. This tuition was to come home to roost with a vengeance in the South China Sea twenty years later!

This is the background to the years 1919-22. Let us now examine in more depth each nation's problems and ideas in this period, to see how the seed began to germinate in some and was neglected in others.

During the grim campaigns fought in 1919-20 to defend the newly established state of Poland against a variety of opponents, the Polish air force, equipped with surplus aircraft from all over Europe, made a lasting impression on friend and foe 17 alike with the effectiveness of its ground strafing. As a result, ground-attack aircraft predominated in the Polish air force from the mid-1920s onwards, culminating in the production of the purpose-built PZL P23 Kara. No interest was shown in the dive bomber until the mid-1930s.

The Red Army had been on the receiving end of most of Poland's strafing attacks and had suffered grievous infantry and cavalry casualties. As a result, the Soviet Union adopted this form of attack wholeheartedly in the late 1920s, developing the technique into the 1930s and largely perfecting air/ground co-ordination. Out of this grew the famous *Shturmovik* units, but the USSR came even later than Poland to dive bombing design and no development took place before the late 1930s.

Japan's embryo army and navy air arms followed the general European trend. The first dive-bombing experiments did not take place until the late 1920s, influenced by developments in the USA. Not until the early 1930s did detailed design and testing of dive bombers take place.

As early as 1917 the German air arm was using to great effect units specially trained in ground attack, the 'battle flights'. After the war all efforts were concentrated on evading the limitations of the Versailles Treaty, which prohibited Germany from maintaining any military arm. The signing of the Treaty of Rapallo with the Soviet Union in 1922 cleared the way for the first exhaustive tests of combat aircraft. Here again the first experiments were directed at development of the strafing role, Dutch-built Fokker D-XIIIs and Heinkel HD17s and 21s being used as fighter-bombers when they failed to perform well as fighters. Work on true dive bombing was hardly possible at this stage in Germany, but it was soon to develop.

One of the three nations which was experimenting with dive bombing was Britain, research was continuous, but much curtailed by the strict economic measures adopted by successive governments. The continued wrangling between the Royal Navy, which wanted the dive bomber, and the RAF, which had little time for it, also caused constant delays. The RAF saw the strategic bomber as its ultimate goal and regarded army co-operation more as a reconnaissance than an attack function, using aircraft like the Audax and similar types. On the other hand, FAA fighter squadrons, under RAF control, but with mixed personnel, developed a form of light dive bombing with the biplane fighters of the period.

Britain's dive bombing units in the 1920s operated the Nieuport Nightjar (1922-4) and the Parnall Plover (1923-4), the former finally being sold to Japan and renamed the Sparrowhawk. By 1926 these types had been replaced by the Fairey Flycatcher, vehicle of the continued development of British dive bombing. Carrying four 20lb bombs on underwing bomb racks, the Flycatcher was used to develop such tactics as the 'converging' attack. By 1928 exercises in the Mediterranean had shown that the 'natural' targets for light dive bombing attacks at sea were aircraft carriers and this continued to be the role of these units in the 1930s.

The earliest French experiments owe much to Lt Pierre Henri-Clement La Burthe. He served in *Escadrille F50* of the Army based at Dunkirk and he put forward as a means of obtaining accuracy, a diving attack placing the bombs plumb on the target, '. . . like a hand'. His ideas were taken up by Lt Teste who modified them in a series of trials in 1920-1 with the ACI Squadron 1 based in the South of France at the St Raphael school.

The most vulnerable part of a modern warship, even a battleship, was known to be the underwater hull, shock-waves from near misses, the 'hammer-blow' of Gen Mitchell, being able to fracture the hull seriously in the right conditions. To achieve the near-miss effect required to detonate these 'undersea bombs' Teste carried out a series of trials using the modern battleship *Bretagne* as a live target.

In the first attack, conducted by Teste flying an HD R39 aircraft, he dived from 1,600m (5,250ft) on the port side of the vessel at an angle of 30^0 then flew horizontally for 100m (330ft) before releasing his bomb. The missile struck the sea about 30m (100ft) from the target which Teste put down to too long an approach.

He began his second attack at an angle of 70^0 and pressed down to 600m (1,970ft), but found that the steepness of his dive prevented him from operating his bomb-release. He tried a third time at an angle of 30^0 again from a height of 6000m. Unfortunately when he tried to open up the throttle again the engine would not respond and he finally crash-landed in the water close to the *Bretagne,* his aircraft capsizing and sinking. Teste himself was picked up unharmed by the destroyer *Potet.* Although he did not have time to work out completely the cause of the accident, the loss of his aircraft did not stop his enthusiasm for the method. He reported that such diving attacks were quite simple to achieve and that great accuracy could be achieved, especially against targets the size of 23,000 ton battleships. He wanted to continue the tests. The C-in-C, Mediterranean Squadron, Vice-Adm Salaun, agreed strongly, stating that the method used appeared interesting and that it could be improved upon.

Teste's experiments led to further and more exacting trials at St Cloud by a commission studying bombing methods for use against targets at sea. The *Commission d'Etude Pratiques d'Aviation* carried out practical trials of three types of attack: 'point-blank', low-altitude and high-altitude. It is the first named — *attaque'a bout portant* — which concerns our story.

It was described as follows: a fast aircraft armed with a delayed action bomb approached at high altitude before diving towards the bows of the target ship. On release of the bomb the aircraft escaped by flying at wave-top level across the ship's bow. The bomb was activated by the shock of striking the water and with a four-second delay fuse exploded against the hull of the ship underwater.

Preliminary trials flown by nine different pilots gave very encouraging results, and the commission asked for material and funds for further work, saying that the method should be carefully studied. Although money was tight, the French Navy remained interested in this method. Pending development of an aircraft designed especially for the role, further tests were conducted with a variety of types, principally the Levasseur PL7, a single-engined biplane which first flew in 1920. The whole design was a left-over from World War I, with a maximum speed of only 90mph. These antiques kept on flying until the late 1930s, so starved of money was the French naval air arm.

It was the US Army Air Force, rather than the Navy or Marines that kept the dive bombing concept alive in the immediate post-war years. The US had in turn been influenced by what it had learned of British methods during 1918. The US *Air Service Journal* of the period reveals the depth of this influence. Commenting on the lessons of World War I, it said: 'There were in use by the British two methods of aiming bombs . . . one of which . . . was to dive directly at your target and release the bombs the instant you are pulling out of your dive. The bombs continue in the line of flight of your dive, which is aimed at the target.'

In a discussion with Marine pilot 'Rusty' Rowell in the early 1920s, Lt (later Brig Gen) Tourtellot of the USAS made the following statements about dive bombing at this time, as recalled by Rowell some years later. Asked his opinion of where the dive bombing idea had originated, Tourtellot said that he had learned the method while flying with the British. In one of the later phases of World War I, when the British had gained air superiority, they had made frequent patrols over German lines without encountering the enemy. To avoid wasting fuel on such missions, two light bombs were attached to the fighters, to be dropped wherever they would do the most good. Tourtellot said that the British pilots found that they could dive on German staff cars and other objectives not protected by AA batteries, and attack by diving their aircraft to low altitudes and drop their bombs by guesswork. These ideas had been adopted by the American pilots working with the British.

Maj Norbert Carolin, referring to the period when he was CO of Air Service Troops at the Aberdeen Proving Ground in late 1919, recalled the following test in the September of that year. He was approached by 1st Lt Lester B. Sweeley, Air Services Reserve, who asked permission to carry out a vertical bombing test. This was granted and the test was witnessed by Lt Col R.R. Studler and Col Stribling.

Sweeley used a DH4B carrying a 300lb bomb in a Mark XVI bomb rack. From between 4,000 and 5,000ft Sweeley dived nearly vertically to within 1,000ft of the ground before releasing his bomb. Although the bomb hit the landing gear and was knocked off its trajectory, it continued towards the target and exploded.

A more persuasive demonstration of dive bombing was described by 'Rusty' Rowell after he had completed an advanced course of instruction at the Army Air Force base at Kelly Field in May 1923. It was here that he first heard of the experiences of Army flyers during the air border patrol of the Mexican frontier during 1919-21. The 3rd Attack Group, flying old de Havillands, had assembled a group of highly drilled pilots who had successfully flown over the desert terrain and in the high altitudes of the border country. When Rowell arrived at Kelly this organisation had four squadrons equipped with DH4s under the command of Maj Lewis H. Brereton (later Lt Gen Brereton, commander First Allied Airborne Army, Europe), and was using typical dive bombing techniques of the period. Rowell describes these as follows.

A pilot-operated bomb release was fitted in the cockpit of the DH4Bs, a novel idea for a two-seater, and the American Type A-3 bomb rack developed just after the war. Each plane carried ten small bombs in racks on each wing, and despite the strains imposed on these old aircraft, by diving steeply and at modest speed, they operated with accuracy and no casualties from accidents whatsoever. The pilots selected a sighting point over the engine using any convenient projection for this purpose according to their eye height above their seat. Using their own judgement visually they attacked in dives of between 60^0-70^0 with 'most impressive' accuracy. Not surprisingly Rowell was impressed by the scope this method gave for attacking similar moving targets, but at sea.

US Marines had first been sent to Haiti in 1915 to restore order to that chaotic island under the Senate's interpretation of the Monroe Doctrine. The 4th Air Squadron of Marines, under Capt Harvey B. Mims, was stationed there from the end of March 1919, disembarking at Port-au-Prince. They were to remain there for fifteen years, operating against the rebel leaders of the 'Caco' group and the like. In 1919 one Marine pilot contributed his own method to the history of the dive bomber.

At this time the 4th Air Squadron was equipped with de Havilland DH4B-2Bs, which were not fitted with bomb sights. The inaccuracy of level bombing prompted Lt L.H. Sanderson to develop his personal ideas of increasing precision by diving on to the target. A canvas mail sack strong enough to take the weight of a bomb was tied at one end to the fuselage and the bomb loaded into it. The sack was then closed by ties of the draw rope leaving it horizontal. The rear end was eventually tied to the rear cockpit so that it could be dropped open in flight.

On reaching his target the aircraft was put into a 45^0 dive down to 250ft. At the judged moment the rear end of the sack was released and gravity carried the bomb down and out, just clearing the propeller. Despite the primitive method it worked quite well, and although subsequent claims that this constituted the true 'invention' of dive bombing are silly in the extreme, it is worth recording these experiments in combat as one interesting sidelight on the development of the technique.

In a series of tests laid on by Gen Mitchell in an attempt to prove his concept of air power as the only defence needed by the US, a succession of captured German warships were sunk by bombers on 13-21 July and 23-6 September 1921 off Virginia Capes, among them the old battleship *Ostfriesland.* Although mainly high level attacks and not dive bombing, one attack was made by 'Turk' Tourtellot who subsequently claimed it did constitute real dive bombing. He flew a British SE5 fighter aircraft with Cooper 25lb bombs in a single rack under the fuselage with a bomb release in the cockpit identical to those used at Kelly. He dived on the *Ostfriesland* in an attempt to prove that by such methods fragmentation or gas bombs could be accurately delivered against exposed personnel aboard such warships. Although he was successful, he concluded that such an attack against a well-armed target would be too risky in real life. This is an argument we shall be hearing a great deal of later.

Thus the spark of dive bombing was kept aglow, albeit dimly, in the immediate post-war years by the Army and Marine Corps in America, the Fleet Air Arm in Britain, and the French Navy. Rowell himself was to take the story on to its next stage with a dramatic flourish. Before turning to that watershed, let us take a brief look at the US Navy's opinion of dive bombing in 1924, as revealed by the following points from the Naval War College lecture, *Aviation,* for that year.

> Another use for fighting planes is ship strafing. The object to be gained is the reduction of morale of exposed personnel, such as those who might be in anti-aircraft gun crews and unprotected tops. However, both material and personnel damage may also be done on the lighter surface craft. Bombing will probably be done at an altitude above 6,000ft. To bomb accurately it is necessary for bombing planes to be making good a course directly over their target at the instant the bombs are released. Pattern bombing will usually be employed, rather than individual bombing.

Such thinking was commonplace the world over in 1924, but the US Navy's experience over the next few years was to alter that picture in a most dramatic way.

In the Virginia Capes bombing trials against old German warships in 1921 Lt Tourtellot made low level runs on the destroyer G-102 in an ex-British SE-5 armed with 25lb bombs. These attacks were later described by him as dive bombing attacks, although not strictly such. One of the planes can be seen just below the smoke of the sinking ship.

4 RE-FORGING THE WEAPON
The US Marines and US Navy flyers take up the running, 1925-29

The first flush of American post-war enthusiasm for the dive bombing techniques taken home from the European battlefields by USAS flyers, died with Mitchell's change of heart under the all-pervading influence of Trenchard. Luckily, Marine Corps Maj Rowell had not forgotten his lessons on the method at Kelly Field, and it was he, almost alone, who nursed the flickering flame. Breathing new life into the technique by gaining actual combat experience, he converted the Corps. The US Navy also began to show interest once again, and by the end of the decade the dive bomber was poised to become the major air warfare development of the 1930s.

Although I cannot go along with the many historians who claim that the United States Marine Corps 'invented' dive bombing, I would certainly agree that the Marines should receive most of the credit for keeping the techniques to the fore and for its remarkable rennaissance in the late 1920s.

When Rowell's period of duty with the 1st Pursuit Group ended he was assigned to the command of VO-1-M, which at that time, the late summer of 1924, was on its way to the mainland after the withdrawal of US occupation forces from Santo Domingo. The squadron was the first Marine aviation unit to be established on the West Coast. Based at Naval Air Station San Diego from August 1924, it was equipped with the old DH4B Liberty. Rowell immediately decided to train his squadron as a dive bomber unit, reasoning that the technique would prove highly effective in support of Marine ground troops.

'I wrote to Lt Walter Peck', recorded Rowell, 'and asked him for sample assemblies of the remote-control gun gear, and at the same time I made requisitions on BuAer [US Bureau of Aeronautics] for the A-3 bomb racks which the Army was then using but which the Navy had not yet procured.'

Although an old-stager like the DH4 might be thought a strange mount for dive bombing trials, the British could claim to have already used the type for this purpose during World War I. One British veteran wrote: 'Even in an aircraft of the last war I remember finding myself actually below ground level, down inside a lock, on the termination of a dive-in attack. Because of the lack of airbrakes and the consequent mush in halting and diverting, the speed built up in the dive. That was in a DH4, a very lightly loaded aircraft by modern standards.'

Rowell described how he personally trained his squadron in dive bombing methods, using miniature racks of the Navy type until the Type A-3 arrived. He recalled that at this time, the spring of 1925, many of the West Coast cities were beginning to open their own airports and that there was a great demand for the air services to give flying displays at the opening ceremonies. This gave Rowell an opportunity to train his unit in the new art and to show off the technique to a far larger audience.

Their combined formation flying and dive bombing exhibitions with smoke bombs went down well and he gained the definite feeling that some naval air officers present were much taken by this form of attack and began to practice it themselves, at North Island base.

It may indeed have been like that, but it is also certain that the Navy ran the Marines very close in this period of experimentation. Another extremely valuable first-hand account of this time comes from Adm F.D. Wagner, one of the pioneer Navy pilots. He stated that in 1925 Capt Joseph Mason Reeves took command of the Aircraft Battle Force on the West Coast and in the summer of the following year had concentrated all Pacific Fleet aircraft at North Island, San Diego for trials. He originated a large list known as 'Reeves Thousand and One Questions' and Lt F.W. Weed began collating their responses. 'To dive down, drop a bomb on a ship and pull away before her guns could be manned became an objective, while a bomb sight accurate enough to make such an attack really effective was still a sort of will-o'-the-wisp', wrote one historian of this era.

Driving forces behind the US Navy dive bomber developments of the 1920s, Rear Admiral Moffett (right) and Captain Reeves (left) aboard the USS Langley in 1925. Reeves developed the dive bomber concept and Moffett showed in exercises what it was capable of

Adm Wagner recalled how dive bombing came to appear high on the list of experiments. Reporting to Capt Reeves in June 1926, when he was in command of VF-2 equipped with Curtiss F6C fighters, Wagner found that one of the questions being considered was how to repel a force trying to land on a beach. Strafing seemed the obvious answer, and VF-2 was investigating a combination of low flying and machine-gun fire. But accuracy proved poor and losses from AA fire seemed likely to be high. Wagner found that:

The answer to the problem lay in approaching at high altitude (above 10,000ft) to attain surprise and avoid anti-aircraft fire, before diving at steep angles (70^0+) to attain very high speed in the dive and to obtain the optimum of accuracy in hitting and in changing the emphasis from machine-guns to bombs.

The squadron knew it had developed a very important form of attack that would be effective against the strongest of targets and one that *in no way resembled the old strafing conception of attack*. We also appreciated the fact that attacks must not all be made from the same direction and that the formation from which the attack started must be a flexible one so that entry into the dive could be made promptly after sighting a target. Accordingly, the Vee of echelon and the ABC formations were developed.

Full of enthusiasm at their 'discovery', the squadrons carried out prolonged trials in the back country of San Diego that summer.

The young pilots, having satisfied themselves that they had perfected their art, were eager to give a demonstration in the hope of convincing others of the value of   23 their new tactic. Accordingly they persuaded Capt Reeves to take up position in the centre of North Island and to act as the 'target' for a simulated attack. This he agreed to do, and the spectacular results made a lasting impression on those there, including Felix Stump (later Vice-Adm). So impressed was he that Reeves had no hesitation in giving his squadrons permission to use their tactic in front of a bigger audience, the US Pacific Fleet.

This was done on 22 October 1926. The fleet had sailed from San Pedro for exercises at sea and VF-2 flew to Long Beach to join in. They arrived over the battleships at 12,000ft undetected and began their dives at exactly the time the fleet had been told to expect an air attack. Screaming down in their dives the aircraft were not spotted until in the final stages of their near vertical approach. They levelled off and, while the battleships were still sounding off 'General Quarters', were landing back at their base.

At the same time, and independently of Reeves and his men, Rear-Adm A.C. Davis and Lt George Cuddihy on the East Coast had been working along similar lines. They reported dives against destroyer targets, flying aircraft equipped with gun cameras to record estimated hits. These trials were conducted by Lt O.B. Hardison, and Lt Cdr Davis of the Bureau of Aeronautics set up improved bomb rack purchases and better equipment for the aircraft generally to take advantage of the technique. The dive bomber had re-emerged, and many old rules had to go overboard as a result. As Wagner recalled, prior to 1926 there had been no provision for dropping bombs from fighters, but that changed completely the following year. The F6C had proved to be well equipped in this respect. Wagner made two other points. First, the fighters that followed the F6C proved to be less sturdy, resulting in some fatal accidents when the aircraft disintegrated during dive bombing. Secondly, the film *Hell Divers,* made by VF-1 and VF-2, was made mandatory viewing for Japanese aviators. The British were equally impressed by it, especially *Flight* magazine and its contemporaries according to Wagner.

Both Wagner's points were introduced to reinforce his claim that the US Navy had invented the tactic of dive bombing in 1926. Although this is not so, there is no disputing that by the summer of that year the US Navy had passed an historic milestone on the dive bomber road.

Turnbull and Lord, record in their history how not all the members of the Bureau shared Cdr Davis's enthusiasm for the new concept. Some had reservations about the suitability of existing aircraft for dive bombing while others opposed the resulting diversion of fighters away from their primary defensive role. A series of tests was ordered in an attempt to settle the matter. These tests proved that dive bombing gave unprecedented results with regard to accuracy and converted many doubters. Dive bombing of unarmoured warships like carriers or destroyers with gas, fragmentation and demolition bombs up to 100lb was considered practicable as a result.

In the 1926 BuAer tests a Chance Vought seaplane, the UO, was used because it was the only airplane that could be fitted with small bombs. The success of VF-1 and VF-2 changed all that and bomb racks were soon fitted on VE-7s, Boeing FBs and the Curtiss F6C. During the initial trials the aircraft dived at 45° from 1,000 to 400ft. The length and steepness of the dive were based on the structural limitations of the aircraft, while the minimum altitude was set to avoid bomb fragments from hitting the aircraft. When other aircraft were fitted for dive bombing, the length and angle of the dive were determined by the CO in the light of structural limitations.

This work led to a feeling that there was no need to develop a specialised dive bomber, since the fighters then available could do the job, and in March 1927 such a view was put from the fleet. But a more realistic approach came from the Taylor

Board, which recommended, for the first time in the world, that such an aircraft should be built.

Tests were carried out at Hampton Roads, Va, in October 1927 by VF-5S commanded by Lt Wallace M. Dillon. The target was a platform towed at 20kts behind a destroyer. The results, confirmed with camera guns, again completely vindicated the dive bombing method and supported the previous year's findings.

There followed further investigations of the bomb-carrying potential and diving capabilities of other types of aircraft, even though the F4B-1 and O2U-2 were strong enough to carry a 500lb bomb and dive with it. By December 1928 a large variety of aircraft had been equipped as bomb carriers by the US Navy.

Table 3: US Navy Aircraft Types Capable of Carrying Bombs 1928		
Aircraft type	Size of bombs (lb)	Number carried
F4B-1	30	10
F4B-1	500	1
O2U-2	30	10
O2U-2	500	1
F6C-1/5	30	5
F7C-1	30	5
FB-1/5	30	5
F2B-1	30	5
F3B-1	30	5
OC-1/2	100	4
OD-1	100	4
OL-6/8	30	10

Also well under way was development of a generation of true dive bombers, as distinct from adaptions from other types. BuAer began the development, at the end of 1928, with the XF8C-2 for carrying a 500lb bomb, and, even more significantly, the XT2N-1 for carrying a 1,000lb bomb. The XF8C-2 was designed to show whether an aircraft especially designed for dive bombing would in fact be better at the job than a strengthened fighter.

This transformation of tactics within such a brief period as demonstrated in the air and on the BuAer drawing boards by the end of 1928, was matched with the formation of the first tentative theoretical doctrines about the uses and advantages of a dive bomber force in a modern fleet. In this the US Navy undoubtedly established a substantial margin over the other leading powers of the day. By 1928 they were in fact, very nearly a decade ahead of the British and Japanese Navies in this field.

This new-found doctrine can be found expounded in a lecture delivered at the time at the Naval War College by Lt Cdr B.G. Leighton, of which brief extracts will serve to show that the trend of though had radically changed since the Bellinger paper of a few years before.

From the point of view of the defence of surface ships against air attack Leighton pointed out that hitherto considerable confidence was held in the ships' ability, especially battleships with their heavy AA batteries, to protect themselves against level bombing attacks. The steady and level approach which was vital to accuracy in this form of bombing, could be accurately predicted by the ships' fire control and could be met by long-range AA fire and massed automatic weapons at closer ranges. But this did not apply to dive bombing:

Many of you are familiar with the so-called 'strafing' form of attack which is now being used by light fast planes in delivering machine-gun, or light bomb attacks against exposed positions on surface ships. In this form of attack the conventional fire control system breaks down, for the plane approaches on irregular courses with rapid and irregular changes in altitude throughout the approach, settling down to a straight flight path in a steep dive for considerably less than ten seconds before actually releasing the bomb. Bombs are released at an altitude of 1,500ft or less. Target practice conducted against targets towed at a speed of twenty knots in the open sea, indicate an accuracy of about 30 per cent hits on a destroyer target, in the neighbourhood of 50 per cent on light cruiser targets and approximately 60 per cent on battleship targets.

As if this was not sufficient food for thought he also pointed out that this was combined with almost complete invulnerability to the attacking dive bomber.

The speed of approach of the plane, due to her diving approach, is upwards of 200mph (or about 300fps). This form of attack gives to the plane unrestricted freedom of movement throughout the approach and until it has reached the final point of release; it makes accurate prediction of future positions impossible; and, if conducted by several planes in concerted attack renders barrage fire completely ineffective.

Leighton then went on to pre-empt claims that light bomb loads, such as those carried by contemporary aircraft, could never be effective against anything other than superstructure and could not sink ships, only damage them. In the case of battleships with their powerful armoured decks this point was still valid, and would remain so, but against all other types of warship it might well apply currently, but would no do so for very much longer. As the bomb loads were bound, on development, to increase in size, so would the lesser ships' vulnerability increase. In fact he told them that work was even then proceeding on just those lines:

The diving form of attack is now being extended to use of heavier bombs up to 500lb weight. We are now putting into the fleet a new type of two-seater machine to replace the old two-seat observation machines which have been operating from battleship and cruiser catapults. These new machines are fitted to be operated as seaplanes from catapults or as straight land planes with arresting gear from the decks of carriers.

The potential of the dive bomber against ship targets was clear for all to see, although a decade of development lay ahead before it was able to prove itself. The equally high factor of the effect of the dive bomber on the morale of land forces, as expounded by Stewart in Britain at the same time, was also being graphically demonstrated in actual combat conditions by the US Marine Corps, even as Leighton was giving his lecture.

5 EMERGENCE OF THE HELLDIVERS
US Marine Corps combat in Nicaragua and subsequent developments, 1927-32

The Marines had been employed in their trouble-shooting role in Nicaragua before in the 1920s but in the middle of that decade the forces of Moncada rose up against the rule of Diaz and to preserve the *status quo,* restore order and stop the fighting from spreading, the US Senate sent in the 5th Marines at the beginning of January 1927 and by 11 May they had been reinforced to brigade strength. Due to the terrain it soon became obvious that they would require air support and in February Rowell's unit, VO-1-M, suddenly received orders to proceed immediately to Nicaragua. Within 48 hours the unit, still equipped with the DHs fitted with the A-3 bomb racks, moved out and by 25 February according to Sherrod (or 19 February according to Rowell) had disembarked at Cortinto. Here they moved up by rail to Managua, hauling their six DHs on flat cars with wings detached.

At Managua they set up their base at the baseball park and were joined by two barnstorming pilots (Mason and Brooks) who were flying old Laird Swallows for the Nicaraguan Federal forces, discards from the Checkered Cab Company of San Francisco! The Marine airmen worked all night assembling this base and their aircraft and were ready to fly within 48 hours of landing. The ground forces were thin and the seven operational DHs finally assembled held the city on their own for a time until Brig Gen Feland arrived from Quantico.

There was complete anarchy in the land and the US Marines held fourteen strongpoints at strategic sections along the vital linking railroad, interposing themselves between the two rival factions. Later they were reinforced by VO-4-M and these two units combined to form an Aircraft Squadron under Rowell's command, flying constant reconnaisance patrols over the two armies while Mr Stimson negotiated an armistice. They had strict instructions to avoid involvement in battle and although often shot at did not fire back. With the signing of the Armistice it seemed that their work was done and troop reductions began in June. But one of the rebel officers, Augusto Sandino, refused to accept the peace agreement as valid and took to the northern mountains to fight on, while the rest of the troops on both sides lay down their arms.

Sensing an opportunity Sandino moved. On the evening of 15 July he launched an attack with several hundred men on the tiny outpost of Ocotal which was defended by thirty-seven Marines under Capt Hatfield, together with about four dozen of the new Nicaraguan guard commended by a Marine NCO, which were cut off from the rest across the town plaza. It was estimated that some 700-800 of Sandino's men attacked at 0300 but were beaten off by dawn. However the town was completely cut off and besieged. The nearest friendly outpost was 125 miles away in direct line, but in terms of land travel by mule trains and bull carts it would take ten to fourteen days for the relieving force of sixty-five Marines under Maj Floyd to reach them. The position seemed hopeless.

Rowell's unit soon made aerial contact, and two pilots of the squadron, now known as VO-7-M, discovered Hatfield's plight at 1010 the next morning and reported back after a daring landing. Rowell had five DHs available for operations and these were immediately despatched. They did not have their full

27

outfit of bombs aboard due to the limitations of the improvised runway, which was only 400yd long, and the need for each aircraft to carry 110 gallons of fuel for the round trip. Nonetheless they all got safely airborne. 'Rusty' Rowell later described the attack in detail. All his pilots had been trained in dive bombing and he determined to test it out. They made their approach at a height of 1,500ft being fired upon without effect as they formed their bombing column.

As the five DHs made the target zone they made one complete circuit of the town to assess the situation and decided quickly where to deliver the attack to do the most good. A tropical storm was threatening and the attack was made as the rain started to fall. Rowell led in diving out of column at 1,500ft and pulling out of his dive at 600ft. The enemy had not been subjected to any serious form of bombing before and exposed themselves regardless. Their casualties were subsequently heavy, it being estimated that between forty to eighty of them were killed outright in this attack. Subsequent dives were made from 1,000ft with pullout at 300ft. The 17lb fragmentation bombs were very effective, and the rebels broke and fled.

Back in the States a second Taylor Board, established in April 1927, reached the conclusion that general purpose aircraft were a waste of money, even if they looked cheaper in theory. Cdr Newton White for example deplored such aircraft condemning them as '. . . an inefficient hybrid in which both types were ruined'. Dive bomber, torpedo bomber and fighter were the three recommended types to concentrate on. But during this early stage of experimentation the splitting of the US Navy dive bombers into 'light' types, fighters which could dive bomb, and 'heavy' types, dive bombers which could also scout, continued and was not halted until the end of the decade. In Britain this habit of building aircraft for more than one function was to have tragic results for the FAA, but the US Navy was more fortunate in that it could control its own destiny with regard to aircraft.

Structural strength remained the chief problem for the designers, dive bombing setting up higher strains than normal on aircraft. The use by the Marines of the Curtiss Falcon (OC-1), which was a Navy-modified version of the Army plane with an air-cooled Pratt & Whitney R-1340 Wasp engine, indicated the need for greater strength and this was incorporated in the XF8C. Even so it was clear that the stress problem was still an unknown factor, for the first XF8C crashed on test flight. Curtiss therefore built a stronger, but heavier, model as a flying testbed and from this resulted the F8C-4.

Martin had similar difficulties with their XT5M-1, for the initial test programme of October 1929 resulting in badly damaged wings. Renewed testing in March 1930 under three different conditions again produced minor distortion of the wings. Even the first production model, BM-1, crashed on acceptance trials and it had to have yet further strengthening before entering service.

Further accidents were involved in the bomb dropping, with the bomb striking the parts of the aircraft on release, while their flight paths were identical during the vertical stage before pullout. In 1929 a string of such accidents, although not fatal, led to a re-appraisal after a small bomb hit the prop of an XF6C-4, and F6C-4 and F3B aircraft had their landing gear struck by their own missiles.

Although it could be proved on paper that in dive bombing the bomb would *always* hit the landing gear of the aircraft due to the relative trajectories of the two, it was already known that in *fact* this only happened rarely, so the problem was not hopeless. Further tests were conducted at the Naval Proving Grounds at Dahlgren, during which dive bombing took place and motion pictures were taken of the bomb leaving the aircraft at various angles. From this a maximum

A view of a Martin BM-1 dive bomber taking off from the USS Lexington *in 1934. The BM-1 was one of the first true dive bombers capable of carrying a bomb load effective against small warships.*

safety angle was deducted but the human element involved in this form of attack was such that it was calculated that the true angle of dive was miscalculated by pilots as much as 15^0-30^0 and a foolproof automatic device was considered necessary to compensate for this human error.

The answer lay, for a single heavy bomb load, in a simple displacing gear arrangement incorporating a bomb-crutch which had two pivoted arms fixed to the fore end of the under-fuselage. On release this mechanism swung the bomb down and out away from the body of the aircraft, thus clearing both the prop-arcs and the bulky undercarriage gear in one quick movement. This invention was the combined work of Lt Cdr A.C. Miles, BuAer, Cdr C.L. Schuyler and Mr George A. Chadwick, BuOrd, and their invention cleared the way for the rapid development of the true dive bomber.

The bomb crutch was tried at the Martin test plant in static tests and then flight-proven at the Proving Grounds on 7 January and 8 January 1931 by Lt Cdr Ostrander in the XT5M-1. There were no snags and this vital piece of equipment became standard fitting to all 'heavy' dive bombers.

A simpler answer was found for the smaller fragmentation bombs which was merely to carry such bombs as far outboard under the wings as possible where they could foul no obstruction on release. In any case the value of such small weapons rapidly declined for use on dive bombers in the decade that followed, as such aircraft were built mainly for 500lb and 1,000lb bombs. An additional safety precaution introduced at the same time was the slow-arming fuse which ensured that the bomb was well clear of the aircraft before chance ignition could occur.

Following the testing of the strengthened XT5M-1 in April 1931 the Martin BM-1 was ordered, but this was only a stop-gap for already the BuAer were looking ahead at a whole range of designs and options.

The first type evaluated was a two-seater, scout and dive bomber. It was this type that was eventually to gain the day at the end of the decade, only to lose it five years after, but in 1932 it was one of many ideas. The designers were required to strive for the following: range with a 1,000lb bomb of 400 miles; with a 500lb bomb, 750 miles. As a Scouting plane the range was to be at least 1,000 miles, with the external fuel tanks being substituted for the normal bomb load. This specification led to the Great Lakes XGB-1 and the Consolidated XB2Y-1.

For the development of the alternative one-seat 'light' dive bomber the Curtiss XF11C-1 and -2 were produced, both of which were capable of carrying a single 500lb bomb, and later the XG11C-3 was ordered. All these aircraft later had their designations changed to BFC-1, -2 and -3 causing some confusion, while the BFC-3 was later to receive the designation BF2C-1.

Thus by 1932 the US Navy was developing six different types of aircraft to perform three main functions, viz: 'heavy' two-seat dive bomber, 'light' two-seat fighter dive bombers; tactical scouts and single-seater fighters.

Of the 'heavies' the Great Lakes XBG-1 incorporated many features of the defunct Martin TG-2 torpedo bomber, when that company was taken into the Great Lakes domain in October 1932 and it proved itself superior to the existing BM-1 and the rival Consolidated XB2Y-1. A dozen of the original Martin BM-1s were in service aboard the carrier *Lexington* by July 1932 and they were followed by twenty-one of the later version, BM-2. Highly regarded in service the Great Lakes design was superior, being both smaller with advantages for carrier operating and stowage, and having a higher top speed (188mph against 145mph) with a higher ceiling (20,100ft against 16,400ft) and thus forty-four of them were ordered, as the BG-1, for the Marines and Navy, entering service in October 1934. A total of sixty were built, but the parent company went out of business in 1936.

With regard to the wider single-seater fighter dive bomber field the situation was similarly resolved. From the Boeing XG6B-1 design the Navy got a 200mph fighter which was designed to double as a dive bomber from the start. In this form it was designated the XBFB-1 but their rivals, Curtiss, made the most lasting impression on this particular field in the early and mid-1930s.

The famous Curtiss F11C Hawks were an adaptation of the US Army P-6E Goshawk and as such they featured a Wright 600hp engine. The first navy Hawks appeared in 1932 as the F11C-1, the export version featuring a Wright Cyclone engine of 700hp, and, although developed earlier, was designated F11C-2. Both aircraft featured the fixed heavy undercarriage and spats, and both of course were biplanes. In March 1934 this aircraft, originally ordered as a fighter, was re-designated to fit its 'light' dive bomber role, becoming the BFC-1 Hawk, similarly the -2 became the BFC-2.

A further refinement of this basic aircraft was the BF11C-3 which had a retractable undercarriage, something quite novel for biplanes. This was also 'made-over' to become the famed BF2C-1 Hawk, the export version of which was sold to Argentina and Thailand as the Hawk III. Twenty-eight of these were delivered to the US Navy in 1933 and joined the Navy's crack *High Hats* squadron embarked in *Saratoga,* but here it served for less than one year.

The impact of the dive bomber was enormous of course in the advancement of the aircraft carrier concept. Now, and only now, the fleet had a fast, handy aircraft that could hurt. The torpedo bomber, although potentially more dangerous against ship targets, was also more vulnerable, for at this time it still had to make a straight low-level run to launch its missile and all warship guns could be concentrated against it. By contrast the dive bomber appeared without much warning in those pre-radar days, from a height to which only the most specialised guns could elevate, and they came in at a speed which limited firing time to seconds. On top of that was its proven accuracy which meant that small ships could be disabled, or even sunk, by this method alone while the battleships could be swamped by a combination of both methods, the dive bomber supressing the AA to enable the torpedo bomber to close in unscathed. The co-ordination of these two methods, although ideal of course, seldom proved possible in combat conditions, but when it did work it was decisive.

With regard to accuracy the first tests had been impressive and in each further dive bomber trial further improvement was shown. The Curtiss F8C claimed a hit rate of 67 per cent on target compared with the horizontal bomber average of 30 per cent, while Lt Cdr Wagner once claimed that in one test his squadron scored '100 per cent' hits on a battleship target.

With regard to the ships' defences the first feelings were that they had little or no chance of stopping a committed dive bomber by gunfire alone and Capt Leahy of the BuOrd was recorded as saying that this type of attack showed great possibilities. But by 1931 the BuOrd was re-asserting its faith in the new generation of close-range weapons to deter dive bombers.

Dive bombing trials against small vessels found that machine-gun bullets could penetrate decks and bulkheads of destroyers, 30lb bombs could wreck torpedo tubes, searchlights and boats and that destroyers were very vulnerable indeed and would need heavier AA weapons and a great many more of them to cope.

Of equal importance, or perhaps more so in the long-term, was the discovery of what naval air power could achieve against land-based aircraft, even as early as the late 1920s. Whereas it was always held by RAF authorities that a land-based plane would *always* be superior to a ship-based one, the US Navy proved in 1929 that this was nonsense. Thus the *strategical* value of the dive bomber was shown in these early exercises as well as its tactical attributes.

This was largely the work of Reeves, now a Rear Admiral flying his flag in *Saratoga*. She was part of the Black (attacking) fleet in that year's war game, their objective being an assault on the Panama Canal Zone which was defended by the Blue forces. The latter had some 145 aircraft at their disposal for defence, including thirty-seven Army and twelve Navy shore based planes in the Canal Zone itself, as well as the carrier air groups from *Lexington*. Against this Black could deploy only 116 aircraft from *Saratoga*, the old *Langley* having dropped out with defects.

Reeves persuaded Adm William V. Pratt commanding Black fleet to allow him to use *Saratoga* independantly away from the battleships, *for the first time*, and she made a high-speed dash through the defenders' screens and flew off her aircraft at dawn. Seventeen torpedo bombers and seventeen dive bombers escorted by thirty-two fighters were despatched, all of which got through.

Complete tactical surprise was achieved. Canal locks and army airfields in the zone were pummelled with both dive bombing and low level strafing attacks. When finally engaged by defending Army aircraft the *Saratoga's* fighters gave more than they got. Pratt termed the strike and the manoeuver that preceded it, '. . . the most brilliantly conceived and most effectively executed naval operations in our history'.

Another account of this notable day in the dive bomber's history concluded: '. . . in theory the simultaneous bombings blew up the Miraflores and Pedro Miguel locks and damaged the airfields at Fort Clayton and Albright. Nine defending fighters came up from these fields but were hopelessly outnumbered and *Saratoga's* planes returned with only one technical loss'. Truly the dive bomber had arrived in the US Navy.

DOUBTS AND HESITANCY
Other nations experiments in the period 1925-32

Chief interest in Britain continued to be shown in dive bombing by the then RAF controlled FAA flights and the famous 'Converging' attacks by the Fairey Flycatchers continued to be the most obvious outward demonstration of this policy. However army co-operation pilots were not adverse to conducting their own 'unofficial' dives whenever they got the opportunity, even if this was frowned upon by the Air Ministry. H.F. King wrote how: 'The conniving squadron commanders might well have known better, but they were always first off the stack'.

Dives in a Hawker Audax might be breathtaking enough, but it was still the Flycatcher which represented the British dive bomber *par excellence* at this time. One of the best descriptions of the method was provided by a former pilot, famous for his record-breaking feats, Lt Owen Cathcart-Jones in his book *Aviation Memoirs.* He described practice attacks against stationary targets with four small practice bombs from 2,600ft. The nose was pulled up into a stall and the aircraft dropped vertically, the target being lined up in the sights. They began to experience the same trouble with bombs hitting the undercarriage as the Americans were to learn.

A new and more accurate method was then adopted which involved a very steep dive from 2,000ft down to 150ft, again with the target lined up in the sights. The aircraft was pulled up sharply at this height and the bomb released within three seconds. Despite the findings at Orfordness earlier Cathcart-Jones recorded that, with practice, this method was very accurate and that direct hits were more common than misses.

The approach and attack saw the flights subdivided into sections of three, in which each circled the target equi-distant but apart from each other. Signal to commence the attack was the leader rocking his wings and starting his own dive. As the leader reached the pull-out position the second machine would commence the dive from a different direction and No 3 would follow in turn from another compass point thus splitting the defensive fire. By the time No 3 had finished the dive No 1 would again be in position to attack keeping the target under constant assault.

The incidents of bombs hitting the undercarriage came to a head in Britain in 1932 following a accident at the Sutton Bridge testing range on 26 September. While carrying out bombing practice over Holbeach Marsh against a towed target in the Wash Flt Lt Henry Maitland King, RN, attached to the carrier *Furious,* was killed when his Flycatcher apparently burst into flames in mid-air and crashed, exploding on impact.

Eyewitnesses told how King had come down from 2,000ft to 1,000ft in an 120mph dive. On straightening out he had dropped two bombs in quick succession. Suddenly flames burst from the fuselage and a second later the machine dived into the bombing range a few yard from the water's edge. There was a loud crash, followed by the explosions of the bombs still on board.

The subsequent inquest returned a verdict of 'death by misadventure' but the truth of the matter came out as follows. The OC No 401(FF) Flt Lt Cdr R.R. Graham, RN, stated that the flight was instructed to carry out live bombing. In

32

the interests of safety he had amended the orders of the previous days trials, on the 23rd, to read '. . . that the height from which the bombs were to be dropped was to be *greater* than 500ft'. Flt Lt King had certainly complied with this. He was no novice pilot, he had experience of using live Cooper bombs in August 1930 and he was in fact Armaments Officer of 404 Flight at the time. Graham emphasised personally the danger of diving too low while live bombing before the attack and he was satisfied that all pilots were fully aware of the danger and the orders not to do so. Asked about any orders as to the angle of the dive while bombing, he replied: 'In discussing this question with other Flight Commanders, I gained the impression that the steeper the angle the greater the accuracy'. No orders or instructions were issued to the flight on the question of angle of dive. King had reported trouble with his bomb racks on the three practices of 23 September however. Other witnesses gave graphic descriptions of the accident, that left little doubt that the bomb had detonated in the air.

AC1 R.A. Blumson of No 3 ARC was employed on the Range Party at Holbeach and noted that . . . on the whole, FAA Flights seem to dive steeper than other units. Similarly Sgt A. Johnstone agreed: 'Lt King was diving down wind, ie from the north-west. I have noticed that FAA pilots dive more steeply than other single seater pilots and I estimated Lt King's angle of dive as between 50^0 and 60^0'.

The Court of Enquiry had no hesitation in deciding that, in their opinion, the bomb when released hit the undercarriage and exploded. They further made recommendations that the method of making 20lb HE bombs 'live' should be investigated and the pistol so designed that the bomb could not become 'live' until at least ten feet below the undercarriage at maximum diving speed. They further recommended that the position of the bomb rack on the Flycatcher be revised and if possible, set back, and that until this had been done or some alternative found, this form of bomb dropping should be prohibited. The Deputy Inspector of Accidents minuted that: '. . . until remedial measures had been taken, the dropping of bombs from Flycatcher aircraft, when diving, be discontinued forthwith'. He added that this type of accident could happen if the aircraft was dived at an agle of about 40^0.

This hardly was encouraging to further experimentation and action was immediate and widespread, as was shown by a Secret Telegram despatched from Air Vice Marshall Dowding at the Air Ministry to Air Marshall Sir John Steel in India: 'An accident has occurred in which a live 20lb bomb released from fuselage rack on a Flycatcher in a steep dive hit the axle and exploded. CAS does not wish to hamper your operations but orders prohibiting diving bombing from fuselage racks with live bombs on single engined aircraft are being issued to other Commands.'

A minute from DTD to AMSR followed in which it was stated that: '. . . aircraft for which steep diving bombing is a requirement, the bomb carriers should be so installed that there is no obstruction on the aircraft in the path of the bomb when dropped at any angle of flight from steep climb to vertical dive'. This brought a list of modifications to current aircraft.

The DCAS had minuted that: 'I agree that diving bombing with live bombs from bomb racks under the fuselage of single-engined aircraft should be stopped for the present, but I do not want to stop this form of bombing with practice bombs if it can be avoided, as this will interfere with the special trials now being carried out by Nos 12 and 40 Squadrons'.

DTD was able to reply that: 'The bomb racks on Gordons are on the wings and consequently they are not affected . . . .' In the case of the Hart: '. . . one of the racks used for practice bombs is under the fuselage but much further back in 33 relation to the undercarriage than in the Flycatcher. The chance of a bomb from this rack hitting the axle or airscrew in diving *is very remote* and only occurs if the angle of dive is over 60^0 . . .' which would seem to confirm that this was not often done in conventional RAF units at that time.

Table 4: Modifications to Allow Forward Dropping Angles to Conform to New Safety Regulations in RAF 1932		
Aircraft Types	Forward Dropping Angle	Side Clearances
Fighters	80^0	10^0
General Purpose	60^0	10^0
Dive Bomber	60^0	10^0
Torpedo Bomber	60^0	10^0
Army Co-Operation	60^0	10^0
Night Bomber	30^0	10^0

Table 5: Recommendations For Modifications to RAF Bomb Racks 1932	
Aircraft	Details
Flycatcher	It is understood that the necessary modications is in hand.
Demon	All new aircraft of this type should be modified to allow a clearance of 60^0.
Wapiti	No action on aircraft of channel type carriers. Angle of 55^0 from carriers under the fuselage can be accepted.
Hart	The light series carriers only in the first 15 aircraft of this type should be re-positioned to give a forward clearance of 60^0.
Hart (India)	No action on aircraft of channel type carriers. Angle of 55^0 from carriers under the fuselage can be adopted.
Horsley	No action owing to obsolescence.
Vildebeeste	No action to existing aircraft. All new aircraft to be modified to clear.

Early post-war German efforts at re-establishment had reached fruition with the secret establishment deep within the Soviet Union for testing designs. A further door was opened with the replacement of the very strict Versailles ruling by the Paris agreement of 22 May 1926. Under this amendment the German aircraft industry was allowed to build a restricted number of aircraft on the understanding that these were not to be employed in a military sense, but for flying club use only. They soon took advantage of this.

Obviously dive bombing aircraft were not a type which was permitted to be studied, openly, but nonetheless between 1925 and 1932 the Junkers company in Sweden and the Heinkel company in Germany was able to make significant advances in this field using the smokescreen of foreign interest and facilities.

Junkers had been early in the field with the production of the successful ground-attack aircraft, the metal frameworked J-1 of 1917 which was a great advance featuring armour protection for the crew and engine. Two hundred had been built and used successfully, fifty of the two-seater type J10, were also produced as an infantry-support weapon in 1918 so this form of aerial warfare was part of the Junkers tradition well before 1920, although they were not dive bombers as such.

In the early 1920s Professor Hugo Junkers had established a Swedish subsidiary, the *AB Flygindustri* at Linhamn, near Malmö as one of the many efforts to get round allied controls. From here came the brainchild of designer Karl Plauth, the K-47, a low-wing, two-seat monoplane fighter. Officially designated as a civilian sports plane and carried under the Swedish civil register as such, it was in fact a very advanced aircraft for its time. Powered by a Bristol Jupiter engine it was specially braced to take the stresses involved in the pull-out from a high-speed dive during fighter operations. Although it proved inferior to biplane types in tests at Lipetzk in 1928 the Chinese authorities had ordered twelve of these aircraft. The Germans themselves rejected it as a fighter and this led to subsequent trials conducted to utilise the K-47's diving capabilities with bomb racks fitted to the machine on sloping struts and, as a dive bomber, the K-47 showed up very well.

Plauth himself was killed in an air accident before the results had come in fully but Swedish Junkers were themselves satisfied enough to continue their development work on the aircraft under a new designer, Hermann Pohlmann, and these efforts resulted in the evolution of perhaps the most famous dive bomber of all time, the Junkers Ju87.

Since the Washington Treaty it was clear to Japanese leaders that the most likely future opponent in any war would be either the USSR or the USA. The general hostility aroused by their Manchurian operations had emphasised this. To the Navy it was the American threat that loomed largest and the key to attacking Japan across the wastes of the Pacific was sea power, or sea/air power, ships and aircraft of the American Navy. The USA already had a 3 to 2 superiority in battleships, and when they called for an expansion of their aircraft strength to a figure of 1,000 planes, Japan at once took steps to build up her own strength, in response with the First Fleet Replenishment Programme. This included provision for the expansion of her own naval air strength.

In 1931 the Imperial Japanese Navy placed an order with the German Heinkel company for the development of such an aircraft. Basic specification called for a two-seater aircraft able to carry into combat a 550lb bomb. As well as being stressed for diving it was to be capable of catapault launched operations from warships, and, with the Pacific islands in mind, to be convertible for use both as a carrier plane and a seaplane. Heinkels fitted the bill having already established a good reputation for the latter.

The result was the Heinkel He50aW, completed at Warnemünde in the summer of 1931 as a twin-float seaplane. The original prototype was under-powered with a 390hp Junkers L-5 engine which was somewhat rectified with a 490hp Jupiter VI engine in the second land-based prototype, He50aL.

Testing in dive bombing configuration followed, with the second cockpit faired over, the methods used involving the dropping of 1,100lb blocks of concrete at floating targets in the Breitling near Warnemünde. Another prototype fitted with a 490hp Jupiter engine was produced for the Japanese contract in the autumn of 1932. This featured a redesigned undercarriage and nose section and was designated He50b, also known as the He66 for export purposes.

The first He50 prototype proved incapable of carrying even a 500lb bomb satisfactorily, but those fitted with the Siemens Jupiter SH22 (later named Bramo 322) engine of 600hp were. Meanwhile the second Japanese prototype was shipped out to the *Aichi Tokei Denki K.K.* in early 1933. The Japanese, in turn, re-engined it with their own Nakajima *Kotobuki II-Kai-1* radial engine of 580hp, and conducted trials in a competition to meet their first dive bomber specification under their *8-Shi* (1933) programme.

The earliest home-produced dive bombers for the Imperial Japanese Navy were the Nakajimi D1A1 Type 94 biplanes. They saw some combat in the early stages of the intervention in China but were not completely satisfactory.

Following the unsatisfactory performance of the Nakajima Type 94 dive bombers, the 8-Shi specification called for an improved type of greater robustness. The Mitsubishi D1A2 was one such contender but proved inferior to the Aichi D1A which was finally selected.

At the conclusion of these trials the He66 export version of Heinkel's dive bomber was selected for production, the Imperial Navy took up the manufacturer's option and the Aichi company was given the contract. This aircraft became Japan's first front-line dive bomber under the designation of the D1A1 Type 94 Carrier Bomber, incorporating several small modifications to undercarriage bracing, tail wheel instead of skid, more sweepback on the wings and other minor changes. Japan was on her way.

Meanwhile back in its country of origin the He50 was demonstrated to the *Reichswehrministerium* at Rechlin in 1932 and contracts were placed for three aircraft fitted with the Bramo engine. These were also completed in 1932 with a three-bladed metal two-pitch airscrew, a feature designed to enable the pilot to

Development of a suitable dive bomber continued slowly in France through the 1920s. Following experimental work in the 1920s the Gourdou-Leseurre GL-430B1 was selected as a suitable mount and was given further trials. As can be seen its World War I origins are only too obvious. Despite its poor performance it was further developed through the GL-432 and this was also a parasol-type aircraft. Four were tested between 1936 and 1940.

select his airscrew pitch before commencing the dive. As a single-seater dive bomber the He50 could carry a bomb load of 1,102lb (500kg).

As a result of these tests the German authorities ordered a batch of sixty of the He50L (later again re-designated as the He50A) for use with the flying training establishments during 1933 and these formed the nucleus of the planned future dive bomber *Staffeln.* The He50A had a maximum speed of 143mph at sea level and a range of 370 miles. In the history of the dive bomber the He50A deserves a notable place for it provided the basis for the subsequent German and Japanese dive bomber expansion programmes. It also saw considerable combat action in China (on *both* sides) and in Spain.

As in the previous period all French development was retarded by insufficient funding, although limited trials continued. However in the early 1930s France could claim it was ahead of Britain in the fact that it had at least produced an aircraft especially *designed* for dive bombing. This was the parasol-wing Gourdou-Leseurre GL-430B1. Powered by a Jupiter 420hp engine it first flew on 26 October 1931 at Villacoublay, but not until 1933 did trials begin to take place in earnest at St Raphäel. It had a maximum speed of 280km/hr at 3,000m altitude, but its performance was not outstanding. The GL-430 underwent progressive development, but not until 1935 can we again pick up the French part of our story, the pace was that slow.

7 PERFECTING THE SKILL
The accelerating development of dive bombers in USA 1932-40

After the great mushrooming of ideas and experimental aircraft types which followed hard on the heels of the US Navy's conversion to the dive bomber concept, as the 1930s wore on this diversification was more and more restricted as the ideal norm was sought. With the bold adoption of the monoplane by that service, years ahead of its rivals, the genesis of the most famous of all American dive bombers was formulated, the SBU. But the road to that final, memorable design was long and complicated.

The six different designs on hand for study were obviously too many and natural selection eliminated three of them early on. Late in 1933 various designs for two-seater dive bombers, each capable of carrying *two* 1,000lb bombs, the XF12C-1, XF3U-1 and the XFD-1, were all converted to scout dive bombers. Of these the XF3U-1 held its acceptance tests, but was then sent back for re-design work and replaced by the XSBU-1. The untested XF12C was re-designed as the XS4C-1 in late 1933, and then became the XSBC-1 early the following year. This conversion involved the replacement of the R-1510 engine with the SR-1820-F, with the installation of a controllable pitch propeller and increased area of the horizontal tail and the release mechanism for a 500lb bomb. From these designs the US Navy ultimately hoped to shortlist either the XSBU-1 or the XSBC-1 for quantity production as a 'standard' type. BuAer planned to take on the production models of the winners and incorporate in them the improvements that had been accepted since the original design was initiated. Exactly the same method was to be applied to the development of the XSBF-1 based on the production SF-2 and, from these two parallel developments, the best airplane of the two would be the dive bomber of the future.

Thus, although in 1935 the Boeing F4B4 was still being employed by the US Marines in the dive bomber role, the aircraft designed for the job more and more began to dominate the scene. The biplane was still in evidence at this stage and the Vought SBU-1 was typical of the aircraft in use in 1935. It was the first to be dubbed SB, Scout Bomber, showing how these two functions were hopefully combined in one airframe. As related this was a reworking of the XF3U-1 fighter with a maximum speed of 210mph capable of carrying a single 500lb bomb. This Vought dive bomber had a composite construction, all-metal body with fabric covered wings and rear fuselage. Although it was highly aerobatic and could be held firmly in the dive it lacked speed and firepower and within a year had been relegated to reserve units, although some still remained in service as late as 1940

Table 6: US Navy Experimental Dive Bomber Designs 1934			
Class	Company	Designation	Notes
VB	Great Lakes Aircraft	XB2G-1	Biplane
VB	Northrop	XBT-1	Low-wing monoplane
VSB	Chance Vought	XSB2U-1	Low-wing monoplane
VSB	Brewster	XSBA-1	Mid-wing monoplane
VSB	Chance Vought	XSB3U-1	SBU-1 modified
VSB	Curtiss	XSBC-2	Replacing XSBC-1
VSB	Grumman	XSBF-1	Modified SF-2

A fine air-to-air view of the Chance Vought SBU-1, 'Scouting Bombing' aircraft in pre-war colours. This shot was taken on 8 February 1940 as these aircraft were being phased out of service with the US fleet.

for training. Its single 800hp Pratt & Whitney R-1535-80 engine gave it a range of 545 miles.

For the 1934 design competitions the US Navy decided that two types were required: the VSB to carry 500lb bombs and the VB, designed to carry 1,000lb bombs. The VSB was to have an all-up weight of 5,000lb, the VB 6,000lb. It was also stipulated that the lighter aircraft was to have a shorter take-off but in other respects the specification was similar. Both were to incorporate dive brakes and have a stalling speed of 65mph.

Here it should be noted how the monoplane designs dominated. Despite the Navy's specification and classification Northrop held firmly that the same design was suitable for *both* requirements. The Chance Vought design was for a biplane version of the SBU-1, but with fully retractable undercarriage. For some reason the Grumman design was not actually submitted to the competition but was proposed anyway. The Brewster company had up to this time merely assembled aircraft but their design had great promise. Unfortunately the new company was fated never to achieve this in the factory or in the sky, despite promise on the drawing board, a fatal handicap that grew worse and eventually resulted in the biggest foul-up in dive bomber history. Curtiss replaced the crashed XSBC-1 with another aircraft of increased performance to meet the new specifications.

Northrop's foresight was reinforced by the identical conclusions reached by both Chance Vought and Curtiss in June 1935 while their own designs were under construction, namely that the *same* design could ably fulfill both functions, and by this time the Navy itself conceded the advantages of such an idea over their earlier duplication of designs. Both firms put forward modified proposals that their XSBU-1 and XSBC-2 should carry 1,000lb bombs or additional fuel, the Navy agreed to this combining of the VB and VSB role and the resultant rationalisation of aircraft types at sea. In the case of Curtiss this meant the replacement of the existing engine in the XSBC-2 with a more powerful R-1525-82, and the designation changed to XSBC-3.

Of further considerable interest is the fact that, in addition to the single-engined designs selected for further development as listed above, the Navy was showing considerable interest in the possible potential of a twin-engined dive bomber at sea. BuAer requested the Naval Aircraft Factory to investigate the possibilities of constructing such an aircraft for dive bombing, with a higher performance than the single-engined type. However, despite some study work 39 no prototype was ever constructed, although different parts were mocked up. The proposal advanced no further.

The biplane configuration of the Great Lakes design failed to meet the tests. It was re-worked as a torpedo bomber, the XTBG-1, but failed in this role also, and with it passed the Great Lakes company, only seven years after taking over Glenn Martin's Cleveland works.

The Northrop aircraft was an entirely different proposition, and here was produced the basic design of the later Dauntless. The Northrop story is, therefore, a unique part of dive bomber history. John K. Northrop is generally acknowledged it have been one of the major innovators of aircraft design in the 1930s, founding his company at Inglewood, California, after leaving Douglas in 1932 having already established a reputation with his mailplane designs. His Gamma mailplane design of 1933 achieved the then sensational speed of 220mph but his first foray into the military field, the XFT-1 fighter for the Navy, failed due in the main to its high landing speed. His next venture was the remarkable XBT-1.

This was in a great part a progressive development of his earlier designs for Army attack bombers, like the XA-13 and XA-16 with fixed undercarriages, which gave strength but caused drag. The XBT-1 first flew in July 1933 powered by a 700hp Pratt & Whitney R-1535-66 engine and had an all-up weight of $1\frac{1}{2}$ tons. It reached a maximum speed of 212mph carrying a 1,000lb bomb load. After testing throughout the winter it was re-engined with the R-1534-94 of 825hp, with a shortened engine cowling, while the tail fin was redesigned to give a more rounded profile and enlarged. The Navy was sufficiently impressed to place a contract with Northrop in April 1936 for fifty-four BT-1s, while the Army took the A-17 version.

The BT-1 had a speed of 222mph and a range of 1,150 miles. It had semi-retractable landing gear but did not have folding wings although designed as a Navy plane. When it entered service in 1937-8 it was a significant advance, indeed it was the *only* plane in the fleet *designated* as a dive bomber. Six embarked aboard the new carrier *Enterprise,* while VB-5 aboard *Yorktown* took further deliveries in 1938. Although the maximum number in service never exceeded forty (in 1940) and by the time of Pearl Harbor had all been withdrawn, the BT-1 nonetheless was a great step forward in this field for the US Navy.

Naturally it had teething troubles. The XBT-1 had difficulties with the new hinged split-flaps attached to the trailing edge of each wing, another Northrop innovation, which, although working well during the dive, tended to cause buffeting of the horizontal tail surface when extended. Numerous provisional alterations had no effect, but the National Advisory Committee for Aeronautics (NACA) solved the problem when Project Engineer Ed Heinemann evaluated the result of a series of large-diameter holes bored in the dive flaps and found that this permitted the flaps to be extended even more in a dive, giving the desired slowing-down effect, whereas with the flaps shut, these holes made no difference to the lift. The version thus modified became the XBT-2 from which the BT-1 was developed.

The first BT-1s embarked experienced landing difficulties of a most serious nature with the bombers crashing into the barriers or going overboard. The Navy diagnosed this to the shortness of the arrestor hook and also noted that the aircraft tended to 'float' when settling down and then to stall violently at the wing tips. This was cured by installing fixed slots in the tips and lengthening the hook. Pilots assigned to the BT-1 underwent a vigorous training programme to familiarise themselves with these unhealthy characteristics. The modifications lowered the stalling speed and increased the lateral control, but it was still a tricky aircraft to land on a carrier for all that.

Solving these problems on a small order proved too much for the young firm and Northrop sold his plant in El Segundo, California, to the Douglas company in January 1938. Luckily the deal included most of the BT design team and Heinemann was therefore able to ensure continuity under the new banner.

Although it was Northrop's revolutionary design that was to prove the ultimate base for US dive bomber development, the second half of the 1930s saw the placing of production orders for a number of alternate designs, albeit in small numbers. Strangely this included an apparent retrogression, in that included in it were numbers of biplanes, despite the general trend to switch to monoplanes everywhere else (save in the artificially retarded FAA of Britain).

Table 7: US Navy Production Orders 1935-9			
Year	Manufacturer	Type	Notes
1935	Chance Vought Great Lakes	SBU-1 BG-1	Additional
1936	Curtiss Northrop Chance Vought	SBC-3 BT-1 SB2U-1	In all cases the production aircraft followed the main outlines of the experimental aircraft, but with a great increase in weight. In the SB2U-1 for example these increases involved an extra 9,171lb over original contract.
1938	Chance Vought Naval Aircraft Curtiss	SB2U-2 SBN-2 SBC-4	
1939	Chance Vought Douglas Curtiss	SBU-3 SBD-1 SBC-4	Additional

Of these types a few were notable, others were obsolete on entering service. The SBN-1 was the Naval Aircraft Factory production version of the XSBA-1. A mid-wing monoplane design, it had the modified dive flaps with Maltese cross type cut-outs instead of circular holes. They were obsolete before delivery, but some operated from *Enterprise* until 1941 before going to training duties. The aircraft had a fully retractable undercarriage. The original Brewster design, the

The Brewster XSBA-1 prototype flight testing on 2 June 1936. From this design, advanced when its first appeared, much was expected, but little or nothing resulted either with the SBN-1 or the Bermuda for the RAF.

SBA, was powered by a Wright R-1820-4 engine and carried its 500lb bomb internally for the first time. Thirty SBN-1s were built, ending their days as trainers aboard *Hornet*. The XSBC-4 and the XBT-2 had been ordered in the same year with the same power plant and hydraulic landing gear, but both were outclassed and were still-born.

The extraordinary story of the Brewster dive bomber spanned two continents and more than ten years and the end result was a huge file, many headaches but few operational aircraft. For a plane that never saw operational service Brewster's long-range 'wonder' dive bomber (known as the Buccaneer in the USA and later as the Bermuda in Britain) was to be unique in the annals of aviation history.

The XSBA-1 when it first appeared, held out so much promise that the US Navy was captivated at once and rewarded the young company with its patronage. It first flew in April 1936 but this product of the Long Island, NY, design team was from the outset beset by problems which led to the Navy taking over its design, and the result, the SBN-1, was a failure. However its successor, the SB2A, promised even more. Whereas the XSBA-1 was the fastest dive bomber in the world when it first flew, at 242mph, the adoption of the Wright XR-1820 engine with a three-bladed propeller pushed this up to 263mph in 1937. It was felt that the SB2A could only be better, and throughout 1939-40 the vastly expanded Brewster works, supported by Navy money, prepared itself for the great mass-production they knew must come. And then, in 1940, came the British, newly-converted by their desperate plight to their own invention of 1917, and Brewster's future seemed golden.

The strange story of the re-appearance, however briefly, of the biplane dive bomber in the US Navy (deliveries of the F4Bs were still being made as late as May 1938), resulted from the earlier period of wide-ranging trials. The final result of this policy was the production orders for the SBC-3 and -4 series, the world's last dive bombers for naval use built as biplanes. Like the earlier Curtiss Helldiver, the SBC-3 began its complicated life as a fighter, but whereas the name Helldiver stuck with the earlier model, and would do also with its World War II descendant, it never took to the SBC and it is always recalled by its initials and mark numbers.

The ancestor of the SBC was the Curtiss XF12C-1 two-seater fighter. Initial design work began in June 1932, resulting in the AF12C-1, No 9225, a one-off plane that combined a number of new and old concepts in an unlikely marriage. It featured a single parasol wing with a monocoque fuselage, but its all-metal appearance belied the fact that the metal covering for the wings was, unlike the fabric covering of the frame, not a solid affair. The control surfaces and wing flaps remained fabric covered. The dual cockpit was enclosed for streamlining and the undercarriage tucked away into the body housing in the Curtiss style. Powered by a single Wright 625hp R-1510-92 twin-row radial engine with flush cowling, the fact that this aircraft was a monoplane fighter at a time when the Navy still held faith with the biplane made it unique, but, by a strange quirk of fate, it then became a biplane as the rest of the world switched to monoplanes. This came about thus.

Test flying of the XF12C-1 commenced in July 1932, just when the first reactions to the biplane were beginning and resulting modifications slowed down progress. A crash a year later halted it completely and by this time the Navy had lost interest in the two-seater fighter. Curtiss re-built it as a scout and tried again, as the XS4C-1 in December 1933 and the next month, as the XSBC-1, with a Wright Cyclone R-1820-80 engine.

In September 1934 another crash took place, and by common consent when

VS-3 wingtip to wingtip. Curtiss SBC-3 Helldivers of VS-3 in immaculate line abreast on 19 July 1938.

re-building, the parasol gave way to the biplane design, the XSBC-2 (Curtiss Model 77). The leading edge flaps were omitted and the lower wing was fabric covered while the upper remained monocoque making it even more of a hybrid. To add to the confusion the aircraft retained the same Navy serial number throughout its metamorphosis. As a scout the second seat was assigned to the rear-gunner and provision was made for the rear part of the long cockpit to fold down into the fuselage. The engine became again the 700hp Wright XR-1510-2 and with this the 'new' aircraft flew in December 1935.

Tests resulted in the replacement of the engine with a 825hp Pratt & Whitney R-1535-82 Twin Wasp in March 1936, the machine becoming the XSBC-3. A production order was placed in August that year for eighty-three SBC-3s and delivery began in July 1937 to VS-5 aboard *Yorktown,* followed by VS-3 aboard *Saratoga* and VS-6 aboard *Enterprise* later. Structural changes and the adoption of the 900hp R-1820-22 engine meanwhile resulted in the XSBC-4, and, despite

Vought SB2U-1 Vindicators on the flight deck of the USS Saratoga *in February 1938. Their pre-war squadron and colour markings are shown to advantage in this shot.*

its obsolete appearance no less than 124 of these tubby biplanes were delivered to the navy between January 1938 and August 1939, the last arriving in April 1940 as the SBC-4. Top speed for the SBC-3 was 217mph and for the SBC-4 232mph; ranges were 560 and 590 miles respectively and normal bomb load was 500lb, although a 1,000lb bomb was carried by some variants. VS-2 on *Lexington* took early deliveries of the SBC-4 and the Marines received fifteen, but most subsequently went straight from factory to reserve units and by the end of 1941 all SBC-3s were ashore. Although the last shipborn SBC-4s served aboard *Hornet* with VS-8 and VB-8 at the time Pearl Harbor occurred they saw no action. But in the interim the European situation had led to a new phase in the SBC story.

A more formidable and workmanlike contender now appeared on the scene, the Vought SB2U-1 Vindicator. The Vindicator was given the nickname 'Vibrator' by Marine pilots who flew it into combat during the desperate days of 1942, but five years earlier when it began to enter service this aircraft was a welcome addition and much admired. It was responsible for some notable 'firsts', being the first monoplane bomber to enter service with the US carrier fleet, and it was fitted with folding wings to facilitate hangar stowage and shipboard usage. It was superior in some ways to its near contemporary, the BT-1, although not so advanced aerodynamically.

Ordered in October 1934 the XSB2U-1 first flew in January 1935. Its airframe was of composite construction, the wings and all movable tail surfaces being fabric covered. The considerable time lag between the testing of the XSB2U and the introduction of the SB2U-1 into service, despite Navy enthusiasm, was due to two main teething problems.

The Navy had been experimenting with a reversible propeller in order to limit diving speeds but, although fitted to the SB2U-1 and -2, it never worked satisfactorily and was never used. An alternative method was devised by Chance Vought comprising a diving flap fitted to the leading edge of the wings, consisting of a number of spars like a 'venetian blind' which were extended to right angles in the dive. Under test they in fact proved *too* efficient and full engine power had to be maintained in normal level flight to overcome this drag effect, even though they lay flush with the wing covering in this configuration. The leading edge air brakes caused severe buffeting in use and their weight, 140lb, further reduced performance. They also proved slow in operation.

The solution adopted in service was therefore to quickly lower the landing gear in the dive and the adoption of a shallower dive than normal to overcome the drag effect. Far more serious a problem was the failure of the R-1535-94 engine during dives. As these were fitted to all the new types of dive bomber then entering service the whole dive bomber concept was threatened and needed a quick solution, for the SBC-3 and BT-1 were also affected.

Under test it was shown that the master rodbearings were failing and the order went out prohibiting the new dive bombers to dive! Single plane tests in 1937 indicated the solution might be the adoption of silver for the manufacture of the bearing and eighteen SBC-3s were thus fitted, but further tests showed that this alone was not the problem. Not until March 1938 was the solution found by Pratt & Whitney who developed silver-lead bearings, and in June these were released for production. Later indium was added to prevent the lead dissolving while the engines were being 'run-in' and these bearings were subsequently used throughout the war in US radial engines.

The SB2U-2 Vindicator had a maximum speed of 257mph at 11,000ft and a maximum bombload of 1,500lb, although 1,000lb was the norm. This version could carry two 50 gallon drop tanks giving a range of 700 miles. A special version (SB2U-3) was developed as a long-range aircraft for the Marines, with extra armour protection and larger extra fuel tanks. A total of fifty-seven of this variant were built, and were in the words of one historian, '. . . literally a flying fuel tank'. Performance suffered accordingly, but this type set another record when the USMC Vindicators made the longest non-stop, overwater mass flight for a single-engined aircraft during a mission to reinforce Midway Island in 1942, when they covered some 1,200 miles.

Altogether 240 production Vindicators were built of the three American variants and various foreign adaptations, of which more later, and it proved a rugged and popular aircraft in service. It was as fast as the later SBD in fact, although not so versatile. The SB2U was in widespread service during 1938-41 and on outbreak of war in December 1941 there were still sixty-two afloat with *Lexington, Ranger, Saratoga* and *Wasp,* with a further forty-five with the USMC. Most saw very little action before being replaced by the Douglas Dauntless, but the Marines flew their Vindicators into immortality at the Battle of Midway.

Meanwhile the transition of the Northrop XBT-2 into what was to become the Douglas SBD was proceeding under the design team of Ed Heinemann, now chief engineer of Douglas. In all some twenty-one different sets of tail surfaces and twelve different lateral control variations were tested during this period. The Wright XR-1820-32 engine was adopted and the fuselage re-designed to accommodate it, giving the distinctive SBD profile. These changes not only added some 35mph to the speed, but also improved handling characteristics. The original Northrop slot arrangement had proved less satisfactory in practice than expected and was complicated to fit, so Douglas therefore developed an alternative wing spoiler, a 1ft half-round rod attached to the leading edges of the wings 3ft away from the fuselage. This was fitted in the XBT-2 and SBD-1 and -2. The testing of the XBT-2 in the Langley Memorial Aeronautical lab wind tunnels resulted in the smoothing of the BT-1 profile into the genesis of the SBD. When in January 1938 Douglas took over the project it was re-designated as the XSBD-1.

The evolution of technique and a careful study of comparative values of dive versus level bombing was to produce the hard facts which further convinced the US Navy that it was on the right track, while, conversely, the US Army continued to blow hot and cold on the subject. The line of thought then developing is reflected in two studies from the late 1930s from which we extract a few relative points.

The ACTS Individual Research Assignment paper by Capt Vernon E. Megee, USMC, is the first of these illuminating studies. It included the following points. On the origins of dive bombing he correctly noted that this began in World War I 'when it was discovered by ground strafing pursuit pilots that releasing bombs during shallow dives was conductive to greater accuracy.' He claimed that little was done during the following decade although a few services toyed with the idea despite the risks involved in terminal velocity dives. He claimed that high altitude, high speed dive bombing originated with the US Navy and the arrival of the Curtiss Helldiver of 1930.

The general lack of interest shown by the Army was noted: 'The Air Corps has conducted some dive bombing experiments with pursuit airplanes in recent years, but has never evolved any tactics for the employment of dive bombers as a class. At present there are no airplanes within the Army Air Force capable of being used as diver bombers.' Strangely enough he claimed that Great Britain and Italy placed, '. . . a considerable emphasis on the employment of dive bombing squadrons for coast defense missions' and that their tactics, '. . . follow closely those in current use by the US Navy'. He could not have been more wrong in his choice, had he picked Germany and Japan at this time his thesis might have stood up better!

Of more interest and accuracy are his descriptions of the individual and unit techniques then employed by the Americans. The first was the 'half-roll'. When the target became visible under the trailing edge of the wing the airplane was rolled slowly into an inverted position and the nose dropped to bear on the target. This permitted abrupt entry into the dive from minimum speed, facilitated smooth control of the airplane during the initial stage of approach and was well adapted for low altitude bombing of precision targets. Its disadvantage lay in lack of surprise and vulnerability to AA fire. The method was considered suitable for individual bombing from column.

Second was the 'push-over'. This allowed a formation to use an initial point for entering the dive at considerable distance from the objective at extreme altitudes. The initial stage was in the form of a shallow dive, or descending spiral of varying radius and speed. When the correct position over the target was reached, at an altitude of around 8,000ft, the airplane pushed over into the final steep dive for aim and release of bombs. 'This is the method in current use by the US Navy for formation dive bombing attacks against naval objectives. It is considered flexible as to direction and angle of approach, and provides the maximum security against anti-aircraft gun fire.'

He revealed that the usual US Navy practice was to release the smaller bombs at about 2,000ft, recovering above 1,000ft; with the larger bombs release was about 3,000ft. Column of sections was the usual bombing formation. In individual bombing from column approach the pilots entered the dive at intervals varying from 5 to 10 seconds and varied the direction of their approach to avoid the slip-stream of preceding aircraft. With formation attacks the wing men fanned out as the initial point was approached and dived with the leader converging on target. The bombs were released in salvo by sections on signal of the leader, or when the leader's bombs were seen to clear the racks. Recovery was made out of AA range, forming up on the leader once more and climbing to high altitude.

This detailed paper then describes the methods used in combat, particular emphasis being placed on the destruction of enemy aircraft carriers, with cruisers, destroyers, submarines and auxillaries being secondary objectives. Against battleships the aim of the converging attack of three or four squadrons of dive bombers was to confuse and flatten the AA positions for the torpedo bombers to deliver the *coup de grace*. Softening up attacks in amphibious landings naturally attracted attention of the Marine pilot and also the value of the dive bomber in annihilating '. . . sensitive points on the enemy's lines of communications, beyond the range of supporting gunfire, important supply installations, massive fortifications and heavy gun emplacements.'

The US Navy viewpoint was that: 'Dive bombers are of particular tactical value against precision and manoeuvering targets. The radius of action, and the tactics employed for this class of bombardment aviation are analogous to those prescribed by the Army Air Corps for attack units.' Stressing the fact that the need to withstand extra stresses had imposed range limitations on the dive bomber type, MeGee stated that, because of this: 'The Army has not felt that the advantages of the dive bomber offset the performance limitations heretofore inherent in the design of the airplane. Consequently, no provision for the inclusion of the type in the tactical organisation of the Air Force *has ever been made.*'

He thought that with the new developments in the pipeline, the Northrop dive bomber in particular, the limitations would vanish. On accuracy MeGee

Table 8: USA Comparison of Accuracy Dive and Level Bombing		
Type of target ship	Percentage of hits Level bombing	Percentage of hits Dive bombing
Battleships (Direct Hits)	13.00	40.00
Battleship (Within 30ft)	23.00	53.00
Heavy Cruisers (At speed)	4.24	18.60
Destroyers (At speed)	1.40	7.80

produced impressive figures on comparative tests with horizontal bombing showing that on average accuracy was three times as great.

The conclusions reached were obvious, dive bombing reduced the radial error of horizontal bombing against *stationary* targets by at least half. Against *moving* targets the difference was even more striking, '. . . the dive bomber is *at least four times as effective* as the horizontal bomber carrying the same weight of bombs.'

On the debit side was the vulnerability claimed against dive bombing, but because of the agreed truth that '. . . the horizontal bomber at 10,000ft, flying a steady course and speed to the bomb release line, is a better target for the director-controlled guns than is the dive bomber during its erratic, high-speed approach and bewildering final dive', the difference was not as great as the USAAF (or the RAF for that matter) continued to claim.

Table 9: USA Comparison of Vulnerability To AA Fire 1937		
Type of attack	Details	Percentage ratio of losses expected
Horizontal Bomber	Above 8,000ft	20
Dive Bomber	Below 2,000ft	30
Dive Bomber	Converging attacks from several different angles to divide the AA fire	15

Even if losses were the same at 20 per cent, the dive bomber for this loss would score at least four times more hits than the horizontal bomber, and, although MeGee did not go into the cost factor of machines and crew totals, it is obvious that both in terms of money and lives, a two-man dive bomber destroyed while scoring four hits is a better return than a seven-man heavy bomber destroyed achieving one hit.

Two years after the appearance of the MeGee paper another attempt was made to analyse the point and counter-point between the two different methods of bombing, this was the Overfield study on dive bombing compared with level flight bombing.

In many of the areas covered Lt Overfield's study goes over the same ground as MeGee. In section 1, Equipment, he goes into greater detail, listing the advantages and disadvantages of the two types, dive bomber and heavy bomber, including variations in range and the effect of the endurance on the crews. On this score he concluded that the range of the horizontal bomber was *twice* that of the dive bomber. However being carrier-based the actual range was potentially much higher than a machine tied to a shore base, although he did not dismiss this vital point. The stress factor would be proportionally higher for carrier-based dive bombers. He also examined the carrying capacity and range figures for both these types.

On size of bomb carried the dive bomber was restricted, but despite all these considerations Overfield still concluded that the dive bomber was the type that suited the Navy best, for the carrier itself gave it the limitless range the 47

Table 10: US Navy : Range and Bomb Load Comparisons 1938						
	Horizontal Bombing			Dive Bombing		
	Patrol Bombers		Torpedo Bombers	Fighters	Scout Bomber	Dive Bomber
Range (miles)	1,200	2,020	600	600	650	500
No of bombs and sizes (lb)	2 x 1,000	2 x 1,000	2 x 500	2 x 100	2 x 100	1 x 500
	4 x 500	12 x 100	1 x 1,000		1 x 500	1 x 1,000
			12 x 100		1 x 1,000	·

At this time the load ration of the USAAF Long-range B-17 was estimated at approximately 4.8 to 2 over the then current USN Patrol Bombers.

conventional land-anchored heavy bomber lacked. (This point was proven in 1942, for only by flying them from aircraft carriers could Mitchell bombers reach Japan.) On accuracy alone it was the best bet, this factor after all being the ultimate facet on which the whole crux of any battle would rest. Penetration power of bombs against battleship armour was not gone into; here the altitude bomber might have the edge, although the dive process itself added to the terminal velocity of the bomb (TV) which made for such penetration. Although he admitted that peacetime data made true comparison difficult, Overfield concluded that on what evidence there was, ie gunnery scores and manoeuver rules, the record of the dive bomber was far superior:

> . . . the dive bomber is superior in accuracy when the fire is directed toward precision targets such as bridges, trestles, cross-roads, single ships at sea etc. The horizontal bomber is effective against these precision targets only by formation bombing when one or more bombs *might* be placed on the objective by means of salvo fire.

On vulnerability from defensive fire, Overfield's opinions were similar to MeGee, both types could gain invulnerability to a similar degree if surprise was achieved, but the dive bomber was the more likely of the two to achieve it. Predicted and directed AA fire was more deadly against level bombers, barrage more deadly against the dive bomber in theory. Touching on combat conditions in the Spanish Civil War he mentioned the engine cut-out, glide-approach method as having some possibilities to this end.

> It is quite obvious that the dive bomber has greater freedom of maneouver and, due to its high speed dive and rapid change in angle relative to opposing guns, is exposed to accurate fire for a lesser period of time.

On actual training methods Rear Adm Holmberg, then a young Ensign, described how he flew a SBC Helldiver in 1940 and they attacked a spar towed by a destroyer off the west coast of California. Such methods were rudimentary but common the world over.

By this date the dive bomber was the backbone, with the torpedo bomber, of the US Navy and Marine Corps air components. They had the modern aircraft coming into service, with even better planes planned. They had the experience of almost two decades of experiment and design behind them and a wealth of expertise. Just as vital as these points, the Navy and its pilots *believed* in dive bombing and they practiced hard at it.

8
A WILFUL BLINDNESS
The RAF experience: Trials, evaluations and findings, 1932-39

At the end of 1932 the Sutton Bridge accident caused a temporary halt to the RAF experiments with dive bombing tests, until safer measures could be adopted. Once the clearance problems with the bomb racks had been solved by new equipment, modifications and rules giving shallow dive bombing only as a requirement, the way was clear for further limited experimentation.

In November 1933 tests were initiated at Martlesham Heath to study the effects of dive bombing with mixed bomb loads, its effects on the stability of the aircraft and on the pilot, and to determine to what extent the bomb-aimer, as in level bombing, was able to aid dive bombing, if at all.

The aircraft used was a Hawker Hart (K2466) and special attention was paid to load distribution and weights to see their effect on the plane's centre of gravity. With a bomb load of four 112lb bombs the Hart's all-up weight was 4,570lb. The limitations of the trials were an angle of dive between 50^0 and 70^0 only, calculated by the bubble inclinometer fitted in front of the windscreen. Maximum crankshaft speed was set at 3,300rpm. In the series of trials carried out in February 1934 no bombs were actually released, only varying loads carried and distributed about the plane to see the effect on a range of tail settings and throttle positions. In each case four bombs were carried. These were distributed equally, with two bombs on the starboard racks and one on the inner port rack and finally with two bombs on the starboard rack, the port rack being left clear.

The Hart was fitted with a non-adjustable Flettner trimmer strip to the trailing edge of the rudder, set 3^0 to port, but this was later removed as it was found that the aircraft had no abnormal turning tendency in normal conditions of flight without it, and once removed there was a marked improvement in rudder control at all speeds. Then the whole series of tests, diving only, was carried out with no untoward difficulties being encountered whatsoever, the report stating that: 'There was no difficulty in operating the tail actuating gear in the dives and no vibration, flutter or control surface instability.'

As for the effect on the pilot, dire warnings of which had been made, the report stated that: 'Accelerations of 5.5g occurred in recovery in one or two cases without the pilot experiencing any discomfort. In an angle of 50^0 at 265mph 5.5g occurred in recovery with a height loss of 800ft and a similar blackout from a 70^0 dive at 280mph resulted in a height loss of 500ft.' This was considered very serious '. . . care must be taken in the recovery from the dive to avoid the imposition of unduly normal accelerations'. It concluded that: 'It is necessary to allow *not less* than 1,000ft for recovery in order that the acceleration shall not exceed 4g.'

This was a limitation of the dive bomber, but not final rejection. The next series of tests was conducted in March and this time bombs were dropped in singles and groups utilising the traditional prone-lying bomb-aimer to effect the drop.

All dives were commenced from 10,000ft and recovery commenced at 5,000ft, some 1,000ft being lost in recovery, so this was really 'high' dive bombing compared to US Navy practice at the same period. In dives of 50^0 235mph was reached, in those of 70^0 a speed of 285mph. In all cases the maximum crankshaft speed of 3,300rpm was met by a pre-setting of the throttle.

Table 11: RAF Trials at Martlesham Heath 1934		
Dive No	Angle of dive (degrees)	112lb bombs release sequence — number of bombs and positions
1	50	1 - port outer
2	50	1 - port inner
3	50	1 - starboard inner
4	50	1 - starboard outer
5	50	2 - port
6	50	2 - starboard
7	70	2 - port
8	70	2 - starboard
9	65	4
10	70	2 - one port, one starboard

The first four dives were made in one flight, the aircraft climbing back to 10,000ft after each release ready for the next, but in dive No 9 the aircraft landed with bombs on the port wing still in place. It was noted that in all these dives the release of the bombs had no noticeable affect on the behaviour of the aircraft. The prone bomb-aimer it stated, was just so much useless weight, for in dive bombing '. . . the pilot automatically becomes the bomb aimer directing the aircraft towards the target'. They noted that there was a strong tendency considerably to over-estimate the angle at which the aircraft was being dived, which could be cured by fitting an inclinometer. Other than that it was suggested that pilots use much shallower angles than those used in the tests. In other words, true dive bombing was out. They also recommended that the bomb-release switch be mounted at the throttle or control column, so that the pilot did not need to take his eyes off the target as he did when it was mounted on the dashboard, and an electrically operated bomb-release switch was necessary.

They concluded that dive bombing depended entirely on the judgement of the pilot to select the correct moment to enter the dive and his own skill at holding the plane on target. Once committed he could not take his eye off the target without seriously affecting accuracy.

The selection of the Hawker Hart for these tests becomes clearer when one examines the design produced by that manufacturer in response to Air Ministry specification G4/31 issued in July 1931. The original specification called for a general purpose light bomber for all-round Army co-operation work, with one of the many requirements being the capability to dive bomb. As the Hart was fulfilling just that function and had shown its ability to dive bomb at angles up to 70⁰ it is not surprising that Hawker came up with what was, in effect, an improved version of that aircraft, but stronger and larger. It had the same bomb load but greater strength to permit this to be used in dive bombing. Thus H.F. King is certainly correct when he states that: 'This two-seater biplane of 1935 can be regarded as Britain's first specialised dive bomber.'

The PV4 first flew at Brooklands on 6 December 1934 by a single 800hp Bristol Pegasus III engine, which was replaced in May 1935 with a Pegasus X of 820hp, and tested at Martlesham between June and October. By the time it appeared however the RAF had decided to drop the dive bombing requirement and this solitary prototype remained the sole example of the Air Ministry's first hesitant step to build a dive bomber as such.

Thus the RAF continued to look upon dive bombing as a sideline which any aircraft designed for general Army co-operation work could perform when called upon and Hawker produced several offshoots of the Hart to this effect. Specification G23/33 of 1933 for example produced the Hardy, a variant of the

What some consider to be the first 'purpose-built' dive bomber for the RAF was the prototype PV4 built by Hawkers in 1934 and tested with two different engines in 1935. It was certainly stressed for dive bombing but, although successful, was not put into production.

Hart day bomber, and Audax Army co-operation aircraft, with tropical equipment for policing the Empire. Forty-seven of these were built and served in Iraq from October 1934. Strangely enough they actually became one of the very few RAF aircraft to carry out dive bombing, but this was many years later with 237 (Rhodesia) squadron in Italian Somaliland and Eritrea in 1940.

Specification P4/34 was the RAF's biggest step forward in securing a high-performance dive bomber monoplane before the outbreak of war. Fairey and Hawker competed and the best design was the Hawker Henley.

The requirement of February 1934 still did not go all-out for a pure dive bomber, but only called for a light bomber for army support. However it *was* to be fully stressed for dive bombing with a full bomb load, and a speed of 300mph was mentioned. As a stable mate of the Hurricane fighter the same power plant was naturally utilised to achieve this, the Rolls Royce Merlin, which, although successful and the logical answer, in effect doomed the Henley for, with limited engine supply and fighters in urgent need, it was not possible to produce both aircraft.

Many of the assembly jigs for the Henley were those used for the Hurricane, but it was not just the shortage of engines but also of the Totol constant-speed propellers. The Henley was a two-seater mid-wing monoplane with capacity for four 500lb bombs on underwing racks. The Merlin II engine of 1,030hp gave it a speed of 270mph and a range of 940 miles, a very advanced aircraft indeed for its day. The first prototype (K5115) flew in March 1937, but by this time the dive bombing aspect was purely academic for the Air Ministry had dropped this part of the specification towards the end of 1935. A total of 200 Henleys were eventually built, but used merely as target tugs while the biplane Hectors went into action!

The promising Henley therefore remained the enigmatic dive bomber that 'might-have-been' for the RAF, as the distinguished historian Owen Thetford was to lament: 'There will always be speculation as to why the high performance Henley (of which the RAF had 122 in service in September 1939) was never issued to first-line light bomber squadrons as it could carry 750lb of bombs and was much superior to the Battle.'

Other designs which fell by the wayside at this time included aircraft like the Westland PV7 built to specification G4/31, which called for a monoplane capable of being utilised as a dive bomber *and* a torpedo carrier. The PV7 was a

51

Another dive bomber project for the RAF which never happened. This is the Westland PV7, shown here without engine or covering. This high-wing parasol bomber never went beyond the initial experimental stage and the whole project was soon dropped as dive bombing fell further out of favour with the RAF in the thirties.

The closest the RAF ever got to producing a first-rate high-performance dive bomber pre-war was the abortive Hawker Henley project. Here is seen the prototype Henley. Finally the overwhelming prejudice against such an aircraft relegated this aircraft to the lowly role of target tug while hundreds of the inferior Fairey Battle attack planes were built instead.

two-seat high-wing aircraft with capacity for two 500lb bombs and two 250lb bombs. In view of the trials already described it is relevant to find that bomb aiming was to be carried out from a prone position below the pilot!

Also rejected was the Fairey P4/34. This company had received similar response to their P27/32 design after carrying out much study into the problems associated with dive bombing. On the PV4/34 the bomb load was mounted on external wing crutches with the carriers themselves recessed, which did away with the heavy ejection gear for under-fuselage designs.

While the Fairey project was still apparently a viable possibility, the lack of any guidance for private firms on dive bombing from the Air Ministry led to an exchange of letters. Thus Fairey wrote: 'The lack of any staff information in connection with the above manoeuvre [dive bombing] has led us to initiate a technical investigation into the problem'.

From experience with the P26/32 and P4/34 Fairey stated that dive bombing with modern high performance aircraft was only possible with the aid of flaps or some other means to restrict terminal speed. For both designs they proposed incorporating a standard form of split flap to reduce this '. . . and if it is desired to reduce the diving speed the obvious course is to make use of the flaps as air brakes'. They realised the additional burden of extra tail weight this would entail, but for the P4/34 for example they pointed out the following: terminal speed with flaps normal: between 450 and 500mph; with flaps down: 230mph.

The methods employed by RAF Hart aircraft in 1935 were listed as follows:

a The aircraft entered the dive at 100-120mph (just below cruising speed) with the throttle left a quarter open in the dive. The tactical approach phase was from 10,000ft down to 5 or 6,000ft. From there the final attack dive went in after the aircraft was correctly positioned in relation to the target. The final dive continued down to 2,000ft when the bombs were released and pull-out started. Entry was usually sideways not by pushing the nose straight down.

b Upper limits depended on visibility, cloud base etc. An undetected approach was the important thing. In clear weather dives from 10,000ft to 5,000ft were found suitable. It was considered that the final attack dive should be as short as possible, 3,000ft being the best.

c On angle of dive it was stated that: 'In the approach phase [the dive angle] is relatively unimportant and is dictated primarily by the need of reaching the required point quickly'. A 25^0-35^0 angle was taken as the mean. In the attack the dive should *not be too steep* as this led to magnification of any initial error '. . . and thus may easily lead to over-the-vertical dives'. Conversely too flat an angle made it harder to keep the target in view. A sarcastic dig at the US Navy methods is found here. 'There appears to be no advantage in the so-called "hell-dive" vertically over the target for this reason among others'. This point is important to understand subsequent RAF attitudes.

d The duration of the dive depended on the speed attained, in the Hart it was 280mph which meant 3,000ft. The shortest time possible was recommended for future work.

e 2,000ft was recommended as the best height for bomb release although it was admitted '. . . accuracy falls off rapidly as height of release increases'.

f Speed in the dive was: '. . . an unnecessary factor since no additional penetration worth consideration can be acquired by bomb dropping by this method. Speed affected vulnerability but a speed of 300mph was considered suitable to cover this factor'.

Mention of penetration power is interesting and we shall return to that point in due course. The minute concluded as it had begun, on angle of dive considerations: 'If this feature can be examined it may be found that future dive   53 bombing (*sic*) attack will allow of flatter angles of dive at speeds of say 350mph, thus easing the loads due to TV speeds and pull out conditions.'

All these points were subsequently incorporated into a memorandum by the Scientific and Technical Branch, which was subsequently modified and amended over the years. The DTS found it '. . . a very useful paper . . . .' More important were his subsequent remarks: 'It is a great disappointment to me that the Vickers 027/34 was cancelled, as this promised to be a really high speed aeroplane, and we should have been able to solve many of these problems with it in a full scale manner'. He did not share fully Ops opinion of dive bombing. 'I have always held the view, which was confirmed as the result of the numerous discussions during my visit to the United States, that really a dive bomber must be *designed* as such. That is, one cannot just take any aeroplane and expect to use it as a dive bomber. The Americans were emphatic about this and I am sure they are right.' He continued: '. . . our new Medium Bombers such as the Battle and Blenheim cannot be looked upon as dive bombers.' He would have liked to have had the chance of pushing ahead with the development of a true dive bomber to explore all the problems involved, 'But for lack of design capacity, and the crowding up of other requirements, I think I should have done this'. He expressed the hope that developments in the Fleet Air Arm would compensate for this lack.

However the DTS viewpoint was a minority one and subsequent developments in this field in the RAF proceeded exactly the opposite to his recommendations with the medium bombers, and especially the Battle, grossly over-produced as it would be in the years ahead, being constantly tried out as make-shift dive bombers, despite his warning that it would not work. A specialised dive bomber was therefore abandoned. Again the lectures delivered at Camberley Staff College between 1931 and 1934, and later expanded and published in book form by Wg Cdr Slessor, more accurately reflect the official RAF line on this subject.

His main thesis was that the aeroplane was not a battle-field weapon. On dive bombers he did at least make an important distinction of the type:

> Assault action, however, should not be confused with dive bombing. The latter is a special technique, wherein the bomber makes his attack coming down from a considerable height at a very high speed, aiming the aeroplane at the target, and releasing the bomb at a relatively low altitude — from 500 to 1,500ft; it is a method which is likely to become increasingly popular for engaging strongly defended objectives where the presence of anti-aircraft artillery makes accurate precision bombing from a height a matter of increasing difficulty and danger; but it is a method quite distinct from assault action . . . .

In April 1936 a further detailed paper was submitted and it is interesting to note how true dive bombing is hardly considered at all, and when it is, usually as something undesirable or impractical. It began by stating that, with the advent of high-speed aircraft of clean aerodynamic design, it was necessary to reconsider the technique of dive bombing attacks. The current position with regard heights and angles were re-examined, bomb release and speed were listed and the following data recorded accurately after recently conducted trials against the Chatham Float target. These were compared with data on the dive bomber fighter designs submitted for the 027/34 specification for the Navy. 'Some very accurate bombing was obtained in these trials, and it would appear that angles of dive between 30^0 and 65^0 in these trials should cover all contingencies of attack in the future.'

Table 12: Comparison of Dive Bomber Designs for RAF 1936					
Flap setting (from 5,000ft)	Aircraft Speed (mph)	Angle of dive (degrees)	Speed attained (mph)		
			Vickers	Blackburn	Avro
Normal	200	30	282	270	255
Normal	200	45	297	300	320
Down	150	70	231	240	215
Increase in weight due to flaps (in lb)			70	150	160

On penetration by the SAP bombs then in use it was estimated that at high speed a 45⁰ dive was the *least* which would bring the bomb within the required angle of strike when released at 1,500ft. The conclusion reached after considering the tactical aspects of diving with the flaps lowered or normal was '. . . with great reluctance, that in diving attacks, aircraft of clean aerodynamic design will reach too high a velocity to make recovery from 1,500ft reasonably safe and certain, and that it will be necessary to apply some form of air brake to check speed.' This meant utilising flaps or lowering the undercarriage as the Americans found later with the Vindicator. It was admitted however that the steeper the dive, within reason, without a substantial increase in speed, the better was the sighting view, which in turn led to increased accuracy of bombing.

It was recommended that in any future aircraft designed with dive bombing in mind it must be capable of making retarded dives from 5,000ft, commencing at 200mph to 1,500ft at an angle of 65⁰ without exceeding an airspeed of 260mph. Trials with a medium bomber produced estimated effects of using split trailing edge flaps which opened equally above and below the chord of the plane and eliminated the torsional stresses. In view of earlier remarks about their unsuitability it is interesting to note that these figures refer to the Battle!

Table 13: Fairey Battle Diving Tests Using Split Flaps 1936				
Angle of dive in degrees	Pullout height (ft)	Speed at pullout (mph)	Height lost in recovery (ft)	Height on the regaining of level flight (ft)
30	3,000	280	230	2,770
30	2,500	296	260	2,240
30	1,500	320	280	1,220
45	3,000	292	590	2,410
45	2,500	308	640	1.860
45	1,500	338	760	740

On 9 April the ninth meeting of the Bombing Committee was held at the Air Ministry and on the agenda was dive bombing. Some revealing statements were made and future policy guidelines issued, from which we shall extract a few of the more notable ones. Although the bombing trials against the target ship *Centurion* had shown great improvement over those of 1935, Gp Capt Guilfoye put this down mainly to the lower release height of the bombs, the flexibility of the methods used and good leadership. Discussing the time interval between individual aircraft Wg Cdr Walker who had led No 57 squadron in the 1934 trials stated he tried for 3 seconds and No 33 squadron practised on the same scale. Flexibility was the main consideration and instead of the normal three-flights-of-four formation, or the newer four-flights-of-three, Walker asked that six-flights-of-two be considered. The Admiralty representatives said that this would certainly make defensive fire more difficult.

On diving angles it was stated that No 801 (FF) squadron with Nimrod and

Hart aircraft were more flexible than No 33 squadron, and their angle of dive was a little steeper. They also favoured attack in succession from astern the target ship rather than No 33s converging attacks by each half of the squadron from opposite directions. On training it was stated that a pilot could attain his maximum efficiency after having dropped 100 bombs in dives. The maximum angle of dive as laid down was given as 70^0 but the DCAS, Air Vice Marshall C.L. Courtney, considered this could be reduced, '. . . as aircraft would very rarely dive at such an angle.' It was therefore agreed that the *new maximum angle* laid down for the RAF should be only 50^0. This obviously ruled out true dive bombing.

Lowest limit for bomb release was fixed at 1,500ft and as for sighting the RAF still regarded that '. . . anything in the nature of a complicated sight for dive bombing was impracticable . . .' according to Mr F.W. Meredith. He recommended a simple method utilising two foresights, one to indicate direction of aircraft the other where the bomb would go. A signal lamp linked to the altimeter would give bomb-release indication and the method would be limited to down-wind bombing. While agreeing this was better than no sight at all the Navy representative held out for a more elaborate sight and a sub-committee was set up accordingly.

Also recommended was an angle of dive recorder and a height recorder. The three Navy men still felt however that '. . . there was a necessity for a more thorough analysis and co-relation of the various factors affecting a successful dive bombing attack.' It was stated that '. . . dive bombing attacks were regarded with some concern by the Army, whereas from the Naval point of view such attacks were considered *easier to repel than those from high altitudes.*' This is rather a different viewpoint than that being expressed elsewhere in the Navy at this time, Capt Stephen Roskill, himself an AA gunnery expert, cites the C-in-C Mediterranean at this period, for example, as recognising that the Navy had no effective defence against the dive bomber, and hard experience in 1940-2 would appear to bear this latter view out.

The use of the Aldis sight again came up, despite the findings of the 1918 trials. Since then the Air Ministry had restricted its use against ground targets below 1,000ft but in 1937 there was a flurry of exchanges on this issue. One Wg Cdr wrote in February 'As diving bombing aircraft pull out of their dives above 1,000ft authority is requested for pilots to use Aldis sights during these dives . . . .' The Director of Training noted that as 'High Diving' bombing release was in fact about 2,000ft there was no objection, while the CO of No 2 (Bomber) Group stated flatly that the use of the Aldis Sight for dive bombing was not considered to be of any practical advantage. He pointed out that accurate dive bombing depended on knowledge of the correct angle of dive, characteristics of bombs and the estimation of wind strength, the latter being a matter of experience which could not be judged prior to commencing the dive and drift could not be observed. The use of the Aldis necessitated a pre-determined point of aim and this would prevent pilots observing their position relative to the target. In dive bombing therefore the use of the Aldis sight '. . . would render dive bombing *more inaccurate*'.

Further 'Urgent Trials' in dive bombing were held by the Special Duty Flight (K1999) and an Audax (K3080). Using LC 250lb bombs the tests were:

a Dive bombing from 6,000ft for release at 2,000ft
b Diving from 2,000ft to 250ft, pulling out and releasing bombs when level.

The bombs were carried on the inner carriers only, diving speed was kept below 290mph or engine speed of 3,300rpm.

On 18 December 1937 Wg Cdr Training, made amendments to standing instructions with regard to the break-away phase on completion of dive bombing:

a On pulling out pilots were not to climb away but flatten out at ground level into a gentle turn, taking advantage of topographical conditions to keep as low as possible to void giving AA defence a nil-deflection shot.
b Straight flight in these conditions was to be avoided and no climb made until well clear of defences.

In 1936 four Hind squadrons carried out high dive bombing tests with angles of dive up to 70^0 and the average result was 41yd error. In 1937 eleven Hind squadrons carried out high diving bombing with the angle of dive restricted to 50^0 as a method of preliminary training for the advent of monoplanes. The average mean error went up to 70yd.

As monoplanes that were in no way designed for dive bombing were all that were available, because of earlier policy decisions, in 1938 six Fairey Battle squadrons carried out high dive bombing tests. The average error bounded up to 130yd. The same year two Blenheim squadrons carried out *shallow* dive bombing (ie at angle of dive under 50^0). The average error went up yet again to 146yd. When two other Blenheim squadrons tried out high dive bombing they brought the average error back to 121yd, but this was still *three times* that achieved three years earlier with more traditional methods. The bankruptcy of the RAF policy to discard building of designed dive bombers was obvious to all.

Table 14: RAF Dive Bombing Trials with Hawker Hinds 1937-8				
Type of target	Angle of dive	Release height (ft)	No of bombs	Average error (yds)
Stationary	Steep	1,000	135	35
		2,000	459	54
		3,000	142	82
	Shallow	1,000	99	38
		2,000	303	61
		3,000	102	98
Armoured Motor Boats (Straight course)	Shallow	2,000	35	44
(Avoiding action)		2,000	63	40
Radio-Controlled Battleship (Straight course)	Shallow	2,000	44	82
(Avoiding action)		2,000	31	53

On 4 February 1938 a meeting was held at the HQ, No 1 (Bombing) Squadron at Abingdon chaired by Wg Cdr E.R. Openshaw with representatives from No 15(B) squadron and the RAE together with Air Ministry officials. Sqn Ldr C.D. Adams described the method of dive bombing used by No 15 squadron during the special trials of 1937-38. He re-emphasised that as *no syllabus of training or any sort of theory existed,* they had evolved their own methods on the spot. Their theory incorporated keeping the altitude of the aircraft constant and determining aiming marks on the ground to allow for the drift of the aircraft during the dive and the 'fall away' of the bomb, and they extended the principal to cover moving targets.

In turn the RAE representative, Mr Meredith, gave an account of the way they were approaching the same problems. They dived their aircraft in such a manner

57

Aircraft placed at point 'X' (starting point of dive) and aimed at point P1, which is a pre-determined distance up-wind from target. Wind was then allowed to blow aircraft towards target. During the whole dive aircraft is *heading* in a vertical plane but *tracking* towards target at an angle dependant on wind strength.

Aircraft is placed at a point in the same vertical plane as the target. Nose is then pointed at point P1, which is indicated by a graticule drawn on pilot's windscreen and which must be kept in position so that it cuts the target during the whole dive. Aircraft then *tracks* towards target and *head* at an angle sufficient to counteract the wind blowing it away. Aircraft is then in a skidding dive tracking towards target.

that the projection of its track on the ground passed through the target at a given height (indicated by a light operated by a contacting altimeter). The bomb was released by a gyro-operated mechanism after the aircraft had pulled out through the angle necessary to compensate for the 'fall away' and they used a scribed grid on the pilot's windshield.

The final suggestion was for a combination of both methods, RAE theory and

No 15 squadron practical experience, to be evolved and a Hind was equipped for a month-long trial period with a graticulated windscreen, sensitive altimeter and indicator lights with an automatic release, controlled by gyro. Following these tests the first RAF *Theory of Dive Bombing* was compiled and issued.

Since 1932 the minimum height regulation for diving attacks had been 1,000ft, but in June 1938 permission was sought for this to be lowered to 500ft '. . . as this form of training is carried out by Hind squadrons.' As late as July 1939 there was an effort to stop camera gun practices involving diving near to airfields, but the majority of groups were against this ban until various trials then underway with *shallow dive bombing* had been completed, it being pointed out that: 'If low level and shallow dive bombing is to be permitted, high level bombing might also be allowed, in which case present practice would continue with the exception of high dive bombing *which is now practically obsolete.*'

Hitler was now doing more or less as he pleased in central Europe and had made no attempt to hide the strength of the Luftwaffe during the occupation of Czechoslovakia or in Spain. At the time of the Munich crisis of 1938 the following appeared in a minute from HQ No 2 (Bombing) Group: '. . . it is pointed out that low dive bombing *does not form part of the syllabus in any kind of bomber aircraft*', and it was added: 'it is appreciated that shallow dive bombing is still in the experimental stage for the monoplane type medium bomber.'

As the last year of peace ran out the RAF spent a great deal of time and effort trying to devise a system whereby its single and twin-engined medium bombers, never designed for the job in the first place, could conduct a limited form of 'shallow dive bombing', despite earlier doubts on both sides of the Atlantic about the wisdom of such a policy.

True dive bombers continued to be rejected officially by the Air Ministry up the very eve of the war. Extracts from the first meeting of the Bombing Policy Sub-Committee on 22 March 1938 revealed some interest in dive bombing but, despite practical experience in America, Germany and Japan, the RAF was still convinced the technique would not be possible for them. C-in-C Bomber Command for example stated that it appeared as if recent developments had put steep dive bombing out of the question. He went on to say that although he would certainly like to have aircraft capable of steep diving, as this method had many advantages, he understood that, for technical reasons, it was impracticable without complicating aircraft and losing other important characteristics and advantages. If this was in fact the case he did not think it worth while following up.

The DTD then outlined three methods which were being developed that would allow steep dive bombing to be tried again:

1 Use of special flaps to retard speed of dive as with the Blackburn Skua.
2 A new type flap being fitted to the Battle which obviated necessity for any increase in strength of tails or wings.
3 An airscrew which would get to a very fine pitch in order to retard speed of dive.

Shallow dive bombing was examined and found to be more their taste, although it was stated that it still required full investigation from the technical standpoint, in the hope that they could use existing light bomber types. The C-in-C stated that: 'He was not clear whose job it was to initiate these investigations or what establishment should undertake them.' It was agreed that tests should be carried out under scientific investigation, but DTD and DDRD/Arm stated that although trials had been on the Martlesham programme for some time no progress had been possible, '. . . *owing to lack of high speed aircraft*'. The italics are in the original and made at a time when the Hawker Henley was in production as a target tug.

Finally they found that it was, even at this late stage, '. . . impossible to reach any solution or conclusions on the tactical or technical advantages or disadvantages of shallow dive bombing consequently recommendations as to the extent to which it can take the place of steep dive bombing attacks are not yet feasible'.

What proved to be the final meeting on dive bombing in the RAF took place in September 1938 with war twelve months away. The Committee painstakingly went over the ground covered by the earlier meetings, but their ultimate conclusions were much the same. These are best summarised thus:

1 That steep dive bombing should not at present be regarded as a requirement for modern RAF aircraft in view of the special devices necessary and the difficulties of bomb release in a steep dive.
2 That shallow dive bombing should be continued without special devices and sights and the most satisfactory methods should be evolved at the Armament Training Camps.
3 That the dive bombing type trials of new aircraft done at A & AE Martlesham Heath were sufficient and that no special dive bombing armament trials are required.

In other words the RAF, luke-warm at best for twenty years and finding insurmountable problems other nations had solved a decade earlier, totally rejected dive bombing. Indeed having decided there was no place for the type or the method they attempted by legislation to purge the very language of the concept, and it was recommended that '. . . this type of bombing should in future be termed "Losing Height Bombing" '! And that, as far as the RAF was concerned, was that.

Table 15: RAF Comparative Shallow Dive Bombing Tests With Light Bombers in 1938					
Type of Aircraft Tested	Battle	Blenheim	Wellesley	Harrow	Whitley
Indicated Air Speed (mph)	308	285	240	220	220
Engine RPM (⅓rd throttle)	3,000	2,750	2,600	2,600	2,450
Engine RPM (open ⅓rd)	3,600	3,120	2,925	2,925	2,940
Max Angle at Which Bombs Clear	80°	30°	54°	30°	30°
Controlling Factors of Dive Angle	Engine rpm	Engine rpm or bombs fouling structure	Engine rpm or wing stiffness (air speed)	Engine rpm	Engine rpm
Height of Start of Dive (ft)	5,000	5,000	-	-	5,000
Height of Bomb Release (ft)	2,000	2,000	-	-	2,000
Dive Angle (⅓rd throttle)	17°	18°	-	-	20°
Dive Angle at Which Target Closed	-	-	-	-	25°
Speed at Entry	150-180	120-160	-	-	120
Speed at Bottom of the Dive	240-285	215-160	-	-	215-220
Height Lost	500-900	500-900	-	-	500

Except of course that dive bombers would not conveniently vanish overnight. Training Command for example did not seem to share the view that dive bombing was either no longer relevant or that the problems could not be overcome. After first repeating yet again that: 'No instructions explaining the theory and principles [of dive bombing] have ever been circulated . . .', they reiterated that a compromise might still be possible. For example modern aircraft like the Battle they felt '. . . can dive successfully at an angle up to approximately 60⁰, it is very strongly suggested that the AGA dive bomb sight referred to by Sqdn Ldr C.D. Adams in his report on his attachment to the Swedish Air Force this year should be purchased and suitable tests made immediately.' They supplied figures to support their case, although the angles used hardly justified the term dive bombing.

The subject was returned to on 20 October when it was stated that although the Air Ministry thought dive bombing was obsolete not everyone shared that opinion in the RAF. It was suggested that the officials might not be aware of the capabilities and possibilities of dive bombing: 'it may not be realised that Battle aircraft can dive at 60⁰ without difficulty and within the limitations laid down. It will be seen, therefore, that if the Swedish sight was obtained and the dive bomb reports of No 15 (Bomber) squadron circulated that we should have very accurate bombing on this type of aircraft in a reasonably short time . . . .'

Further backing was given in a memo of November 1938. The points made were that shallow dive bombing was valueless, despite the RAF's concentration exclusively on that type, and the angle of dive to be efficient had to be at least 45⁰. The overwhelming advantages of steep dive bombing from 6,000ft were considered to be so great as to justify its retention, if a suitable aircraft could be obtained. Finally if it was shown that even the Battles could be dived steeply then all Battle squadrons should be trained in this technique.

But it was all too late. The RAF, by rejecting a purpose-built dive bomber with the Henley or the other alternatives of 1934-35, had committed itself to the rejection of true dive bombing and all else was compromise. The overwhelming power in the upper echelons of the heavy bomber lobby carried all other considerations before it, and by the eve of the war the equally neglected fighter arm was crying out for what spare design and building capacity there was to make good its own deficiencies. There was no room, even if the Air Ministry had been willing, which was far from the case, to add a dive bomber programme as well at this late stage. And so the ill-conceived Battles went to their doom in low flying suicide *en masse* in those desperate hours during the Battle of France in May and June 1940. Years later Sholto Douglas admitted that the pre-war policy of the RAF had been wrong: '. . . it would have been so much better, if, some years earlier, we had developed a dive bomber along the lines of Ernst Udet's Stuka, instead of devoting so much of our resources to the design, development and the production of those wretched Battles.'

9 AGAINST ALL ODDS
Naval Dive Bombing — the British experience 1932-39

The result of having the air arm of the Royal Navy under the control of the RAF between 1918 and 1938 was an absolute disaster. This is best illustrated by contemporary comparisons of strength between the principal navies of Great Britain, USA and Japan. By as early as 1933 the Admiralty, which in 1918 had established an overwhelming lead in sea-air power, was bewailing the fact that Japan, the most likely enemy in any foreseeable naval conflict at that date, was, after twelve years of peace, far ahead of Britain. The British lead of 1918 in aircraft, men, carriers and expertise had been allowed to wither away through lack of funds and interest.

A minute from DNAD revealed the sorry picture at the end of November 1933. 'It is desired to draw the attention of the Board to the situation regarding Japanese Naval Aircraft which will arise when certain expansion programmes now proposed for the future are completed.' The facts showed that with regard to shore-based naval aircraft the programme of seventeen squadrons for Japan was completed in 1932, while the 1st Replenishment Programme proposed to increase that total by a further fourteen squadrons, which gave the total number of combat aircraft estimated to be in service with the IJN by April 1937 as 472. Nor was this all for the 1934-5 programme provided for a further eight new squadrons on top of these, giving the IJN a grand total of 590 shore-based aircraft by 1938.

With regard to ship-carried aircraft the IJN would have 329 by April 1937 including reserves. Two new carriers were under construction and aircraft provided for in the same estimates would give them a total of 500 ship-borne aircraft of all types by 1938. He continued: 'The full measure of the weakness of our air power in the Far East will be realised when it is pointed out that our one carrier in China has a capacity of only twenty-one aircraft, and that the total of ship-borne aircraft is only twenty-six on that station. At Singapore there are only four flying boats and twenty-four bombers of the RAF (not under naval control).'

The result of such a state of affairs should war break out over China were not difficult to predict: '. . . air superiority, with all its great advantages will go to the Japanese fleet. This will entail continuous T/B and dive bombing attacks . . . .' Adm Rawlings was very prophetic and he warned that '. . . these figures showed we cannot afford any further to delay the development and expansion of the FAA.'

Nor were the Admiralty any less alive to the developments taking place across the Atlantic. Comparisons of strengths and methods were produced in January and December 1936 which showed that the gap was increasing if anything in relative strengths of naval aircraft.

It was further estimated that the US Navy had some 1,218 aircraft on hand against a Royal Navy allocation, *requested only,* of 305. More important, the British figure included no specialised dive bombers at all. The Admiralty was pressing for such aircraft, indeed strongly recommending them, but not getting them. In a minute of 1933 the DNAD made some very sound recommendations: 'In general, sufficient evidence is availale to indicate that dive bombing is likely

Table 16: Comparative Strengths of Naval Aircraft USA/UK 1936					
Date	Service	Carrier Based (All types)	Land Based		
			F/B	Scouts	T/B
1/1/36	UK	180	34	-	36
	USA	455	154	31	42†
1/12/36	UK	198	40	54	40
	USA	475	158	31	45†
† In both cases this figure included 18 Fighter Dive Bombers					

to be far more effective than high level bombing against any target, and "B" [bombs designed to explode underwater creating a 'water-hammer' effect] development is likely to accentuate this since, owing to the increased time of flight high level bombing with "B" bombs will be the easiest type of attack to avoid unless complete surprise is achieved.'

The minute continued: 'So long as the FAA has no aircraft capable of really effective dive bombing attack with heavy bombs, the torpedo is the only weapon of attack which can be pressed home sufficiently to obtain results commensurate with the effort and probable losses. It cannot at present be anticipated that any developments in dive bombers, even with "B" bombs, will entirely supersede the torpedo . . . .' On the other hand '. . . the torpedo is not the most effective initial weapon of attack on enemy carriers, *which will usually be our primary objective.* At least in the first attack, which is designed to stop all flying operations, there is little doubt that dive bombing with SAP bombs *should form the main part of the attack.*'

The Royal Navy cannot therefore be faulted in their correct appreciation of sea/air warfare as it actually took place in combat ten years later, and their thinking was on a par with American and Japanese ideas. Obtaining suitable aircraft from the RAF was something else again, as Adm Sir Dudley Pound later explained: '. . . the navy only receive from the RAF in the way of services that which the RAF is prepared to give. Symptomatic of the latter was the failure of the RAF — who had no interest in dive bombing — to produce a dive bombing sight at the Admiralty's request in the six years between 1932 and 1938.'

The most important development for the navy in attaining the kind of aircraft it required to catch up with foreign rivals was initiated at a meeting held at the Air Ministry in November 1934. The chairman, Air Marshal Sir E.R. Ludlow-Hewitt, DCAS, expressed the view that '. . . a considerable change of policy was involved in the Admiralty proposal to introduce a Fighter Dive Bomber, and that as far as he knew no official letter on this aspect of the matter had been sent to the Air Ministry. The question had in fact arisen out of the discussion which had been going on with regard to the Osprey replacement. It had not been considered by the Advisory Committee.' He went on to reveal that he had only discussed the matter informally at the Admiralty the day before and he then outlined the Navy's reasoning behind it for the benefit of the Committee, which is of considerable interest for it reveals how the Royal Navy was viewing the dive bomber in the mid-1930s.

They felt that there was insufficient room aboard carriers to provide for both the defensive and the offensive aircraft needed in required numbers. The proposal was an attempt to secure protection against air attack by an aircraft that might combine both duties but, as he emphasised right at the start: '*The first of these was dive bombing against hostile carriers,* the second was the attack of enemy aircraft in the air.'

On the feasibility of producing an aircraft which would be an effective fighter as well as a good dive bomber Mr J.S. Buchanan of DDTD said that due to the weight problem and need for high wing loading, the radius of turn would be very poor as a fighter. The replacement envisaged for the Demon fighter would not fit the role as the requirements were different, but the Hart replacement might fit the bill as the aircraft would be able to do dive bombing and fly at 250mph. But after discussion it was rejected as unsuitable. As a fighter movable front guns or a very powerful armament of front guns was asked for, but Buchanan stated that if four were required there would be great difficulty in finding room for them, and they would be heavy.

The chairman stated that it was no good giving the fighter dive bomber adequate armament unless it had the performance necessary to engage the enemy. The essential factor was therefore performance, and this was what they also wanted from the dive bomber point of view. He was inclined to conclude that there was no particular difficulty in producing a dive bomber with the necessary performance, a somewhat different viewpoint to that being expressed at the Air Ministry at the time (see Chapter 8). He continued: 'It was quite clear that in any one aircraft it was impossible to combine high qualities as a dive bomber with equally good qualities as a fighter.' (Eight years later the Air Ministry were arguing the opposite as a reason for not wanting dive bombers.)

The naval representatives then made it crystal clear that if it was to be a choice they would prefer dive bomber qualities to be emphasised rather than fighter qualities. Buchanan said that the experimental aircraft could not be expected before about the middle of 1936, and that no service unit was likely to be re-equipped with them before 1938. The Committee finished with a series of decisions with regard to the new aircraft, which can be summarised as:

1 To recommend the issue of the specification of this aircraft, with a view to adoption, if successful, in place of present fleet fighters.
2 To include in the specification a suitable description of the purpose and function of the aircraft.
3 To specify two front guns only.
4 To leave it to contractors whether it be biplane or monoplane, in either case wing-folding must be as rapid as possible.
5 To have landing speed of not more than 60 knots.
6 An overall length of not more than 36ft, with 33ft as ideal.
7 To leave the remainder of the specification as previously drawn up by the two staffs.

It can thus be seen that *from the very start* the Skua was to be designed as a dive bomber *first,* and as a fighter only as a secondary consideration. This is a fact which is continually ignored in the post-war evaluation of this aircraft, which is invariably judged on its fighter performance rather than as a dive bomber. This unfounded criticism of its capabilities continues up to the present day.

One historian did however get the right perspective, the former editor of *Flight International* stated that: 'It was the first specialised dive bomber to enter British service and has been accorded (the present writer feels) less than its deserved acclaim.'

This major point of emphasis of role was restated in the resulting full specification (027/34) issued on 12 December 1934. The main details agreed were:

1 It was to be a single-engined ship-plane either monoplane or biplane for FAA, to operate from carriers, and its role was defined as: '(a) to disable the opposing FAA by dive bombing attacks on hostile carriers and other vessels,

and to undertake such other dive bombing as may be required. (b) to engage hostile aircraft in the air.'

2   Dimensions were a height of 14ft 9in, a length of 33ft, span of 46ft, with wings folded this to be 16ft only. Half a minute was given as time to fold mainplanes.

On the tendering for the aircraft Mr Buchanan recommended to AMSR on 13 December 1934 that only three firms be asked to tender, and tenders to be due one month from date of issue. Most suitable firms were Hawker and Fairey, next most suitable were Gloster, Vickers, Blackburn, Westland, Bristol and Arm-

The concept of the 'light' fighter dive bomber was the only one to hold sway in the British forces in the 1930s and the Fairey Flycatcher tradition was continued with the Hawker Nimrod, shown here being rocket assisted off the flight deck of a carrier.

One of the early Blackburn Skuas, K5178, on the ground with the old-style cockpit etc. A 1937 view.

65

strong, but due to other commitments this was whittled down to Blackburn, Hawker and Vickers, while Armstrong, who had already submitted proposals for an aircraft of this type fitted with the Hyena engine, could have their aircraft evaluated in the same tests.

In the interim period before the arrival of the dive bomber proper into service a hotch-potch of aircraft continued to be utilised by the FAA for 'light' dive bombing work. Although the much-loved Flycatcher had continued in service with the Royal Navy it was finally declared obsolete in April 1935. Its successor was the trim and pleasing Hawker Nimrod, first introduced in 1932. A single-seater biplane with all-metal structure but composite wings, it was powered initially by a 525hp Kestrel II MS and later by a 640hp Kestrel V engine. Based on the RAF Fury, but with a greater wingspan as well as the extra naval equipment, the Mk1 had a top speed of 181mph, the Mk2 195mph at 14,000ft. It was originally called the Noorn and came down by way of the Hornet and the Hoopoe. The Nimrod was fitted with either the Aldis or the ring-and-bead sight and they were interchangeable. Dive bombing capability was limited by the provision of light series carriers under the starboard wing in which four 20lb bombs only could be stowed. With such weapons its role could only continue to be the limited one of the disruption of enemy warships' AA fire, and this at a time when in the USA the Curtiss Goshawk was taking four 116lb bombs into action.

Deliveries of the Hawker Nimrod to the FAA began in 1932. In the same year it was joined by the Hawker Osprey, a two-seat derivative of the Hart, the later RAF workhorse in dive bomber trials. Like all FAA aircraft, the Osprey was intended to fulfil a number of functions ranging from fighter to light bomber. It had folding wings and, powered by a Kestrel V engine, reached a maximum speed of 176mph at 13,210ft. In 1938 the Nimrod and Osprey joined the new carrier *Ark Royal* on her maiden voyage.

These were the two main types in use in the mid-30s but mention should also be made here of the two Fairey stalwarts that came along at the end of that decade, the Swordfish and the Albacore. Although their principal forte was torpedo bombing, they had, perforce, to double as dive bombers from time to time and for that reason deserve passing mention. The Swordfish of course, became immortalised in its designed role, but tests utilising this aircraft as a dive bomber were carried out in 1939 against the target ship *Centurion* with quite reasonable results while embarked on the carrier *Glorious* in the Mediterranean.

Table 17: Dive Bombing Trials with Fairey Swordfish 1939			
Height of release (ft)	Angle of dive	No of bombs dropped	Average Error (yds)
1,200	70°	61	94
1,300	70°	54	49
1,700	60°	72	80
1,500	70°	72	95*
1,800	60°	54	44*
1,200	67°	53	75*
* Target ship taking avoiding action			

During the war the Swordfish was frequently called upon to perform in a dive bombing role, mainly due to the lack of anything more suitable afloat at that time. As for the Albacore, emphasis was placed *in its original design* on limited dive bombing capability, and was not just an after-thought, and, as H.F. King remarked, the Albacore should be thought of as a complementary aircraft to the Swordfish, rather than as its replacement. In the event the Swordfish outlasted the Albacore in operational use, but nonetheless, post-war judgements are often harsher on this aircraft than they need to be. Although obviously obsolete compared with every foreign contemporary, the Albacore could dive bomb well, even if this fact was rarely acknowledged. For example in the Western Desert operations of 1942, Albacores of No 821 and 826 squadrons worked with great effect in this role, making 471 sorties between June and November. One historian noted how: 'Their accuracy in dive bombing was proverbial. Yet, swamped by the numerically much greater effort put up by the RAF, and ignored by the Admiralty, who were moved at one point to enquire to what extent they were being employed, it was hardly known they were there.'

Despite the (perhaps unsuspected) merits of these two contenders it is a fact that it was on the Nimrod, Osprey and later, Skua, that the Royal Navy's experience of dive bombing was based in the immediate pre-war years 1935-9, and first-hand accounts by the pilots themselves stress that the constant practice of this method achieved very good results on all three types. Damage to enemy carriers remained a priority, although when the Skua entered service with its more powerful bomb load serious thought was given to just how effective dive bombing might be on heavily armoured warships. Any thought of sinking battleships of course was merely post-war bravado due to the many factors involved in penetrating the armoured decks of such vessels, but severe damage could be done to upperworks and gun turrets of the lighter weapons carried by such ships, while other surface ships, from heavy cruiser downward, stood to be badly damaged by dive bombing as it had by then developed.

A great deal of study pre-war went into the effects of bombs on battleship armour, and a whole series of tests was conducted up to the outbreak of war. The ABE Committee was set up in October 1936 to study this question, and was known as the 'Sub-Committee on Bombing v Battleship Experiments', which in March 1938 changed to 'Sub-Committee on Bombing and AA Gunfire Experiments'. The Admiralty constructed a full-scale model representing one part of a section of a modern battleship (it became known as the 'Chatham Float') and this was used for trials from 1934-5 onward in the River Medway. RAF aircraft attacked this with 250lb and 500lb bombs and the FAA used "B" bombs. One result from this was that no bomb *ever* penetrated 4in of armour.

Table 18: Heights at Which Deck Armour Could be Penetrated by Bombs				
Armour Thickness (in)	2,000lb AP Bombs	1,500lb AP Bombs	1,000lb AP Bombs	50lb AP Bombs
7	9,000ft	13,000ft	immune	immune
6	7,000ft	10,600ft	15,000ft	immune
5	5,000ft	7,800ft	10,500ft	immune
4	3,000ft	5,000ft	7,000ft	12,000ft
3	1,000ft	2,500ft	4,000ft	7,000ft
2	-	-	2,000ft	3,200ft

Penetration depended on impact velocity and terminal velocity. Terminal velocity is the maximum speed any object achieves after accelerating at about 32ft/sec/sec, when the air resistance drag eventually balances the force of gravity. In practice the TV of almost all bombs was never reached, as this would have necessitated dropping them from over 50,000ft. Impact velocity is the speed that each bomb reaches on striking the target, which dive bombing added some initial velocity of the aircraft, although not enough, in the Air Ministry view, to be worth the effort. Again the attacks delivered at angles of less than 40⁰, although accurate, would greatly increase the chances of the bomb 'skidding off' the armour decks because of its shallowness. Maj C.S. Parsons, BSc, came to different conclusions in his later study. He found that in comparison with 67 horizontal bombing with a 40° dive the impact velocity from 1,200ft was 173 per cent greater. At 400ft it was 250 per cent greater. With a 60° dive the figures for the same heights were 215 per cent and 349 per cent respectively. There is no doubt therefore that dive bombing was more effective with the same weight of bomb than any level method at that time, and it would have been far more accurate.

Table 19: Velocities of Bombs; Comparison of Dive and Level Bombing					
Dive Angle 75° Initial Velocities	Speed 420mph (Vertical 595ft/sec) (Horizontal 249ft/sec)				
Height (ft)	Time of flight (sec)	Target distance on release (ft)	Horizontal distance travelled (ft)	Distance of impact from target (ft)	Vertical impact velocity (ft/sec)
1,200	1.95	322	485	+163	657
1,000	1.63	268	406	+138	647
900	1.47	241	366	+125	642
800	1.31	215	326	+111	637
700	1.15	188	286	+98	632
600	0.99	161	246	+75	627
500	0.83	134	207	+73	622
400	0.67	107	167	+60	617

The tests themselves incorporated both high level and dive bombing and were also carried out for accuracy estimation by the squadrons embarked aboard the *Glorious,* although for the tests they were disembarked and operated from Hal Far airfield, Malta. The Nimrod and the Swordfish were used by the FAA (see Tables 17 and 20).

Table 20: Dive Bombing Trials with Hawker Nimrods 1939			
Height of bomb release (ft)	Aprox angle of dive	No of bombs dropped	Average error (yd)
2,400	62°	48	84
2,000	65°	48	67
2,400	65°	48	72*
2,000	66°	47	54*
2,300	67°	48	64*
2,300	67°	48	73*
2,000	68°	44	51*
* Avoiding action being taken by target ship			

Among the conclusions reached by the Admiralty and RAF from these figures were that a very marked improvement in the standard of dive bombing was apparent. It was noted how pilots who had bombed the same target ship the year before, at once showed not only superior results to those only trained against splash targets, but also over their own previous figures. Those pilots unaccustomed to bombing such a large target as a battleship were deceived by the great size of *Centurion* which they imagined would be an easy target after small armoured motor boats, but they found this was not so until they had learned the trick of selecting a small point of aim rather than the whole ship, when their accuracy improved. Pilots of No 812 and 823 Squadrons were instructed not to dive below 1,000ft but those of No 825 Squadron only had a 600ft limit, '. . . as this is the minimum height allowed in war'. In view of earlier comments it is interesting to note that the report stated that while this restriction was observed at first, pilots tended to disregard it in the later series. This resulted in an increased number of hits, several of which should be discounted.

On steepness of the dive there was a variance of opinion. One CO stated that: 'It was noticed that those TSR pilots who favoured a steep dive angle did not get such good results as those who favoured a more shallow dive', while another said: 'The steeper the dive the less skill is required to judge the exact moment of release.' The obvious conclusion was arrived at, that a compromise between these two extremes would probably produce the best average results.

On the vexed question of bomb release height the summary of these tests read:

> While the accuracy of dive bombing increases as the height of release is reduced, there must be a height for any given target in which the increase in percentage hits obtained is over-balanced by the casualty rate suffered. This height will depend on the variations in accuracy with height of release, and will vary with the extent of the AA defence and the degree to which surprise is achieved, but it is obvious that a lower height of release is possible and desirable when attacking a small lightly defended ship, such as a destroyer, than when attacking a capital ship or a carrier. In attacks on capital ships or aircraft carriers the release should not be nearer than at 1,000yd slant range from the target, in present circumstances.

These figures, obtained with biplanes, were similar to the results of dive bombing tests conducted by aircraft of No 100(TB) Squadron, RAF, in the Far East during October 1938. Their old Vildebeest biplanes were the approximate equivalents of the FAA aircraft in appearance and capability, on paper anyway, and reflect another area of neglect. Dive bombing carried out by this squadron was studied but considered of little value in assessing the dive bombing capability of modern light bombers:

> The *maximum* angle of dive laid down in F406 (1939) for medium bombers is approximately 30^0 according to the limitations of the aircraft. It seems therefore that this method of attack carried out in the Vildebeest does not to any extent simulate the 'shallow' dive bombing of twin-engines aircraft. If the correct angle of dive is maintained the high speed must, of necessity, be sacrificed and the angle of dive is such that, in a Vildebeest, the practice becomes normal dive bombing.

The RAFs conclusion was: 'It is intended that all aircraft should carry out dive bombing at the angle most suited to the type . . .' and, as they had no true dive bomber, there the matter ended.

10 ACHTUNG — STUKA !
Germany re-enters the field, 1932-39

The initial build-up for the German Air Force had begun with the introduction of the He 50a as related, and this was to be an interim measure until stage 2 of the planned expansion could be implemented. All this initial work was well in hand prior to 1933 and the advent of the Luftwaffe as such, but of course with the arrival of Hitler and Goering on the scene in January of that year the increase in all armament research gained new impetus and the tempo of the programmes was rapidly increased.

In October 1933 the fighter unit Jagdgeschwader 132 was given prime responsibility for dive bombing training. They were already equipped with Arado Ar 65 and He 51 fighters, and, to carry out their new duties, were allocated the first He 50As off the production line.

In a further expansion initiated on 1 January 1934 another fifty-one of these aircraft were ordered and, although these were mainly for service with the flying training schools, they did form part of the equipment of the first German dive bomber unit to be establishment, the *Fliegergruppe Schwerin.* With further ambitious expansion planned even these were in short supply and the He 51 was also utilised in this role for a short period. A British report of 1936 pointed out: 'The He 51 forms the equipment of No 132 (*Richthofen*) *Geschwader* (nine squadrons) and also as a temporary measure of No 162 (*Immelmann*) and 165 (six and three squadrons respectively) *Geschwader,* which are intended for Low Attack of Dive Bombing.'

So pressing was the need for such aircraft that at one point in 1935 export models for the Chinese Air Force were held over for Luftwaffe use for a six month period. Renamed *Stukageschwader* I/StG 162 was formed from *Gruppe Schwerin* in April 1936, II/StG 162 at Lübeck-Blankensee and I/StG 165 at Kitzingen, three He50As being allocated to each *staffeln* at this time.

Although the He50A then began to be phased out to the training schools they did see operational use during the occupations of the Rhineland on 7 March 1936, when I/StG 165 moved two *staffeln* to Frankfurt/Main and the third to Mannheim soon after this re-organisation. As Hitler's bluff worked, these half-trained infant dive bomber units were not called upon to go into battle, which was just as well. Nonetheless the Luftwaffe's first dive bomber soldiered on well, remaining in the training role as late as 1943, and even seeing combat later in the war on the Eastern Front when an Estonian-manned *Nachtschlachtgruppe* (NSGr11) used these elderly biplanes against the advancing Soviet forces until October 1944.

In order to act as an operational stop-gap in squadron service the next stage of the dive bomber plan initiated a requirement for aircraft capable of this role which would be both cheap, and more important at that time, quick to produce. The basic design was for a single-seater biplane of all-metal construction and the two aircraft proposed in response to this specification were the Fieseler Fi98 and the Henschel Hs123. Very similar in some respects, they were to have widely differing fates.

Designed by Reinhold Mewes for the Fieseler Flugzeugbau — which was the firm of Gerhard Fieseler, a contemporary of Ernst Udet, and with the latter's enthusiastic backing — the prototype Fi98a flew for the first time in early 1935. Powered by a 650hp BMW 132A-3 radial engine it had a maximum speed of 183mph and was fitted to carry four 110lb bombs under the lower wings. Of conventional construction, the Fi98 was flown at Rechlin and performed well enough, but its rival was considered ahead in design and performance. The second prototype was never built, and, after attempts to interest the Japanese had met with similar lack of interest, this one-off dive bomber passed from the scene.

By contrast the Henschel Hs123 was the greatest success. The Henschel Flugzeugwerke had only come into being in March 1933, with Erich Koch as Chief Engineer and Friedrich Nicolaus as Chief Designer under Oskar Henschel, their factory at Schönefeld near Berlin opening in December 1935. Nonetheless the design the young company came up with was outstanding. Although employing the same power unit as the Fi98, the Hs123 featured some radical advances, the most obvious feature being its clean aerodynamic design which, unlike the strut-cluttered Fieseler, showed only as a single streamlined interplane strut with no external bracing. In the original prototype the BMW 124A-3 engine (a licence-built version of the Pratt & Whitney GR-1690 Hornet), was encased in a large-diameter smooth cowling and had a fixed, spatted undercarriage like the Fi98.

It was in performance that it showed up against its rival to advantage. The first prototype, Hs123 V1, was put through its paces at Johannisthal, near Berlin, only three days after it had been unveiled, on 8 May 1935. The man putting the machine through a series of stiff dives was Udet himself and in his hands the plane performed gloriously, attaining a maximum speed of 220mph at 4,000ft, although without any armament aboard at that time.

Enthusiasm was such that two more prototypes quickly followed that summer, the Hs123 V2 with the long smooth cowling replaced by the distinctive short cowl with eighteen little blisters enclosing the valve gear, and the Hs123 V3 which had a three-bladed, adjustable-pitch airscrew. Prolonged testing followed at Rechlin which ended in tragedy when two of the aircraft broke up in mid-air, due to the diving stresses being too much for the centre section struts. Both pilots were killed and it appeared that the Luftwaffe dive bomber programme, already in the doldrums, faced termination. However considerable strengthening of this weak area was made on the Hs123 V4 and when this prototype was tested in 80° dives at Rechlin that autumn it came through with flying colours.

The future of the Hs123 was therefore assured and a small pre-production batch of Hs123A-0s for evaluation showed little change from the V4. In 1936 the Hs123A-1s began to roll off the assembly line, joining squadron service the following year. Main alterations in these were the adoption of the 880hp BMW 132Dc engine, tailplane struts instead of bracing cables as in the Hs123 V4 and a completely metal-skinned fuselage of oval cross-section. As a dive bomber it could lift a single 550lb bomb in a crutch and four 110lb bombs under the wings. The Hs123A had a maximum speed of 248mph and a range of 530 miles. It was not of course fitted with dive brakes and had a designed diving speed of 350mph.

It should not be thought from this brief description of the German dive bomber programme up to 1936 that the proponents of this form of bombing had things all their own way at the RLM. There were many in Germany who held the same viewpoint as the British air chiefs and were vehemently opposed to vertical attack for the same reasons. One of the chief opponents was also the man in the position to do the most to retard development, for Wolfram von Richthofen was appointed Head of the Technical Office and he harboured grave doubts all along. He held that for any aircraft to dive below 6,000ft in the face of heavy AA fire would be nothing less than suicide. He felt that the return in terms of accuracy would not be compensated for by the enormous casualties such aircraft would incur.

His viewpoint must be taken in the *context of the state of the art,* both for offence and defence, and in the mid-1930s it had some validity. At that time the cost-effectiveness of producing cheap dive bombers, able to do with accuracy what a whole squadron of expensive horizontal bombers could only achieve by saturation of the target, was very alluring in terms of man-power and speed of production. Bomb sights were primitive and would remain so for almost another decade and Germany had no *need* for long-range aircraft, as all her immediate potential enemies were on her doorstep. Richthoften assumed always that the enemy armies would deploy their anti-aircraft batteries in the same density and with the same attention to mobility as did the Luftwaffe's own flak arm, but this proved illusory. Both in terms of accuracy and power German light automatic weapons and heavy AA artillery remained supreme throughout the war.

Be that as it may the German Stuka programme several times came close to termination in the 1930s and the fact that it was saved must to a large extent be credited to the intervention and single-mindedness of one man, Ernst Udet.

This colourful character has been the subject of several books so only the salient details of his involvement need be re-stated here, along with the demolition of the myths. Of the latter it would seem that Ullstein correspondent Walther Kelffel was the first German to bring back detailed word of American progress in dive bombing in the air shows of 1930. After seeing the Helldiver in action he submitted a report to the Air Travel Department praising its virtures. The German dive bomber programme was already under consideration at this time and no doubt Kleffel's report provided more food for though.

It was not until the Cleveland demonstration of 1931 that Udet was similarly impressed and was allowed by the Americans to try the Helldive himself, being given *carte blance* by Doolittle and the Curtiss-Wright company after the US Army had rejected the Helldiver themselves. The American company offered to sell Udet one aircraft for $14,000 in talks soon afterward and, on his return to Germany in October 1931, he took up the championship of the dive bomber with some fervour, but as a civilian his arguments did not carry much weight. He discussed it with Goering but the latter did not then have the power to help him.

Eighteen months later it was a different story and Goering was not only pressing Udet to join the Nazi party but the new Luftwaffe as well. On 25 March 1933 Udet, as a honorary Air Vice Commodore of the German Sports Flying Club, had a position, and that summer he was back in the States. BuAer had given permission for further demonstrations and sales, and, on 19 October that year, two crated Hawks arrived at Bremerhaven as Udet's personal property. They were named *Iris* and *Ilse,* manufacturer's Nos 80 and 81 respectively, and had cost Goering $11,500 each in the end — an expensive indulgence, but one he no doubt considered worthwhile for the end result was that Udet joined the Luftwaffe and became the chief 'prophet' of the dive bombers already undergoing evaluation.

Udet himself flew the Hawk in a demonstration at the Rechlin Test Centre in December 1933 and then at Staaken. But his audience of high-ranking officers, including Milch, watched his performance in stony silence. The Hawk performed well in four power dives, but they remained unenthusiastic and the planes were released back to Udet, flown to Tempelhof and stored. One later crashed in 1934 and the other finished up in the Berlin Museum pre-war, its final resting place being the Air Museum at Krakow in Poland.

There seems little doubt then that the Hawks themselves had little or no effect on the Luftwaffe dive bombing policy at that time, which, as we have seen, was already set on its pre-determined course with indigenous machines. But in gaining Udet the Luftwaffe had also got a man who now put every effort into seeing that the dive bomber programme was a success, often at the risk of his newly-obtained job and upsetting his superiors. Thus, at the age of forty Udet became a Luftwaffe colonel with the post of Inspector of Fighters and Stukas in January 1936. Here he found two men who shared his enthusiasm, Maj Gen Wever, Chief of the Air Staff, and Col Wimmer of the Technical Branch. Richthofen was still opposed, but when Wever died in an air crash at Dresden in June of that year Udet took over Wimmer's position at the Technical Office and was then in a position to really push the dive bomber programme ahead.

Two things resulted from this: one was his flight testing of the Fw56 *Stösser* and the growth of a legend-within-a-legend, the other was a competition to initiate stage 3 of the German air armament programme and the first full-scale production of a satisfactory dive bomber for the Luftwaffe.

One of the first aircraft Udet examined in his new role was the Focke Wulf Fw56 *Stösser* (Falcon). Its origination is well-documented in the story of its designer, Kurt Tank, but it was *never* a dive bomber. Tank became Technical Director in 1933 and the Fw56 was his first major aircraft for the company. It was designed as a fighter for Home Defence (*Heimatschutzjäger*) and first flew that November. The Fw56 was an advanced design monoplane, featuring the parasol wing, but initial prototypes were shown to have weaknesses here and the V3 was much strengthened. With the Fw56 V4 dive brakes were first introduced to improve performance as a fighter but thereby it became a suitable vehicle in Udet's eyes as a dive bomber *trainer*. He flew the second prototype when he visited Johannisthal and was impressed with the *Stösser's* diving performance — its speed of 300mph and the ability of pulling out of a terminal dive from 6,500ft. He therefore requested that the Fw56 V2 be modified so that further diving trials could be held.

This was done, the aircraft being fitted with the vane-operated variable-pitch airscrew and with light underwing bomb racks capable of carrying six 2.2lb smoke bombs. In this configuration *Flugkapitän* Wolfgang Stein held a series of trials in which an average of 40 per cent of the bombs hit the target. Udet, according to one biographer, did rather better with cement bombs, scoring 50 per cent direct hits. Nonetheless, despite its attractive diving ability the Fw56 was rejected as a dive bomber trainer and saw service solely as a fighter trainer.

During this time the Junkers team had been pressing on with their own experiments after their K47 experience. Development was still continuing when Henschal and Fieseler competed, but by the end of 1935 satisfactory progress had been made with the first prototype of the Junkers Ju87 designed by a team led by Herman Pohlmann. In fact the year before the RLM had given their sanction for the construction of three prototypes and in January 1935 issued their official *Sturzbomber* specification, drawn up heavily around the Junkers proposal to other firms. These however went their own ways in their interpretation of what was required and the Ju87 remained unique.

The Ju87 V1 was ready by March that year at Dessau and embodied most of the radical features called for in the definitive stage of Germany's three-part programme. Junkers, from their long experience in the field, introduced innovations of their own within the basic concept. The finished design was a single-engined, two-seater monoplane featuring the inverted gull-wing, and a very sturdy undercarriage enclosed in a trouser-type fixed fairing, similar to the racing aircraft of the day.

The distinctive wing, which was to become the hallmark of the Stuka, had its 73 centre part built integral with the oval-section fuselage of all-metal construction and was again built for strength. The first prototype had a twin tail to give the rear gunner a clear field of fire and the crew were housed back-to-back under a spacious canopy which gave an outstanding all-round view. It was powered by a Rolls-Royce Kestrel V, a twelve-cylinder water-cooled engine rated at 525hp for take-off, driving a two-bladed fixed pitch airscrew of wooden composition. Air brakes were to be a feature of the design, but were not ready when Ju87 V1 undertook its initial trials at Dessau in the summer of 1935. This probably contributed to the vibration suffered during diving tests which culminated in the collapse of the tail section, and the aircraft crashed.

As a result the tail section was re-designed as a single-fin unit, the aircraft now featured under-wing dive brakes which consisted of a hinged slat that could be turned to 90^0 during the dive, effectively keeping the speed of decent down to around 375mph, the limit the Pohlmann team felt the aircraft could withstand. The Ju87 V2 also had a new power plant, the Junkers Jumo 210A 610hp engine with a three-bladed variable-pitch airscrew. The third prototype was almost identical, but with the engine lowered to improve pilot visibility, while the tail fin was enlarged and fitted with small endplates. The radiator was also enlarged to combat heating problems and the basic profile of the Stuka was complete.

All was now set for the comparative trials but, on 9 June 1936, von Richthofen issued a confidential memorandum recommending the immediate halting of the dive bomber development in one last attempt to reverse the current policy. He was thwarted in this by the fact that the very next day Udet took over his job and immediately concelled his predecessor's instructions. The programme went ahead as planned.

Although the Ju87 was the most favoured contender for the position of Germany's final phase of dive bomber programme, comparative tests were held in June 1936 to evaluate it in competition with several rival designs. The main contenders were the Heinkel He118, the Arado Ar81 and the Blohm und Voss Ha137, the latter being something of an outsider for, whereas the specification had called for a two-seater, the Hs137 was a single-seat aircraft. Nonetheless it included some advanced features that appealed to the Richthofen concept of ground attack rather than dive bombing and so the Ha137 was allowed to compete.

One of the unsuccessful contenders against the Ju87 during the Rechlin trials to select Germany's dive bomber type in June 1936 was the Arado Ar81. Tests with the V-1 showed that further strength was required and the second prototype, featured here, had bracings to the tailplane but this proved still insufficient.

Of all the designs considered the Arado probably stood the least chance of all for selection as the new Luftwaffe's next *Sturzkampfflugzeug*, or Stuka as it was subsequently abbreviated world-wide. The Arado design presented rather a hotch-potch appearance, as if spare parts from a number of aircraft had been thrown together. An equi-span biplane, it had a fixed undercarriage and a twin-fin tail. The two-man crew were seated in tandem behind a long nose which housed a Jumo 210C engine driving a three-bladed airscrew. The Ar81 had a span of just over 36ft and a maximum speed of 214mph and could carry a single-crutched 550lb bomb on the swing arm mounting to clear the airscrew like the latest American designs.

Despite its odd appearance the Ar81 was, of necessity, a strongly-built aircraft but its old-fashioned struts and bracings stood out in marked contrast to the sleek designs of its rivals. The Ar81 began its flight tests late in 1935 and encountered similar stability problems with the twin-finned tailplane that had beset the Junkers prototype. The Arado 81 V2 featured a brace tailplane section with inverted vee-struts, although subsequent testing showed this was insufficient. As a result the third prototype featured a re-designed rear fuselage and tail assembly and a deeper, stronger body with a Jumo 210Ca engine driving a two-bladed variable-pitch airscrew.

The Blohm und Voss Ha137 had not grown out of the *Sturzbomber* programme as such to start with, credit being given to designer Richard Vogt for initiating it as a testbed for his new wing form, the inverted gull-wing configuration which he had pioneered while working in Japan on the Kawaski Ki-5 fighter. Indeed Blohm und Voss was not even asked to tender for the final stage of the programme. Nonetheless they pressed on with their own concept in the hope that the inherent strength of the new tubular wing form would attract attention.

Not surprisingly then the Ha137 presented a similar outward appearance to the Ki-5 and was also a single-seater design, final choice of power plant being the Pratt & Whitney Hornet radial built under licence. The result was an attractive low-wing monoplane of all-metal construction with heavy trousered under-carriage fairings and an inverted gull-wing similar to the Ju87 but otherwise very different in appearance and conception.

The Ha137 presented a rakish appearance and was aerodynamically cleaner than either the Junkers Ju87 or the Arado Ar81. It featured an open cockpit and the BMW 132A3 engine gave it a maximum speed of 205mph, less than its rivals. It could only carry a light external load of four 11lb bombs on underwing racks, although provision was made for the fitting of 20mm cannon for the ground-attack role more favoured by the Richthofen faction at the RLM.

The most serious contender to the Stukas crown at the Rechlin trials was the Heinkel He118. This photo shows the first prototype, V-1, fitted with the Rolls-Royce 'Buzzard' engine.

The first prototype flew at Hamburg in April 1935. Although the Ha137 V2 followed quickly the unpalatable fact that a two-seater was required meant that this aircraft never really stood a chance in the tests. Vogt knew that to re-design it would cripple its performance but the RLM continued to give backing to the project with a view to utilising it in the *Schlachtflugzeug* role which had many supporters, and a further three aircraft were built powered by the Kestrel V, this version being designated Ha137B. A two-bladed variable pitch airscrew replaced the three-bladed metal one at the same time. Tests in the autumn showed that the aircraft performed quite well and the Ha137 V3 was selected to take part in the Test Programme the following year.

The most advanced design of all was the Heinkel He118, and to many people it was a mystery why this aircraft was passed over for the Ju87 which it outshone in almost every way.

The designers, Walter and Siegfried Günter, prepared the drawings for their dive bomber hand-in-hand with their new fighter design, the He112, and this showed up in the sleek and graceful product that finally emerged. Advanced features were apparent everywhere. A clean monoplane designed to the latest concepts in construction, with an oval-section all-metal fuselage carrying a crew of two in a semi-enclosed tandem cockpit, the He118 featured such innovations as an internal bomb bay capable of housing a single 1,100lb bomb if flown as a single-seater, or a 550lb bomb if both crew members were carried; fully retractable undercarriage, which was also fully enclosed; and an aerodynamically clean silhouette, marred only by a small chin radiator, designed to complement the new Daimler-Benz DB600 twelve-cylinder liquid-cooled engine. It looked, and acted, like the thoroughbred it was. Like the Hawker Henley in Britain at the same time, this completely deserving aircraft was shunted to the sidelines by an official policy that ignored its virtues and emphasised its faults.

It was a larger aircraft than its rivals, having a span of 49ft 6½in and an all-up weight of 9,082lb. This was deliberate policy in order to ensure sturdiness and it was anticipated that the new engine would more than compensate. In fact the maximum speed for the version fitted with the DB600 was a good 245mph at 19,685ft, far in excess of the others.

The first prototype however featured not the DB600 but an imported engine, the Rolls-Royce Buzzard of 845hp and it flew in the winter of 1935-6, some time behind the other contenders. However the He118 V2 carried the designed engine and quickly joined in the trials, claiming speeds of 270mph in level flight which

The second prototype of the Heinkel He118.

seemed then to indicate Heinkel had found a winner. This was sufficient to narrow the pre-trial choice down to the Heinkel He118 and the more well-established Junkers Ju87, the Ar81 being retained as a back-up, with the Bv137 more or less out of the running before the trials commenced. A more powerful engine, the DB600C, was fitted to the He118 V3 and orders for ten pre-production aircraft were placed at once. A modified tailplane assembly was introduced and a reduction in wing span achieved by clipping the original elliptical design somewhat. In this form the Heinkel was ready for the contest.

Some people are convinced that the trials were only a showpiece and that the result was a foregone conclusion, certainly the odds were heavily weighed in favour of Junkers who had a long head start, but in the event the choice was narrow.

The Ha137 was no longer a serious contender and with Udet's sudden take-over from Richthofen any hopes Blohm und Voss might have had for a dramatic change of policy in favour of the fighter type ground-attack design were dashed, Vogt being informed that they were not being awarded any production contracts. The last faint anticipation that this aircraft might be adopted for carrier purposes when the laying down of the *Graf Zeppelin* for the Navy was announced, were also short-lived, the Ha137 not having the range considered necessary for maritime operations.

The Arado Ar81 performed well during the tests reaching a speed of 373mph during its dives and pulling out without ill-effects, and its accuracy and general performance equalled, indeed out-shone according to some reports, the other aircraft in the role for which it was intended. Its outmoded design was however a fatal handicap and the Ar81 was doomed by its late arrival for the tests; by the time it was performing the die had already been cast and the Arado followed the Ha137 into oblivion.

The He118 entered the lists with great hopes based on its earlier superlative performance. However its reputation had been based on overall figures and although advanced as an aircraft, the He118 fell down in the vital role for which the whole programme had been brought about, dive bombing. Flown by *Flugkapitän* Heinrichs the He118 did not exceed 50^0 in any of its dives, whereas the Ju87 went in almost vertically. This was the factor above all else that decided the competition in Junkers' favour, but it was not the cut-and-dried decision often claimed.

The final decision was still in doubt when Udet himself elected to give the He118 a last chance to prove itself, *at his hands!* On 27 June he took off in the third prototype from Marienehe to put it through its paces. Fitted with an interconnection of the airscrew pitch change with the flaps/dive brakes which was still not perfected, the He118 he flew required careful handling. Before the flight chief test pilot Nitschke had explained that before going into the terminal dive the airscrew must be changed to a coarse pitch, but Udet, impulsive as ever, sped down the runway without apparently taking this fact in. The result was predictable. The He118 Vs was thrown joyously into a dive by the Inspector, who forgot to carry out this simple procedure. Coming down from around 13,000ft the propeller took off on its own, taking the reduction gears with it. The tail broke off and, managing to get out, Udet followed the plunging bomber down to earth in a more dignified manner by parachute. His fault or not, the hopes of Heinkel went up in flames with the funeral pyre of his He118!

This was not quite the end of the He118 however, and Heinkel, who had been selling his designs to Japan since 1935, was approached, quite separately, by both the Japanese Navy and Army on the potential of this aircraft. We shall follow its fortunes in the next chapter.

With the elimination of the He118 the selection of the Junkers Ju87 for the last phase of the Luftwaffe's pre-war build-up underway with production initiated at Dessau. Indeed all preparations had been made in 1936 when the first ten pre-production machines were ordered. The most significant part of the German dive bomber story now began, for, with the outbreak of the Spanish Civil War the new aircraft, and the 'new' techniques, were to be given a perfect setting to evaluate their merits.

The Ju87 V4 differed from earlier prototypes by having a swinging bomb crutch as in the Ar81, designed to lower the bomb clear of the airscrews before release. The crutch could take either a 550lb (250kg) bomb with normal crew of two, or, with the aircraft flying as a single-seater, a 1,000lb (450kg) bomb. In pre-production batches the Jumo 210C replaced the earlier engine and a more simplified wing construction to facilitate rapid assembly was introduced.

In 1937 the first of the production models, the Ju87A1 (*Anton*) started to roll off the line and join squadron service, the first unit to replace their Hs123As being I/StG 162 *Immelmann* in the spring of that year. It saw its first service during the occupation of Czechoslovakia and differed from the pre-production Ju87A0s in having the Jumo 210Da engine of 635hp, which in turn was replaced by the Jumo 211 late in 1937. After some 200 Antons had been completed this version was phased out and a complete re-working of the basic design was initiated, resulting in the Ju87B (*Bertha*) all the Antons having been relegated to training units by September 1939.

After the establishment of the *Legion Condor*, a *kette* of Ju87As were despatched to Spain from StG 163. Although only three of these aircraft were used their crews were rotated so that a constant supply of battle-trained veterans returned to the Reich to pass on their knowledge. There was still uncertainty about the precise role of the dive bomber, but it was felt to be more a weapon for back area bombing than for close support, the *Nahkampfkorps* rather than the *Schlachtflieger,* although combat soon proved it was suitable for both roles. Evaluations were made by the He50A and He51 fighters, the Hs123 as well as the trio of Ju87As in this theatre.

The He51 soon found itself outclassed as a fighter and these aircraft, which had already doubled up once in the dive bombing role during the earlier build-up phase, were again fitted with racks to carry ten 10kg bombs for low-level attack. The Hs123 was fitted up to carry out similar duties after the appointment of Gen Richthofen as the *Legions* Chief of Staff and five Hs123s arrived in Spain in

The 'Little Angel'. The HS123B was so dubbed by Spanish pilots who flew them during the civil war in 1938-9. The Germans used them themselves in World War II in the ground-attack role and not as true dive bombers.

December 1936 at Seville for use in their dive bomber role, but it was mainly as *Schlachtflieger* that they were employed. Rugged, reliable and able to absorb punishment from ground fire, simple to operate and maintain, the Hs123 proved very popular. Franco's airmen were equally delighted, dubbing the aircraft *Angelito* (little angel.) In response to their requests a further eleven were shipped out and in 1940 the surviving fourteen from both batches were handed over to the Spanish Air Force where they remained in service for many years. The Hs123 equally commended itself to German pilots in this role and although its replacement by the Ju87 continued unabated, it was to earn new acclaim both in Poland and France in 1940 and resurrected from training schools, to serve on in the grim wastes of the Eastern Front until 1944.

The Ju87A1 was no 'little angel', indeed its crews promptly gave it the sobriquet of *Jolanthe,* after the pig in a German stage comedy of the time, and a pig was duly painted on the wheel spats of both the Ju87A1s and, subsequently the early Berthas which arrived in Spain later. The pig motif remained the Stuka mascot throughout the war also, but this name did not reflect on its flying qualities, for it was a joy to handle, being very sensitive to the controls, rock-firm in a dive and having a wide all-round vision that delighted those flying it after the cramped cockpits of earlier types.

As a combat aircraft the Stuka was efficient, accurate, rugged and totally reliable. Although the Hs123 claimed to be one of the few dive bombers that could really be dived vertically, the Ju87 was equally at home at 90^0 and soon proved itself in action, seeing combat at Teruel, Ebro and in the Catalonian campaign. In Spain too its accuracy found reflection in attacks on shipping targets, at which, of course, the dive bomber excelled. Strangely enough this feature seems to have passed unnoticed by the Royal Navy who were very active around the Spanish coast at the time. At all events the ship-killing capabilities of the Stuka appeared to come as a nasty shock to the Royal Navy in the years ahead.

In October 1938 the new Ju87B arrived in Spain and special Bomber Group K/88 conducted operations with it with increasingly good results, five aircraft being the permanent establishment. A modified Ju87A1 formed the basis of the B series, being fitted with the Jumo 211 engine early in 1938. This was followed by the Ju87V6 with altered airframe and ten pre-production machines and the new jigs were assembled at Tempelhof. By the autumn of 1937 the first aircraft were coming off the line. The Ju87BO featured an entirely new body line and cockpit, and had the clumsy undercarriage fairings replaced by spats.

The increased lifting power of the new engine enabled the 1,100lb bomb to be carried with a normal crew, an alternative load being a single crutched 550lb bomb with four 110lb bombs on underwing racks. In parallel with the enormous growth of the Luftwaffe, production of the Stuka rose from 395 in 1938 to 557 in 1939. A rapid change in organisation had taken place in these years to accommodate this expansion.

A total of nine *Stukagruppen* were equipped with the Ju87B by September 1939 divided into twenty-seven *Staffeln* with an establishment of forty aircraft. II (*Sturzkampf*)/LG1 had twenty-five aircraft and in addition to these were the modified Ju87Cs (*Cäsar*) allocated for the Navy's future air arm as 4(ST)/TrGr 186 (*Trägersturzkampffflieger*) and the last Hs123s, thirty-six aircraft forming II/(*Schlacht*)LG2 at Alt-Rosenburg.

This impressive force was ready for action when war broke out with Poland on 1 September 1939 and with Britain and France two days later. Only one untoward incident marred the remarkable growth of the German dive bomber force and it proved a sobering blow.

Table 21: Growth of German Dive Bomber Units 1935-9		
Month and Year	Units in service	Equipment
March 1935	I/StG162 (*Schwerin*)	Hs123
August 1936	I/StG162 (*Schwerin*) I/StG165 (*Kitzingen*) II/StG165 (*Wertheim*)	Hs123
April 1937	I and II/StG162 I/StG262 III/StG165	Ju87A
	I/StG165 II/StG165	Hs123
September 1939	I/StG1 I, II and III/StG2 (*Immelmann*) III/StG51 I/StG76 I and II/StG77 II (Sturzkampf)/LG1 4(St)/TrGr186	Ju87B
	II (Schlacht)/LG2	Hs123

In a final period prior to moving up to their war stations *Generalleutnant* Richthofen, who, although still harbouring some misgivings about dive bombers, had nonetheless been appointed to lead them into battle, had laid on a demonstration for the benefit of assembled Luftwaffe leaders, including Sperrle and Loerzer. This was to take place at the Neuhammer training ground with a mass Stuka attack using smoke bombs. Three *staffeln* were to take part led by *Haupt* Sigel of I/StG 76, followed by I/StG 2, both units attacking in sequence.

The ill-fated Stukas had been instructed to approach the target at 12,000ft then to dive through a cloud-layer, reported to have been identified between 2,500 and 6,000ft, although there is some doubt whether the reports of the latter were ever transmitted, and release their bombs at 1,000ft. The official version was that the doomed Gruppe of StG 76 failed to realise that a ground mist had formed and they dived into this mistaking it for the higher cloud layer which had subsequently dispersed. Whatever the truth one whole formation of Ju87s tore straight into the ground at full speed, only a few aircraft from the second flight realising the error in time and pulling up, and many of these failed to clear the surrounding trees. In seconds the testing ground was littered with the exploding debris of thirteen Stukas as they hurtled down to their destruction at Neuhammer. Nonetheless, after landing and a brief rest, their compatriots carried out the scheduled attack later that day on the direct orders of Richthofen. Within a fortnight the survivors of this carnage were spearheading Germany's opening attacks on Poland and the start of World War II.

11 THE RISING SUN

The expansion of the Japanese Naval Air Arm, 1932-39

With the adoption into service if its first dive bomber, the Nakajima Type 94 D1A1, the Japanese Navy soon began to flex its muscles. Their relationship with Heinkel in Germany continued throught the 1930s but the Japanese always adapted the German designs to fit their own special needs. Although dive bombing did not form a very large part of the requirements of the Japanese Army Air Force, they too maintained a continued interest in new designs, completely separate from the Navy, which gives good insight into inter-service relations in that, and other, nations.

The Nakajima 94 was soon taken afloat aboard Japan's growing carrier fleet and sea trials began in earnest. From what they learnt from these tests the D1A1 was further developed into the Type 96. Largely similar to the original He50A Japanese version, a two-seater biplane with a 550lb bombload, it was re-engined with the 600hp Hikari engine to improve performance, giving it a top speed of around 140mph, becoming the D1A1.

Joined by the Mitsubishi Type 96 by the outbreak of the so-called Sino-Japanese incident of July 1937, which led to the start of permanent Japanese expansion on the mainland of China, the dive bombers were serving with the fleet in reasonably large numbers.

Table 22: Japanese Dive Bomber Units in Service July 1937		
Carrier or Unit	Equipment	Complement
Ryujo	Nakajima Type 94	15
Kaga	Nakajima Type 95	12
12th Air Corps (Shanghai)	Nakajima Type 94	12
13th Air Corps (Shanghai)	Mitsubishi Type 96	12

These units saw entensive action for the next three years in that theatre. The development of expertise in the dive bomber arm of Japan followed that of the general trends elsewhere but with the added degree that Japan was the first nation, other than the US Marines small-scale activities, to test their men and machines in hard action, which no exercise, however extensive could hope to simulate sufficiently. It is not surprising therefore that Japan's naval air arm was a superb weapon by 1941-2 for they had been given six years combat experience to perfect their techniques.

A large proportion of Japanese air effort was solely devoted to the direct support of land operations. This was especially noticeable with the Army Air Service, but the Navy also carried out this type of warfare. In fact a over-proportionate percentage of what long-range bombing there was was carried out by the Mitsubishi G3M 'Nell' bombers of the Japanese Navy flying missions, averaging 1,250 miles from both Formosa and Kyushu, Japan, against city targets like Shanghai, Nanking and Hangchow.

For attacks on ships a report stated: 'It is not possible to say whether the Japanese prefer the torpedo or the bomb as a weapon against ships. Pilots are trained to use both. Much attention has been given to dive bombing practice, and the Naval Air Force have had considerable experience in China of both dive and level bombing against stationary targets.'

With regard to attack of enemy sea-borne trade, it was admitted that: 'The Japanese have shown themselves to be particularly ruthless during the China campaign, and there is little doubt that they would make air attacks on enemy sea-borne trade, without regard to the safety of the crews of the vessels they attacked . . . .' Naïve wording, but highly accurate. With regard to the tactical employment of aircraft in co-operation with the Army, the report goes on: 'The Japanese evidently consider this method of employing aircraft to be useful and effective.' The surprised tone is apparent, contrasting as it did with RAF doctrine of the time. All types of aircraft were employed thus, and all types of tactics used: 'Level bombing from medium or low altitudes, dive bombing and low flying tactics with light bombs and machine guns are the normal practice. Aircraft are frequently used as an adjunct to artillery in the bombardment of enemy strong points or artillery positions.'

The analysis of dive bombing is worth quoting in full:

> Dive bombing is carried out by light bombers and fighters and is particularly favoured when no AA resistance is expected. One of three methods may be adopted; single aircraft attacks, attacks by two aircraft, or attacks by flights in 'V' formation or in line astern. Against moving targets on land such as motor cars or mobile guns, two aircraft are normally employed; the first dives and opens machine gun fire causing the abandonment of the target; the second aircraft then makes a dive bombing attack on the then stationary target. Dives are normally made at an angle of about 60^0 and bombs are released at about 800ft.

But it was not only small-scale targets which were selected for the dive bombers attention in this campaign. During the Japanese assault on Nanking for example, which commenced on 18 September 1937, it was the dive bombers of the Second Combined Air Flotilla commanded by Rear-Adm Mitsunami, which, heavily escorted by Mitsubishi A5M 'Claude' fighters, carried out repeated raids on the city which was defended by Chinese pilots flying all manner of foreign fighters. The success achieved by the dive bombers of the Imperial Navy are even more worthy of note, when it is remembered that their training was designed for use against warship targets at sea, not land targets. Thus Nanking fell to the Japanese in December.

The importance the Japanese Navy attached to the dive bomber is illustrated by the fact that some 428 Aichi 'Susie' aircraft were built, at a time when the US Navy's counterparts were only being ordered in batches of two dozen or two score and the Royal Navy still had no real dive bombers at all in service.

In the summer of 1936 the Imperial Japanese Navy had issued its next expansion programme included in which was the *II-Shi* specification for a dive bomber to replace the 'Susie'. Although Aichi, Nakajimi and Mitsubishi all submitted their tenders, having all built models for the fleet, the latter was passed over due to its heavy commitment in the field of the Zero-Sen fighter, and the Navy placed orders for two prototypes from each of the other two companies.

If the Type 94 had derived from the ideas of the Heinkel company, then it can be claimed, to a lesser extent, that the Heinkel He70 *Blitz* influenced the design of the Aichi D3A of Type 99 'Val'. Indeed the Navy had purchased an example of the He70 earlier, flying it under the designation LXHe1, but no further orders had followed.

Nonetheless when the Aichi team of designers under Tokukishiro Goake commenced work on the new specification for the Am-17, a few features of the He70 attracted them even though their finished product was completely dissimilar in appearance. Once more the design called for ruggedness and strength, common factors in all specialised dive bombers and particularly so in those designed from the outset to operate from aircraft carriers.

The first prototype was completed and flew in January 1938, a single-engined monoplane with fixed undercarriage that gave it a superficial resemblance to the Stuka from some angles, but this was merely coincidence. The power-plant selected was the 710hp Nakajimi Hikari 1, a single-row nine-cylinder radial, but this proved to be insufficient once serious trials commenced. External dive brakes were fitted under each wing, hydraulically operated, but the original design did not prove outstanding. The crew of two were seated in tandem and a single 550lb bomb was carried in the by-now normal crutch with provision for bombs under each wing. It was the first mainly metal dive bomber constructed for Japan, although the control surfaces were fabric-covered.

Because of the relatively poor showing of the first prototype considerable re-engineering was done on the second aircraft. For a start the Hikari 1 was replaced by the 810hp Kinsei 44 fourteen-cylinder radial engine. The wing and tailplane were increased and an improved type of dive brake was incorporated. This improved version was designated D3A1 and in the usual comparative trials proved itself winner against the Nakajima D3N1. Aichi was therefore awarded the contract for the Type 99 carrier dive bomber and six pre-production models were ordered forthwith.

Japan took advantage of previous close connections with the Heinkel company when both the Japanese Navy and Army expressed some interest in the He118, despite its rejection by the Luftwaffe. Here the V-4 prototype is seen assembled in Japan for trials. Despite this the type was not further developed there but may have formed the genesis of the later Yokosuka D4Y dive bomber concept.

Meanwhile Heinkel had appeared on the Japanese scene more with his big He118. Already rejected by the Luftwaffe, the RLM had given the Heinkel team permission to try and sell the He118 abroad and with his previous connections Heinkel naturally contacted the Japanese Naval attaché. It appeared the right moment for such a move and, once again, it seemed that success was assured, for already the Imperial Navy were looking beyond the Type 99 into the future. The Army Air Force, by this time no doubt influenced by events in China, also indicated interest in the Heinkel design and separate negotiations were conducted in the 'normal' manner with both services by the German company. The result was that *both* placed orders for single aircraft, the Navy for delivery in February 1937 and the Army for October the same year. The Navy also acquired the manufacturing licence for the aircraft without waiting for evaluation tests. This proved somewhat premature, but they had already paid out 530,000 RM.

In the event it was the He118V4 version that was shipped out on the freighter *Kagu Maru* from Hamburg on 1 February and re-assembled at Yokosuka under the designation DXHe1 for flight testing. The He118V4 was powered by a DB601A engine, with a 1,175hp take-off rating, from which great things were expected. Preliminary plans were made for the Hitachi Seisakusho to undertake manufacture. Then came the tests.

These proved to be as big a blow as had those conducted at Rechlin the previous summer. Again, although the He118 showed a superlative turn of speed in level flight, 260mph being touched, it crashed during further evaluations, breaking up in mid-air, and, for the second time Heinkel had lost out. Although the He118V5 was shipped out on 15 September 1937 for similar trials by the Japanese Army nothing further resulted and the He118 dive bomber, outstanding in everything *except* dive bombing, had reached the end of the road.

It is doubtful whether the Heinkel company derived much satisfaction from the fact, but the Japanese Navy were still impressed with *some* of the design features of the ill-fated He118, but whether it influenced the final design of the Yokosuku D4Y is open to question. At all events they decided to go ahead with their own interpretation of what was required.

At the First Naval Air Technical Arsenal in Yokosuka a special design team was assembled under Masao Yarmana to translate the Navy's future requirements into an advanced dive bomber for the fleet. The specifications called for a top speed of over 280mph and a range of some 800 nautical miles with a 550lb bomb. This materialised in November 1940 as the D4Y1 *Suisei* (Comet) prototype, a really first-class dive bomber by any standard.

An all-metal low-wing monoplane, the D4Y had a retractable undercarriage, internal weapons bay with the crew of two seated in tandem under a streamlined canopy affording good all-round vision, important for both dive bombing and deck landings at sea. With a span of 37ft 8¾in the new bomber was compact enough to dispense with the complicated folding wing structure and this added to its strength. The diving brakes were of the electrically-operated slotted flap type, fitted forward of the landing flap. Its all-up weight was 8,047lb. Originally it was intended to fit a licence-built version of the DB601A, the Aichi Atsuta, but in the event this was not ready in time and a 960hp DB600G engine was imported. Four prototypes later carried the same power plant.

The D4Y1 first flew in December 1940 and hopes were high that full-scale production would quickly follow to allow the replacement of the 'Val' now that the war clouds were darkening, but this was not to be. Diving tests had shown up weaknesses in the wings under stress. Although limited production continued, the new dive bomber, like the American Vindicator earlier, was not allowed to carry out its main task, and was used for reconnaissance missions only. A further

Japanese Navy VALS taxiing out in readiness for a sortie on an island airstrip on 23 April, 1943. Taken from captured Japanese film

three years were to pass before the 'Judy', as it was code-named by the Allies, was able to take its place in the battle line of the Imperial Navy and meanwhile much had happened.

No such hold-ups were affecting the Aichi 'Val' however and with production lines in full swing this aircraft rapidly replaced the other types at sea and in front-line units in China. September 1940 saw the first combat mission of this dive bomber with the 12th Air Corps. This unit launched the first air raids against Chungking deep in the heart of China, from their base at Ichang on the afternoon of 3 September 1940, heralding an even deeper penetration of Japanese forces into the heartland of China. Part of their immunity was attributed to the fact that the sky was clear of Chinese aircraft, for, with the arrival of the 'Zeke' or Zero-Sen fighter in the skies above the battlefields, all opposition was annihilated and the 'Vals' were able to cruise to their targets and carry out their precision attacks undisturbed by anything other than primitive flak.

Fresh targets in south-western China also became available to the Aichi D3A when the Vichy French Government allowed the Japanese to operate from French air bases in Indo-China, the 'Vals' of the 14th Air Corps flying in October. On the seventh of that month Kunming airfield was brought under dive bombing attack, four Chinese aircraft being destroyed on the ground while the escorting fighters disposed of those that ventured aloft. No dive bombers were lost.

This pattern was repeated on 12 December when ten D3As raided Siangyun with similar results. At sea the new dive bombers joined their squadrons aboard the carriers after detailed deck trials earlier in 1940 aboard the *Akagi* and *Kaga*. In September 1941 all D3As were pulled out of China however. Events were rapidly building up to the long-forecast showdown with the United States and the Navy's front line dive bombers put in a period of intensive training against ship targets. There was no doubt that the really vital decision, when it came, would find the D3A operating against this type of opposition, a somewhat different proposition than the poorly defended Chinese airstrips. 85

The Japanese Army Air Force continued to show interest in dive bombing from time to time. The events in China and the continued tension with Soviet Russia along the Manchurian border, which led at times to all-out, if undeclared and unpublicised, war gave them further pause for thought in the late 1930s and designs were finally pressed forward for a dive bomber of their own. Two widely different designs resulted.

The Mitsubishi Type 99 *Guntei* was born directly out of combat experience in China and was the brainchild of the long-distance record holder Capt Yuzo Fujita. He saw considerable action in a ground-support role and was eventualy killed in combat. He saw the need for a small bomber which could be mass-produced to cary out the combined functions of tactical reconnaissance in advance of the forward troops, coupled with dive bombing ability to offer immediate pinpoint support against strongpoints which it had spotted which might delay any advance. To carry out such a combined mission it had to be agile enough to avoid enemy fighter opposition, but at the same time be sufficiently stressed to carry out dive bombing. It seemed an illogical combination, but the resulting Mitsubishi design fulfilled both roles well.

The Ki51 was a two-seater, low-wing monoplane and carried its bombs externally under each wing, but, in its primary role as a scout the bombs were light. It was powered by a single 900hp Kinsei Ha26 engine. Its *forte* was its good performance at low altitudes and for this it was fitted with small slats on the leading edge of each wing. Its radius of turn was around 500ft. Designed to operate close up with the leading troops from improvised airstrips it featured a take-off distance of only 540ft and a landing distance of 910ft.

Dive bombers over China. The sturdy, stubby shape of the Mitsubishi Type 99 Guntei was built as a cheap, reliable, short-range dive bomber to operate in the rugged terrain of mainland China. Code-named by the Allies as Sonia it saw extensive service during the war.

Over 1,470 of these aircraft were eventually built by Mitsubishi and Kawasaki, production continuing until July 1944; its main operational use was in China. Code-named 'Sonia' by the Allies, the Ki51 was a very successful type in its limited dive bombing role, even when used in the more mountainous regions of central China.

An attempt to improve on its performance led to the Manchurian Aircraft company producing an experimental version of the 'Sonia', the Ki71, powered by the Ha112 engine. It featured a retractable undercarriage and was armed with fixed machine-guns in the wings as well as ten small bombs. The fuselage was elongated and the wing featured a straight centre section with a dihedral angled outer section. However the Army showed no interest in this version. In common with most older types it found a limited employment as a suicide bomber at the end of the Pacific War, but was really too slow for effective operational use. Although outclassed by most contemporaries and not a true dive bomber in every sense of the word the 'Sonia' is deserving of this passing note in our story.

Of more interest was the Army's concept of the large, twin-engined dive bomber conceived at the same time. This was drawn up in response to the Army's need for a more powerful aircraft with a descent range to tackle the very likely possibility of war with Soviet Union along the Manchurian border. Not originally conceived as a pure dive bomber type, but termed the Ki48 light bomber, the specification called not only for an internal bomb bay capable of housing 880lb bombs but was to feature a mid-lower gun turret for ground straffing as well.

Powered by two 1,000hp Ha25 engines and with a crew of four the Ki48 was a mid-wing monoplane. The initial trials took place between July and November 1939, during which extensive flutter was encountered. To alleviate this the tailplane was raised by 15½in and the rear fuselage was considerably strengthened. The result was the Model 1 and some 550 of this type were built between July 1940 and 1942. Although it was used extensively in China it was not a great success in this form, being too heavy for its power plant. As a result the model 21A was brought out featuring two of the improved Ha115 engines. This version first appeared in April 1942, but of particular interest to our story was the model IIb which was specially designed as a dive bomber variant.

Air brakes were added to each wing and with these this heavy aircraft was capable of diving at 60° which was satisfactory from the Army's viewpoint. A fin was added in front of the tailplane for further strength in this role in some of the later models. Code-named *Lily* by the Allies during the Pacific War the Kawasaki Type 99 was one of the very few twin-engined dive bombers to see extensive war service (the others being the German Junkers Ju88 and the Soviet Pe2.) The Ki48 served in both China and the Pacific, but was not an especially brilliant aircraft, its maximum bomb load of 1,000lb being low for an aircraft of its size. About 2,000 were built before production terminated in October 1944. Both these types were not built originally as dive bombers but were adapted later, but experimentation continued by the Army and war experience showed that the need for dive bombers was valid. The result was the experimental Ki66.

The first directive for initiation of design and construction of the Army Air Force's first *real* dive bomber was issued in September 1941, after extensive studies of the Navy dive bombers. The Army decided, as in the case of the Ki48s to opt for a twin-engined aircraft. As this was the first such aircraft Japan had produced to be fitted with air-brakes, extensive wind-tunnel testing was carried out and, as a result, a multi-strip, semi-retractable air brake was selected for use. These were both effective and stable and one was fitted under each wing.

Work proceeded but slowly with the outbreak of war. The first Ki66 was not completed until November 1942 when it underwent a two-month test programme. Joined by a second and third prototype it was sent to the Army Experimental Command in February from which the aircraft emerged as an entirely satisfactory dive bomber but sadly deficient in speed.

Two further prototypes of a more powerful and faster version were commenced but in October 1943 all work was halted after a total of six aircraft had been built. This was not the final Japanese Army interest in dive bombers, but on the eve of the Pacific War the main strength of Japanese aircraft of this type rested with the Navy. By December 1941 this had reached a formidable degree of expertise.

Table 23: Japanese Navy Dive Bomber Strength December 1941			
Carrier based	No embarked	Shore based	No on strength
Akagi	18	Yoksuka Air Corps	12
Kaga	18	Saeki Air Corps	16
Hiryu	36	Usa Air Corps	36
Soryu	36		
Shokaku	27		
Zuikaku	27		

12 CONVERSION TO ACCURACY
Other nations developments and operations, 1932-40

Interest in the dive bomber not only encompassed the major naval powers like Britain, USA and Japan and the new Luftwaffe of Germany, but spread to other nations who experimented in their own ways at this period. The other two major powers who adopted dive bombers in limited form were France and Italy, while Soviet Russia failed to develop any interest until very late in the day. Lesser nations either copied or bought versions of the main types available, but some, like Poland and Sweden carried out their own research into the problem and came up with some novel answers.

In France the testing of the Gourdou-Leseurre GL430B1 continued throughout the mid-1930s and, at the end of 1935, this company received a small order from the French Navy for four aircraft derived from this design, these being designated as the GL432. The GL432 was a single-seat parasol-wing monoplane like the earlier experimental machines and could carry a single 150kg (330lb) or 225kg (500lb) bomb under the fuselage instead of the 50kg (110lb) missile of the prototype. Designed for carrier work it had a wingspan of under 13m (43ft) thus eliminating the need for folding wings aboard France's only operational carrier, *Béarn*. This aircraft flew for the first time on 28 January 1936 and trials continued into the war, the last flight being on 7 May 1940.

Four prototypes were constructed and a great number of tests were conducted in a four-year period, but aircraft were never actually embarked aboard the *Béarn*. Their ultimate fate is obscure but one was captured at Orly by the Germans and then destroyed, while another was seen at Bretigny at the beginning of 1946.

A further development of this design with a more powerful engine was the GL521 which had a maximum speed of 300khp (186mph). The first prototype of this version arrived at Villacoublay in March 1937 but during subsequent testing at St Raphaél it crashed into the sea. A second model was accepted in December 1938 and continued trials led to a new aircraft altogether.

It can thus be seen that between the wars the French Navy had put a great deal of thought into the dive bomber with nothing to show for it. Subsequently the only attack aircraft embarked aboard the *Béarn* between the summer of 1927 and the autumn of 1939 were Levasseur torpedo bombers, which doubled as limited dive bombers from time to time, like the Levasseur PL7 and PL101, both of which were three-seater biplanes with poor performance and only capable of shallow diving.

Like most Army Air Forces the French flirted on and off with the dive bomber concept between the wars, but was never really convinced of its potential until too late. Typical of this attitude was their attack bomber Bréguet 690. A twin-engined two-seater with clean lines, it was originally designed as a three-seater fighter, making its first flight in March 1938 and joining squadron service as the Br691AB2 in October 1939. After the Polish campaign there was a re-study of the dive bomber in most air services and an investigation was conducted into the feasibility of converting this aircraft to the dive bomber role, as the Br698, but France's collapse terminated all such projects before they had progressed very far.

The second prototype LN-40 dive bomber for the French Navy which was later designated the LN-401.

And so it was that the *Aéronavale* alone continued to seek a satisfactory dive bomber of their own pre-war. The design for a modern aircraft came from the Societe Anonyme Loire-Nieuport designer M. Pillon. His earlier two-seater shipboard fighter for the Nieuport company, the Ni140, had not entered service but he gained insight into the special problems of the Navy during its development, while his single-seater land fighter, the Ni161, although similarly not adopted, gave him expertise in stress problems.

Work on the first prototype LN40 commenced in 1937 and it flew for the first time in June 1938. At casual glance it owed a good deal to the Ju87, featuring similar gull-wing configuration, but it was much more advanced and had a fully retractable undercarriage. Powered by a 690hp Hispano-Suiza 12Xcrs engine it was an aerodynamically clean single-seater. The lower portions of the single rudder were split vertically, dividing right and left and serving as additional dive brakes. Six pre-production models were ordered in 1936, and, after trials this was increased by a production order for the LN410 for the Navy.

Meanwhile events in Spain had aroused the Army's interest and a land-based version was built, the LN411. The *Armeé de l'Air* in fact ordered three LN40 prototypes in August 1938, the initial Navy order for seven LN410s followed on 26 August and the following year, on 3 July 1939, for another batch of thirty-six. The Army order for the LN411 came in September 1939, but almost at once they decided it was under-powered for their requirements and required an engine of at least 1,000hp to make it viable in their eyes. In the event they turned to American builders for their dive bomber needs.

But it was not just the LN411 that the Army Air Force could not decide upon, it was the dive bomber as a whole. Indeed despite the purchase of foreign aircraft being approved the Army Air Force came out quite firmly against dive bombing on 14 September 1939, and re-affirmed this policy even after the fate of Poland and on the eve of their own lesson, 25 April 1940!

Of the forty LN411s ordered and completed, thirty-nine were handed over to the Navy when all Army interest officially ceased at that date. The solitary remaining exception was retained by the Army, who planned to develop it further and work continued for a while until surrender forced it to be hidden away. The original airframe was fitted with the 1,100hp HS12Y-51 engine and had a re-designed wing structure. Not until after the liberation did the solitary LN42 prototype, as it was designated, continue development. The decision to hand over the LN411s to the Navy was taken on 13 October 1939 and welcomed by the Navy, still critically short of modern aircraft, their own modest orders being only slowly fulfilled. In fact by the time of the French surrender in June 1940 only twenty-eight had been completed in addition to the three LN40 prototypes. In September 1939 there were just *three* LN410s in service!

With its own programme in total disarray as war drew closer the French Navy urgently cast around for a solution. They found it in the Chance Vought SB2U Vindicator. Although the Vindicator was in service with the US Navy as its first monoplane dive bomber and was popular and well-tried, by late 1938 it was beginning to be phased out as the new Douglas SBD came along and both the US Navy (and the Vought company) were wondering what to do with surplus aircraft in the near future. This dilemma coincided with the French need and both came together at the Paris Air Show of November 1938 with the V-156 (as the export version of the Vindicator had been designated).

It had been planned to take the V156 around Europe after showing it in December at the *Salon Aeronautique International,* but when the French expressed interest this plan was dropped. The French Government had decided as early as May 1938 that the Vought V156s were necessary and planned to order ninety of them (although only forty were ultimately delivered). The prodding behind this decision by the Navy was the fact that the whole LN401 programme of tests was coming apart at the seams, airframe failures had developed in those aircraft that got off the runways and production problems and accidents were multiplying.

The American sales team of Lyman Bullard and Earl Irwin spent two months at Orly airfield, while technical changes were itemised for the Vindicator to fit in with French service requirements and handbooks were translated. In February 1939 they returned to the Chance Vought plant at Stamford, Connecticut, with the prototype. Here the company was already hard at work turning out production models of the V156F to French requirements.

The actual modifications were in fact few, the French version featuring a reverse operating throttle, finger type diving brakes (the Americans were lowering their undercarriages during dives due to the failure of their own dive brake system), and instruments graduated in the metric system. A French radio was fitted, plus French machine guns (which had an alarming habit of jamming after twenty rounds!). Although the standard US Navy bomb crutch was retained, capable of lifting bombs up to 1,000lb, the French rarely used such large missiles for their dive bombers.

The first deliveries began just before the outbreak of the war, five Vindicators being shipped out to Orly for re-assembly in July 1939. Ensg Boone T. Guyton had left the US Navy and joined Chance Vought that month as a test pilot. With his vast expertise of Vindicator operations he was a natural choice as the liaison test pilot and he went to Orly to join Capt Gerald Mesny, the French Project Officer, in getting the aircraft operational.

The French V156 first flew over its homeland on 6 August 1939 and by the outbreak of war six were ready and tested. After 3 September 1939 the US neutrality laws caused complications, but a compromise agreement enabled Guyton to go on flying and testing the dive bombers as manufacturer's property before they were officially handed over to France. After nineteen had been handed-over assembly work moved to Brest for safety and the first squadron formed under Capt Mesny, followed by a second later at Cherbourg. By April

1940 the first batch of forty V156Fs had joined the French navy and the American technicians left, there being no immediate sign of the second group of fifty arriving, nor, in fact, did they ever arrive in France.

Meanwhile the decision had been taken to replace the American bomb crutch with the bigger French Alkan type. This involved modifications to the fuselage to enable the bomb to clear the propeller arc, but by May 1940 this had still not been carried out, so in true dive bombing runs only underwing bombs could at first be used. The heavier bombload could therefore only be utilised in a more shallow dive with consequent lack of precision. The French Navy V156Fs carried a single 450kg (1,000lb) bomb under the body, or else two or three 150kg (330lb) bombs (one under each wing and one amidships), on their combat missions.

With the formation of the first units elementary exercises commenced and, never having had modern equipment, these had to start almost from scratch. In November 1939 the first aircraft went to their war stations, although the sole French aircraft carrier *Béarn* was rarely used operationally. In September 1939 she had aboard nine Vought 156Fs and four LN401s but, of necessity, had to land them to ferry other aircraft from the USA. In March 1940, following several such trans-Atlantic trips, the *Béarn* was employed in conducting deck landing trials off Toulon, as a result the French Navy dive bombers were used mainly as land-based combat planes.

Out of the first batch order of forty V156Fs, only twenty-four were eventually operational and they were organised in five *Escadrilles* with the available LN401s and LN411s.

Table 24: French Navy Dive Bomber Strength April 1940			
Unit	Commander	Aircraft type	Complement
Escadrille AB-1	Lt-de-Vaisseau Mesny	Vought V156F	12
Escadrille AB-2	Lt-de-Vaisseau Lorenzi	Loire LN-410	12
Escadrille AB-3	Lt-de-Vaisseau Pierret	Vought V156F	12
Escadrille AB-4	Lt-de-Vaisseau Laine	Loire LN-410 & 411	12
Escadrille AB-5	Lt-de-Vaisseau Dupont	Loire LN-411	12

Of these the fifth *Escadrille* had been formed at Houtin in April but was still not equipped and trained. Five more Vought V156Fs were at Hyeres in southern France awaiting the return of *Béarn* for deck trials, but she never came. The reason for her absence was the further order of dive bombers made by the French Army Air Force during one of their earlier bursts of temporary enthusiasm for the type.

Although even more outdated than the Vindicator, the Curtiss SBC4 was still in production for the US Navy in 1939 for reserve units. Early in that year, the French Army Air Force had placed an order for ninety Curtiss 77s (the export version of the SBC4) to be delivered as quickly as possible. The US Government had sanctioned the deal, despite the many complications involved regarding neutrality, and in order to speed up delivery the US Navy took fifty of their own SBC4s out of service and Curtiss refurbished them to French requirements. The US Navy deficit was to be made up from the last fifty aircraft of the French order later.

Modifications to these SBC4s were simple: a new seat to take the French type parachute B and fitting of French machine guns, and was carried out at Wright Field, Dayton, Ohio. The aircraft were then flown to Houlton, Maine, for transshipment by road, across the Canadian border, to Dartmouth, this devious route being used to avoid infringing neutrality laws too obviously. From Canada the dive bombers were transported to Halifax, Nova Scotia and loaded aboard the *Béarn* for ferrying to France.

This all went almost according to plan. Of the fifty aircraft duly refitted, one was lost in a snowstorm *en-route* (NXC21) and its American pilot, B.R. Wallberg, killed. The remaining forty-nine reached the border intact and were duly wheeled over to Dartmouth, fully camouflaged and with French nationality markings already painted on. However the *Béarn* could only accommodate forty-four aircraft and these were duly embarked in June 1940. The remaining five aircraft (NXC48, C49, C51, C53 and C54) remained at Dartmouth until August, when they were taken over by the British. On 17 February 1941 these ex-French SBC4s were delivered to Rissington airfield in the UK for training FAA engineers after the RAF had tested them and stated that they were unfit for European combat. These machines were allocated the British serials AS467-471.

To conclude the story of these French dive bombers, on the German invasion of France *Béarn* was diverted to Fort-de-France, Martinique and there all forty-four SBC4s were disembarked under the control of the Vichy French authorities. The aircraft were parked out in the open and slowly rotted away in the humid temperature. By 1942 the majority were unserviceable but when the island finally went over to the Allies, pro-Vichy individuals blew many of them up with explosives.

Italian experience largely followed that of France in belated attempts to produce an indigenous dive bomber. All aeronautical development was in the hands of the *Regia Aeronautica* and the Navy had no say in the matter, so dive bombing languished. It was not until the sanctions and possibility of war with Great Britain in 1935 over the invasion of Abyssinia that the need for a precision bomber to attack the British Mediterranean Fleet initiated a fresh look at this neglected form of bombing attack in Italy.

As a result of this crisis preliminary plans were put in hand for the rapid development of a dive bomber by the Italian *Stato Maggiore dell'Aeronautica* to the SIAI Marchetti company. Their specification called for a single-seater dive bomber to carry a 500kg bomb and the airframe was to withstand stability tests

A fine study of the first Italian designed and built SM85 dive bomber. Its wooden framed box fuselage and unmistakeable shape can be seen. It suffered from poor pilot visibility, and was grossly underpowered despite being a twin-engined design.

in dives from 40⁰ to 90⁰. Alessandro Marchetti thought that an aircraft fitted with two 460hp Piaggio PVII engines should be able to conform to these instructions and design work commenced at once on 'Programme R'.

The first result was the prototype SM85 which first flew on 19 December 1936 (MM374) and was a twin-engined monoplane with a cantilever wing and retractable landing gear. It featured a very simple box-type fuselage with a marked upward sweep to nose and tail and earned it the unofficial title 'Flying Banana'. A single-seater, the original had an enclosed cockpit housed well forward with a simple fairing behind it and had a very restricted view. First flown by test pilot Adriano Bacual this aircraft was delivered to the Furbara test centre on 27 April 1937. Designed to operate against an enemy fleet, the early trials, held that spring, were against warship targets underway. Many high-ranking Air Force and Navy officers attended, as did Mussolini himself, because it was he who was pressing hardest for such an aircraft to further his ambitions at this time.

Two further prototypes joined the first at Furbara (MM385 and MM386) and these were flown in March and April 1937, both featuring small improvements and a better designed cockpit. Although not too impressive in its performance an initial production order was placed for ten (Type B) and this was followed by a second order for a further twenty-two (Type C) in which visibility for the pilot was increased by completely re-designing the cockpit as a raised 'bubble' type forward with a 'glasshouse' extension aft.

These first S85s (re-designated in June 1938 as the SM85) were delivered to the experimental Italian dive bomber unit *Reparto Sperimentale Volo a Tuffo,* commanded by Capt Ercolani, for evaluation and development of techniques. They discovered, after repeated testing, that although the S85 handled well enough in horizontal flight, its speed was insufficient in the dive to be effective and listed among the many other faults found by this unit during the next year was insufficient power, weak landing gear and the need for variable-pitch airscrews. In short, the plane was *not* a success and although proudly displayed as an operational dive bomber to visiting officials like Germany's Erhard Milch

A one-off refinement of the 'Flying Banana' was the SM86. It incorporated many refinements over the SM85 and its designer had greater faith in its abilities than the Italian Air Force itself. Flown on combat missions against targets in Malta and Greece with Ju87 units, its test pilot was finally killed in a Stuka and the SM86 was laid up and then written off for good.

in March 1939, it was never likely to be! However Benito Mussolini expected a dive bomber squadron to proclaim to the world, so one was formed.

This was the 96⁰ *Gruppo Bombardamento a Tuffo* (BaT) established on 20 March 1940 with two *Squadriglie,* 236 and 237, and a total strength of nineteen aircraft. However all SM85 production had ceased after the thirty-sixth aircraft in December 1939 and on Italy's entry into the war in June 1940, this *Gruppo Autonomo* was transferred to the island of Pantelleria to await its chance to attack the British Fleet.

The improved SM86 was a direct development of the SM85. It is true to say that many of the lessons learned from the earlier effort were put right in the prototype (MM397), for example stronger landing gear, better vision and the like, but it was no more a success than the SM85. More powerful 600hp Walther Sazitta engines were the major refinements, driving three-bladed variable pitch propellers, but the drive system remained the same.

This prototype was delivered to the 1⁰ *Centro Sperimentale* at Guidonia on 10 May 1940 by test pilot Elio Scarpini after its maiden flight had taken place at

The Italian Breda Ca65 was utilised by the Italian contingent of the Intervention Forces during the Spanish Civil War in the dive bombing role with some outstanding successes to its credit although not built for the role. Here the rough forward airstrips of Spain hold three being serviced ready for another mission against Republican forces. Although receiving less publicity than the Condor Legion of Germany in the same conflict the Regia Aeronautica contingent was far larger.

Vergiate on 8 April 1939. Testing by the experimental group pilots resulted in very luke warm reports about this aircraft's capabilities. Not satisfied with the adverse reactions, Savoia asked the Ministry to test the aircraft in combat. The SM86, piloted by Scarpini, was therefore sent to join 96⁰ *Gruppo* at Comiso, along with several Ju87s, arriving on 4 September 1940 to await its chance to prove itself, flying with 236 *Squadriglie.*

Apart from these custom-built dive bombers Italy conducted other experiments and learned from combat in the Spanish Civil War. Italian participation in that conflict was more widespread than that of Germany and Italian aircraft were early in the field on Franco's side, among them being a section of Breda 65s serving with 65⁰ *Squadriglie Assalto* based at Puig Moreno. The Breda 65, designed by Giuseppe Panzieri and Antonio Parano, was one of the most important designs of the pre-war *Regia Aeronautica* in that it introduced to that service all-metal construction and retractable landing gear. Of some interest to this story is the fact that during the Aragona offensive of July 1938 three of these aircraft were employed as dive bombers. They carried out their attack on the bridges at Flix across the Elbro River in dives of 80^0, and succeeded in destroying these very important targets outright. In all eighteen Breda 65s were used in Spain, only two being lost.

In early 1939 an Italian aviation team visited Germany and observed the aircraft being produced by Junkers and Heinkel, including an impressive tour of the Ju87 assembly lines at Dessau. They returned with new demands for the Italian industry to develop the dive bomber and a competition was set up. They also recommended that the Stuka itself be tried out for the *Regia Aeronautica*. Whether or not the Stuka design impressed itself upon Italian manufacturers as the ideal at which to aim is not certain, but certainly the design ultimately produced by the Breda team of Vittorio Calderini and Mario Pittoni bore a marked resemblance to that aircraft.

It was on 28 August 1939 that the Italian Air Ministry announced the competition for dive bomber designs open to either single or twin-engined aircraft. The single-engined Breda 201 was more streamlined than the Ju87, but featured the inverted gull wing configuration. It was powered by a Daimler-Benz DB601 engine, had retractable undercarriage and slotted dive brakes of the Northrop principle on the inner surfaces of the trailing edge of each wing, with small underwing dive flaps on the inner edges. The tailwheel was fixed. The Breda 201 first flew, piloted by Mario Acerbi, on 3 July 1941.

Caproni's entry to the competition was the Ca335 *Tuffo,* designed by Cesare Pallavicione. It was developed in conjunction with the Ca335 and powered by a single Isotta Fraschini IF *Delta* RC35 of 700hp. The Ca335 *Tuffo* was a single-seater of all-metal construction, had retractable landing gear and could carry a single 500kg (1,100lb) bomb. Flown by test pilot Ettore Wengi this prototype was evaluated during January 1941 and delivered to Guidonia for testing, but no orders resulted.

The CANSA Fc12 was really designed as a dive bomber trainer and was a private venture by Fiat's CANSA subsidiary. A monoplane, it was fitted with dive brakes under each wing, fully retractable landing gear and a light bomb rack under each wing. It first flew at Cameri in 1939 and underwent trials until 1940 but was never evaluated by the Air Force.

Another design was the IMAM Ro41. A single-seater fighter, this aircraft was serving with 5^0 *Stormo Assalto* and was used to conduct a special study of ground attack utilising a diving angle of 45^0 by 98^0 *Squadriglie,* 7^0 *Gruppo,* 5^0 *Stormo* when they formed the *Nucleo Volo a Tuffo* under Capt Ercolani. It was used as a dive bomber trainer during the war.

The IMAM Ro57bis was originally conceived as a twin-engined fighter and designed by G. Galasso. Powered by two 870hp Fiat A74 RC38 engines, the prototype (MM407) was modified as a dive bomber at Guidonia in the summer of 1940 by the addition of two dive brakes under the wings, a bomb rack for a 500kg (1,100lb) bomb under the fuselage and an extra bomb-aiming window cut in the fuselage. With these alterations it underwent testing at the hands of Aldo Ligabo and Cdr Mantel. Although, as a dive bomber, it was really underpowered and of limited range, the Ro57bis was nonetheless offered to the Air Force and 200 were ordered in 1942, (subsequently reduced to ninety). Although far from outstanding, the Ro57bis is worthy of note for it was to achieve the only big Italian success in dive bombing with their own aircraft during the war.

Another contender for the competition was the twin-engined Piaggio P122 dive bomber powered by the Piaggio PXI RC40 radial engine of 1,000hp. It was developed from the P108 through to the P133, but was not accepted into service. As well as this assembly of testbeds the Italian, in common with most other nations, tried to adapt existing aircraft to perform dive bombing of various types. Pre-war experiments of this kind included the Fiat Cr42 AS Falco. This famous little biplane fighter (the Italian equivalent of the Gloster Gladiator), was adapted to a ground-attack role in 1940. The possibility of it carrying 250kg bombs was investigated and during the Greek Campaign a few were used as glide bombers with anti-personnel bombs (*spezzoni*).

At Guidonia in the autumn of 1940 dive brakes were tested on the Caproni Ca310 in the somewhat optimistic hope that it would thus somehow transform itself into an Italian equivalent of the Ju88! The brakes used were the Ballerio SCA but, not surprisingly, the results were abortive.

Similar thoughts were entertained with the Breda Ba88, with, perhaps, rather more chance of success. A number of these twin-engined, high-wing monoplanes were modified as a dive bomber trainer. Tested thus in 1940 in diving missions, they were further modified with enlarged wing areas, more powerful Fiat A74 engines and all defensive armament removed. Dive brakes were fitted under each wing, but the aircraft were not successful and used operationally only for a brief period.

Yet further experiments of a similar nature were tried later in the war and will be described in their proper place, but it can be seen that, if anything, the *Regia Aeronautica* was even less well equipped for dive bombing than either Britain or France on the outbreak of war. It is little wonder then that they quickly turned to Germany for help to solve their problems in this field.

In Poland, we have already seen how the final commitment to a ground-attack policy had resulted in the PZL P23A Karas aircraft which entered service in the Polish Air Force and was replaced in the same role by the improved P23B, but this was of course by no stretch of the imagination a dive bomber, nor was there any call for one initially. World events however influenced Poland as they did other nations but the original thought behind Poland's first dive bomber design was the replacement of the P11 single-engined fighter. Seeking to remedy a deficiency in both these types led the Polish Department of Aeronautics to study the possibility of combining the functions of both as an economical and quick answer, on the lines of the FAA Skua. The result was the P38/39 concept.

The idea was not exactly the same as the Skua however; the Poles instead, planned to produce a basic airframe that could be completed either to perform as a two-seater fighter, the P39, *or* as a dive bomber, while another version of the same aircraft would be completed as an attack plane or long-range escort fighter. It is the former that we are concerned with here, for the P39 designation was later dropped and both versions were designated the P38, later given the name *Wilk* (Wolf).

The P38 was in fact a remarkable aircraft for such a nation as Poland, not rich or technically advanced, to produce for itself. It was an all-metal, cantilever monoplane with retractable undercarriage. It was originally to be powered by either the Hispano-Suiza or the Foka V-type engine, but these plans fell through. It was felt undesirable to produce the Hispano-Suiza in Poland and their own Foka engine in turn proved unreliable in testing during development work.

Instead the Gnome-Rhône double-row radial engine was selected, but negotiations for the licence to manufacture dragged on until 1938, while the plans to adapt the P38, re-designed the P38-Lampart, were even more sluggish. As it was the Ranger powered Wilk second prototype was not completed until the spring of 1939 and neither of the two aircraft produced had even conducted their trials when war broke out on 1 September.

97

Therefore the only aircraft found by the advancing German forces that resembled dive bombers in Poland were some 250 PWS26 single-engined biplane trainers. They had been hastily adapted to carry two 26½lb bombs on underwing racks, but, in the event, there was not time for them to be used in combat.

Dive bombers of various kinds and adaptations served with most of the minor powers pre-war. Probably the most active were those employed in China and Spain.

In 1934 the Chinese Central Government had placed orders with Heinkel for twelve He50a biplanes, similar to those used by the Luftwaffe, but powered by the more reliable Jupiter VI engine and designated He66aCH. These dive bombers were shipped out that summer. A repeat order was placed for a further twelve a year later, and these had the SAM22B radial engines as in the Luftwaffe version. Known as the He50bCH these machines were completed in the spring of 1935, but held up for six months due to the Luftwaffe's own shortages in this type of aircraft. They finally arrived in China in January 1936.

These He50bCHs were assembled at Peking in the summer of 1937 and had their tail surfaces painted yellow to avoid confusion with the Japanese D1A1, but they only saw active service for a short period before being relegated to training duties.

The use in Spain of the Hs123 has already been mentioned and, as the popular *Angelito* they performed well. Another aircraft, the British Hawker Fury fighter, also saw limited service in the same conflict. Three of these biplane fighters were ordered in 1935. Powered by a single Hispano-Suiza 12 XBrs engine they were first flown in Spanish colours in July 1936 and actually arrived in that country on 11 April 1936 in company with an Osprey from the same company.

A week later the Civil War commenced and the Fury aircraft (4-1, 4-2 and 4-3), became split between the opposing forces, two being flown by the Government and No 4-2 by the Nationalists. They appear to have changed hands from time to time before being written off, but one, (4-3) was reported to have been used as a dive bomber before being finally destroyed in 1938.

Away from Europe Argentina took delivery of the Hawk III, the export model of the US Navy's BF2C-1, while Thailand also purchased a number of Hawk III dive bombers before the end of the war and may have used them against the Vichy-French in their brief conflict during 1941.

But of the smaller nations it was Sweden who made the greater strides, initiated the greatest research and evolved the most-advanced theories of the dive bomber idea during the 1930s and 1940s. Their detailed studies resulted in the AGA dive bomb sight which aroused even the interest and admiration of the RAF when Sqdn Ldr Adams served as liason officer with the Royal Swedish Air Force in 1938-9.

The Royal Swedish Air Force (*Flygvapnet*) had not been formed as a separate service until 1 July 1926 and only reached an establishment of eighty aircraft by 1931 instead of the planned 229. This state of affairs continued until further agitation led to a reorganisation under the 1936 Defence Resolution when the *Flygvapnet* finally became truly independant of the Army and Navy.

Sweden, during this period, relied on the import of foreign aircraft for most of its front-line strength, and in 1934 they purchased three Hawker Hart day bombers from Britain, along with some Osprey's for naval co-operation work. At the same time talks were opened on the possibilities of the manufacture of these aircraft under licence at the ASJA Linköping, the forerunner of SAAB, the AB *Götaverken,* Gothenburg and the CVN (Central Maintenance Depot) at Malmslätt, under the designation S7. With the receipt of intelligence of dive bombing developments abroad, Maj Gyllenkrook of the *Flygvapnet* sought to

Ready for action, which never came. A Wing of Royal Swedish Air Force B5 licence-built Hawker Harts, which formed the basic dive bomber strength of this neutral nation squeezed between German threatened Norway and Soviet dominated Finland in the uneasy winter of 1940.

silence continued naval opposition to the Air Force's expansion plans by practical demonstration of the accuracy of dive bombing against naval targets, and the three Harts were selected as suitable aircraft for this purpose.

The first dive bombing trials were conducted by No 4 Wing at Frösön in northern Jämtland and showed that the Hart was both capable of withstanding such dives and of hitting the targets. 'Sensational Swedish Dive-bombing', ran one press headline at the results. The tests were expanded by No 4 Wing during the early spring of 1935. Of interest during these trials of 1934 however was the fact that the German Junkers team were testing the K47 at Frösön at the same time as the first Hart trials there. The Limhamn-assembled K47 was conducting rocket-bombing tests and the Swedish and German teams had the opportunity to study each other's tests in detail.

During February and March 1935 comparison trials with horizontal bombing and dive bombing were conducted here too, and again the dive bomber results came out far superior. All three British-built Harts were used in these trials, which were led by Capt Paul af Uhr from F3 Malmslätt and among other experts were Capts Alf Svenzén and Hugo Svenow, while the more notable junior Lts were Ragnar Carlgren and Nils Selander. At the same time they were re-designated as the B4 Light Bomber and delivery of fifty licence-built Harts from the Linköping ASJA factory were well-advanced, these Harts being fitted with the 590hp Nohab Mercury VII radial engine built under licence at Trollhättan.

The initial tests proved very satisfactory, Lt Carlgren reporting that after intensive training he could maintain a diving angle of 80-85°. In the summer of 1935 therefore the F1 Light Bomber (Attack) Squadron was set up at Västeras under the command of Carl Bergström with dive bombing as its main programme. Continued training in this form of attack continued the following winter, and in all, fifteen to twenty pilots were put through the course. Swedish dive bombing was therefore well-established. We shall return to the Swedish developments in this art in later chapters.

13 THE WARBIRDS PREPARE
The main contenders pre-war: Aircraft, training, tactics 1939-41

The five principal dive bombers in service with the major powers on the eve of World War II were the German Ju87 Stuka, the American Douglas SBD Dauntless, the Japanese Aichi D3A1 'Val', the British Blackburn Skua and the French Loire-Nieuport LN-410. Just entering service was the German long-range Junkers Ju88, while the American Curtiss SB2C-1 Helldiver and the Japanese Yokosuka D4Y 'Judy' were under development.

Table 25: Basic Details of the Six Main Dive Bombers in Combat Service 1939-41						
Aircraft	LN410	Skua-II	D3A1 'Val'	Ju87B	SBD Dauntless	Ju88A-1
Country	France	Britain	Japan	Germany	USA	Germany
Engine (hp)	1 x 690	1 x 905	1 x 990	1 x 1,100	1 x 1,010	2 x 1,200
Span (ft/in)	45' 11¾"	46'2"	47'7¼"	45'3½"	41'6"	59'10¾"
Length (ft/in)	32'0¾"	35'7"	32'4¾"	36'5"	32'2"	47'1"
Height (ft/in)	11'5¾"	12'6"	12'7½"	13'2"	12'7"	15'11"
Max Speed (mph)	220	225	240	238	253	280
Weight (lb)	6,250	5,490	5,309	5,980	5,903	22,500
Ceiling (ft)	31,168	20,200	30,050	26,250	29,600	27,500
Range (miles)	746	760	915	370	860	1,553
No of Bombs	1	1	1	1	1	4
Bomb Load (lb)	496	500	551	1,100	1,200	3,969
Crew	1	2	2	2	2	4
Designed Base	Carrier	Carrier	Carrier	Land	Carrier	Land

The only true British dive bomber in service at the outbreak of World War II, the Blackburn Skua, deserves special attention for that very reason. From the original confusing specifications the company, beset by enormous difficulties, produced a very good dive bomber whose fighter performance was, *and was always intended to be,* a secondary consideration.

The design team led by G.E Petty at Blackburns quickly responded to the order issued by the Air Ministry in April 1935. The first prototype (K5178) flew in 1937 and was shown at Hendon display that same year. The second prototype soon followed (K5179) differing only in having an elongated nose. Both were powered by the Bristol Mercury XII radial engine and with these they conducted their trials.

As a result of quantity production orders placed by the Air Ministry for 190 Skuas to a modified 25/36 specification in July 1936, a major change in these aircraft from the initial pair was the adoption of the lower-powered Bristol Perseus XII sleeve-valved engine and these became Nos L2867-L3056. The first Skuas began to join squadron service with No 800 Squadron at Worthy Down in the autumn of 1938, six being sent initially.

The main features of the Skua are of interest. The fuselage was of metal monocoque structure in two sections which were joined forward of the fin. Alclad frames, stringers and special sections riveted together, held the flush-riveted plating surface. Special attention was paid to buoyancy in the event of ditching in carrier operations at sea. Two water-tight compartments were built into the main structure, one forward under the pilot's floor and the other aft behind the cockpit.

The whole after section of the fuselage carrying the tail unit and tail wheel was detachable and built in the same manner as the main section to which it was bolted. A light metal fairing was carried underneath for the fixed tail wheel. The tail unit was fixed and cantilever. The elevators had inset-hinges and trimming tabs with irreversible controls operated from the cockpit. The cantilever fin was detachable from the fuselage. The rudder was horn-balanced with inset hinges and the balance tab operated automatically.

The wings were in three sections, centre and two outer with the former detachable, being bolted under the fuselage so the upper surface formed the bottom of the front watertight compartment of the fuselage. The wing-tips were upswept at the tips and watertight compartments were built into each wing. The flaps were all-metal. The undercarriage retracted outward and upward into recesses in the other main planes. The hydraulic system operated the retractable undercarriage units and the flaps on the wings. The pneumatic system comprised an engine-driven compressor, air reservoir, oil reservoir and trap, air filter and pressure gauge.

The flying control surfaces were operated by a normal system of cables, pulleys and levers, the control-column had a knuckle-joint so that lateral movements of the upper portion controlled the ailerons.

The Bristol Perseus XII air-cooled, sleeve-valve, radial engine was fitted with a controllable pitch three-bladed airscrew. It provided 830hp for take-off and was rated at 745hp at 2,400rpm at 6,500ft. It was cowled by a fairing ring and the cooling was controlled by gills.

The crews were accommodated in a long enclosed cockpit with a transparent cover. The pilot was over the centre section and had an excellent outlook in all directions, especially for landing, in a heated cockpit. The observer-gunner was seated well abaft the wings, the glass was strengthened and special frames protected both from rolling-over accidents.

The Skua was fitted with fixed machine-guns in the leading edges of the wings firing forward outside the airscrew disc, and a single moveable machine-gun on a special mounting at the back of the cockpit. Provision was made to mount a camera gun on the starboard side of the centre-section controlled, like the wing guns, by the pilot.

The method and details of a typical Skua attack plan are shown illustrated in Diagrams 3-5 and are based on sketches made for the author by Skua pilots. Again these varied according to a number of conditions including weather, type of target, bombload carried, whether surprise was achieved and the like.

Given this aircraft in sufficient numbers the FAA was confident of showing just what up-to-date dive bombing could achieve at sea. They quickly got their chance.

The Luftwaffe's dive bomber units had, by the autumn of 1939, completely re-equipped with the Ju87B-1, the establishment totalling 336 aircraft of which 288 were immediately available for operations. At this time the B2 replaced it on the production line at the *Weser* works.

Refinements over the B1 were restricted to minor items, the chief of which was a broad-bladed airscrew, while the *maximum* bombload could rise to 2,200lb

Diagram 3: Moving to attack in *en echelon* vics

Flick over

A Flight

B Flight *en echelon*

Flick over

Into dive position — in Flights or line ahead of squadron.

Each flight C.O. on reaching this point, climbs, rollsover and was on the dive path on target.

C Flight

Flight in vic moves up *en echelon* to port or starboard.

Diagram 3b:
Skua attack sequence

Around 800ft release bombs, up flaps 'drop like a brick' increasing speed at target, then away, with Nos 2 & 3 following up. (Pilots noted each others hits). Flak has little or no time to lock on 1 before 2 & 3 are at bomb release point.

Diagram 4: Lining up target vessel with electronic ring and bead sight. Gunsight used for dive bombing.

Target ship

Ship turns

Skua rotates in dive so ships track remains along the gun sight fore and aft.

NOTE: The ball of the turn-and-bank indicator *must be centred* otherwise the ordnance will fly off at a tangent, resulting in a complete miss.

(A)

(B)

(C)

Aim off to allow for estimated ship speed and wind.

Down to 800 feet.
OFF BOMB!

Target getting larger in sight - tracking along ship's course, *Skua* follows by rotating its turn.

(D)

(E)

Diagram 5: Final attack dive

Observer/gunner tries to hang on (he had a harness with a clip tying him to the floor) so as not to be thrown out.

Aircraft speed now steady.
Pilot hangs on his straps.

Gunsight

500 LB bomb swung down and out to avoid prop.

Target ship

with the second crew member deleted and other modifications. Variants of this subtype included:

Ju87B-2/U2 with improved radio communications equipment.
Ju87B-2/U3 incorporating additional armour protection.
Ju87B-2/U4 an experimental modification with skis instead of wheels; it was not a success.

The intended strike group for the aircraft carriers Germany had under construction or planned, were to be equipped with the Stuka, and special pre-production models stressed for catapult launch and fitted with arrester hooks were designated the Ju87C (*Cäsar*). A further refinement of this type with folding wings and jettisonable undercarriage for sea ditching became the Ju87C-T (*Trägerflugzeug,* carrier aircraft). When the project was later cancelled and work stopped on the *Graf Zeppelin,* most of these carrier Stukas were re-converted back to Ju87B-2 standard.

Another development which paid handsome dividends was the Ju87R (*Richard*), which, like the above variations, was introduced early in 1940. It was a long-range modification for anti-shipping strikes featuring drop tanks and extra radio equipment, while the R2 was a further improvement on this type.

Training for Stuka crew was tough and detailed in order to produce first-class air groups for precision work. The first *Stukaschule* was set up at Kitzingen, and later *Stukaschule 2* was established at Graz in Austria. As a temporary measure there were also *Stukavorschulen* for preliminary Stuka training, but these were disbanded on 17 November 1942. All operational units had *Ergänzungsstaffeln* replacement sections mainly deployed at the home base in which new personnel were trained to operational readiness as far as possible. From 17 November 1942 these sections were organised to *Ergäzungsgruppen* one for each Stuka *Geschwader.*

Familisation training in 1939 was done with the Hs123 and the Ju87A, during which formation flying, fighter tactics to elementary standard and dive bombing were carried out averaging about thirty sorties in all or just over fifty hours actual flying time

Whereas the dive bombers of most other powers were *naval* weapons first and foremost and concentrated their training on anti-shipping tactics, the exact reverse was the case in Germany, but nonetheless specific training against ship targets was carried out, especially of course in the carrier-destined units. A wooden cross anchored off-shore was one basic target in order to assimilate crews with the special difficulties of estimating height and wind-drift at sea.

Just prior the outbreak of war the existing formations of nine *Sturzkampf-geschwader* were authorised to be expanded to twelve in addition to *Träger-gruppes* I and II/186; the first of the latter formed at Burg near Magdeburg and the second was in the process of formation at Kiel. This was never completed and the naval units were re-converted back to normal Stuka duties early in 1940, but not before they had seen action in Poland.

Each *Geschwader* was divided into a staff flight (*Stab*) and three or four *Gruppen.* A *Gruppe* comprised three *Staffeln* of nine (operational) and three (reserve) aircraft each, with airborne *Staffeln* subdivided into *Kette* of three aircraft each. Typical attack formations at this period were stepped up echelon and similar basic methods common to all air forces.

Apart from the Stukas which formed the backbone of the dive bomber forces in Germany in 1939, the most advanced German twin-engined attack bomber was undoubtedly the Junkers Ju88, dubbed the 'Wonder Bomber' by Goering. It was far in advance of its rivals in both Germany and abroad and great things were expected of it. The Ju88 did indeed prove itself the main workhorse of the

Diagram 6: Cruising formation of a Stuka Staffel. 'Vee' formation in three *Ketten*

Diagram 7: Approach period - *Staffel* adopts triple *Ketten* en echelon

Diagram 8: Over Target ready to commence Dive. *Staffel* is stepped up echelon. Following signal from *Kettenführer* each aircraft peels off into the attack dive.

105

Luftwaffe, adaptable in the extreme and an enormous number of derivations were evolved from the same basic airframe over the years. It was as a dive bomber that it first made its mark however, and this is the role in which the Ju88 excelled and which concerns us here.

The Ju88 stemmed from a 1935 requirement for a *Schnellbomber,* a hard-hitting medium bomber that could outpace any fighter then being conceived. Design work by W.H. Evers and Alfred Gassner, who had gained considerable experience in the American aircraft industry, commenced in January 1936. The original project studies were designated Ju85 (with a twin fin/rudder assembly) and Ju88 (with a single fin/rudder), and detailed design work on the selected version started at once. The first Ju88 prototype was completed in record time and was first flown by test pilot Kindermann on 21 December of the same year. The design was an obvious success and was developed through several further prototypes. Once the early teething troubles had been overcome no time was wasted to demonstrate the potential of this new bomber to the world, and in March 1939 the specially modified fifth prototype (Ju88V5) established a new world speed record of 321.25mph over a closed 621 mile circuit carrying a 4,409lb payload. Of course the initial production series, completed early in 1939, were nowhere as fast but nevertheless returned excellent performance characteristics. Series production of this new bomber was initiated at several plants, by which time the decision had been taken to adapt the Ju88 for dive bombing. Apart from some re-stressing this involved the fitting of slatted underwing dive brakes outboard of each engine nacelle. These brakes hinged under the front spar and initially caused some problems in such a highly stressed aircraft when extended.

A special unit, *Erprobungskommando 88,* was set up in summer 1939 to test the new bomber under service conditions and provide the initial trained crews. The first operational unit, I/KG25, was formed in August 1939, and redesignated I/KG30 in September, was soon in action. Due to the unexpectedly slow deliveries of the Ju88A-1 series this unit included several pre-production and test aircraft to bring it up to strength.

In American the Douglas XSBD-1 was accepted by the US Navy in February 1939, and two months later the naval authorities placed orders with the parent company for 144 Dauntless dive bombers, of which fifty-seven SBD-1s were for the USMC and eighty-seven SBD-2s for the Navy. The Navy version differed from the initial series principally by having an additional machine gun in the rear cockpit, bullet-proof windscreens and some armour protection for the crew. The production Dauntless was also fitted with self-sealing rubber-lined fuel tanks and provision was made for two 65 gallon fuel tanks in outer wing panels for increased range. The offensive load was augmented by adding underwing racks for 100lb bombs.

Contrary to normal practice it was the Marines rather than the Navy who took the initial deliveries of the new dive bomber, and June 1940 saw the first SBD-1s entering squadron service with Marine Air Group (MAG) 1 based at Quantico, Virginia. The first Dauntless dive bombers joined the Navy in November of the same year and all eighty-seven had entered service by May 1941. The first carrier air group to completely re-equip with the Dauntless was VB-2 commanded by Lt Cdr H.D. Felt aboard *Lexington.* With the new aircraft this unit participated in the annual Army manoeuvres held at Lake Charles, Louisiana and also took part in a mock attack on Oahu in May 1941!

Further variants entered service during 1942 onward, these being the SBD-3 and SBD-4. The SBD-3 had been ordered in June 1940 by which time the power of the dive bomber had been strikingly demonstrated in Europe. 174 aircraft were asked for and deliveries began to the Navy in March 1941. The new version featured such improvements as twin guns in the rear cockpit, self-sealing fuel tanks and extra armour. The power plant was the major modification with the adoption of the Wright R-1820-52 engine which gave a maximum speed of 250mph. The electrical system was modified at the same time. This version was to be the major type used in the Pacific campaigns of 1942. After Pearl Harbor additional (500) SBDs were ordered.

The SBD-4 came in much later and differed in the installation of extra radio equipment, radar and the fitting of a Hamilton Standard Hydromatic constant-speed propeller. Some 780 of this type were ordered, deliveries commencing in October 1942 and continuing until the following April.

Normal pre-war training in the US Navy consisted of fifty practice dives, or ten flights with five dives in each sortie. Automatic pull-out devices were not used, although tested at the Patuxent River Centre in 1944. They were not popular with the crews however. The US Navy used the eighteen-plane squadron formation with three divisions of two three-plane sections and the normal cruising altitude was 18,000ft. Attack dives were initiated by the leader from down-sun and upwind and the push-over was made from 15,000ft, peel-off commencing from top of the stack and followed down in sequence. An unbraked Dauntless would achieve a speed of 425mph but the air brakes held this to a normal speed of 276mph. The SBD was stressed up to 4g and normal angle of dive was 70^0.

The diving sequence for the Dauntless compares interestingly with the Stuka method. The leader signalled the moment of attack, not by waggling his wings as was the British practice, but by kicking his rudders. The pilot then throttled back and lifted the nose of the SBD slightly above the horizon to stall position. The lever marked D at his right hand was then operated, opening the dive and landing flaps. The plane was then pushed over on its side towards the peel-off direction of the leader and at a 70^0 angle dived toward the target. The crutch gear was released, swinging the bomb out and down to clear the propeller arc.

In the half-minute or so of the descent the target was lined up in the crosshairs of the sight, wind deflection and drift being calculated and then translated into action by a touch on the ailerons to regain alignment selected by the pilot's judgement. The engine was kept revving over, just sufficient to ensure instant pick-up when required. At the selected height, usually between 1,500 and 2,500ft, the manual bomb release was operated for either the fuselage bomb or the entire bomb load including the wing racks. This was done either manually or electrically, this extra equipment being fitted later in the war. Most pilots also operated the manual gear to make quite certain of release.

On release of the bomb, the throttle was opened up and the stick pulled back, the dive brakes retracted and the SBD hurtled out and clear of the target to re-form away from the action zone. Pilots at this stage were experiencing 5g or more. Although, as Holmberg explained, automatic pull-out devices were scorned in the US Navy the Luftwaffe, in contrast, had tested these in the 1930s and had fitted their aircraft with the *Askania* auto-pilot, tested by Melitta Schiller on the ten pre-production Ju87A-0s. This could be over-ridden by the pilot manually and was not fitted to later marks, presumably for the same reason as in the United States.

Although considered by some past-war critics to be obsolete before America entered the war in December 1941, the Dauntless was the most modern dive bomber available, equipping two-thirds of the carrier groups and steadily replacing the Vindicator in the others during the first half of 1942. Like the Ju87 it was to make its mark in no uncertain manner in the years which followed. In all

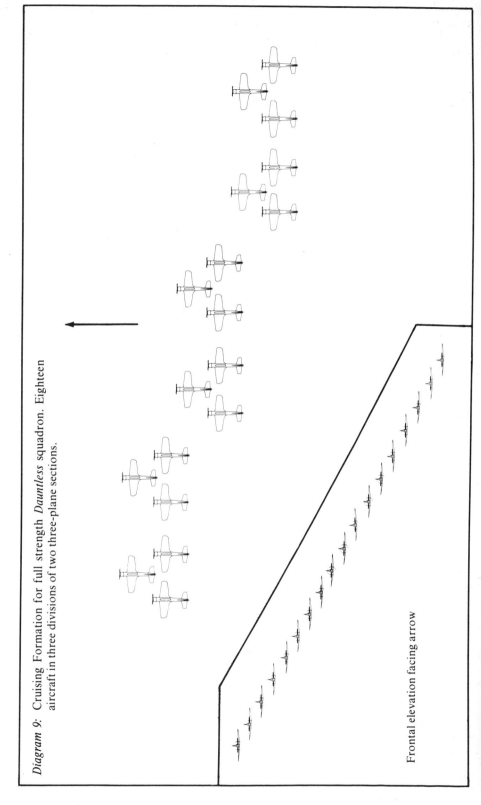

Diagram 9: Cruising Formation for full strength *Dauntless* squadron. Eighteen aircraft in three divisions of two three-plane sections.

Frontal elevation facing arrow

some 6,000 were built.

The US Army interest in dive bombing had just been about nil from the 1920s onward, the strategic doctrine of Trenchard and others dominating all else as in the RAF. But the stunning work of the Stukas led to some hasty re-thinking while others remained blinkered throughout. As a result policy resembled a see-saw over a number of years. One convert to dive bombing was Gen George C. Marshall, then Chief of Staff, and he initiated a crash programme to equip the Army with no less than sixteen dive bomber groups in the great expansion programmes of 1940.

The bulk of the first order was for a variant of the Dauntless, known as the A-24 Banshee, an appropriate name for a dive bomber. However almost at once the Truman Committee set up in 1941 to study future requirements reversed this policy, recommending that in the Army Air Force the dive bomber did not merit funding to any large extent. The US Navy wisely ignored this banality but the Army, being no doubt further influenced by the RAF boasts to have 'exploded the myth of the Stuka' in the Battle of Britain, decided upon the abandonment of the complete programme and Gen Orvil A. Anderson deleted the entire project.

The vacillation continued. Gen Marshal was *not* impressed by Anderson's claims that although fighters could dive-bomb, dive bombers could not fight. It was perfectly true of course, but he was more impressed by what dive bombers were *actually* doing in the Balkans, the Mediterranean and Russia in 1941, than by what fighters *might* be able to do at a later date. He therefore restored the programme and the production of the Banshee went ahead, the first seventy-eight being the equivalent of the Navy's SBD-3.

Unfortunately the Army were to find that you did not just need the hardware to construct a good dive bomber force, you had to have the enthusiasm and expertise as well and this they just did not have. To catch up on twenty years' neglect of the type, they called in Navy and Marine airmen to advise the newly forming groups.

The first batch of Banshees, the A-24, differed little from the Navy SBD other than the arrester hook was removed and the solid rubber tyre replaced by a pneumatic one. A further ninety A-24As (SBD-3As) were converted from existing Navy orders. The first unit to take delivery for Army service were the 27th Bombardment Group in the Philippines, to whom some fifty-two were shipped out to in November 1942 from the States. But they never reached their destination.

Meanwhile the new dive bombers ordered in response to the Navy's August 1938 specifications were on the drawing boards to replace the Dauntless. These were the Curtiss SB2C Helldiver and the Brewster SB2A Buccaneer. Unfortunately although both designs promised the ultimate in engineering and refinements, with internal bomb-bays, increased speed and range, air-cooled radial engines of greater power and reliability, retractable landing-gear, de-icing equipment, armour protection and so on, they were having great difficulty in transferring these ideals from drawing board and factory floor to sky and squadron service. Both designs were big aircraft by dive bomber standards of that time and were beset by totally unforseen snags that meant delay after delay.

In January 1939 the go-ahead was given for the two companies to proceed with the development of the XSBA-1 and the XSBC2-1, and contracts were awarded in May. The Brewster plant in consequence, was expanded but could never settle in its enlarged status — problem after problem cropped up on the shop floor and dragged on.

The XSBA-1 weighted 3,695lb when completed and with the Wright XR-1820 engine reached 242mph. This was not good enough and the machine went back to the factory to be fitted with the improved XR-1820-22 engine and a three-blade propeller. This improved performance to a top speed of 263mph, making it the fastest single-engined dive bomber in the world at the time. All seemed set, and the subsequent enormous British orders that followed this impressive display in 1940, appeared to indicate plain sailing for the new company. But the Buccaneer's problems were not in the air but on the ground.

Curtiss were no more fortunate, although their problems were the reverse of Brewster's, after all they had built dive bombers before, Brewster had not. It was when the Helldiver was aloft that the problems started. A new plant was laid out at Columbus with the latest equipment and the Navy and Army placed order after order for the Helldiver, but the 'Big-Tailed Beast' would not co-operate. Already a hefty animal, the replacement of the magnesium alloy by aluminium was necessitated early on and still up went the weight. Changes in the cannon armament called for the re-design of the wings, wind-tunnel tests resulted in a large increase in wing area, despite the fact that the original specification called for two Helldivers to be accommodated on the 40ft by 48ft lifts of the new *Essex* class carriers then building, and these could not be altered.

The XSB2C-1 made its maiden flight on 18 December 1940 at the hands of test pilot Lloyd Childs, and trials ran through to February 1941, terminating abruptly on the ninth of that month when the plane crashed and broke in half. Rebuilt in May and tested at an increasing tempo with the orders building up behind it that summer, many changed were made in the design and not until November were the first dive tests made. Then a second crash in December halted the entire development.

At this stage, December 1941, a total of 578 Helldivers were on order for the Navy, but after Pearl Harbor this was increased to 3,000, of which 450 were for the RAF to be built under licence in Canada. In addition the Army had ordered its own version as the A-25, but not until 30 June 1942 did the first production model, SB2C-1, take to the air. Two more followed and testing continued throughout the summer and autumn. More aircraft followed, and more tests and modifications, and it was not until 1943 that the first Helldiver joined a combat squadron, VS-9, aboard the carrier *Essex*. Even then the tale of woe was not at an end. We will return to the Helldiver/Buccaneer saga later in our story. It was perhaps fortunate that across the Pacific the Japanese were having no better fortune with their Aichi D3A 'Val' replacement, the Yokosuka D4Y 'Judy'.

As recorded earlier the prototype Yokosuka D4Y flew in the last month of 1940 and hopes were high that it would replace the Aichi D3A before outbreak of war. But like the Dauntless the 'Val' was destined to soldier on and carry the bulk of the air-sea war in the Pacific on its own. The reasons were very similar to the American difficulties.

The testing of the five Yokosuka D4Y prototypes fitted with the Daimler-Benz engine had shown marked wing flutter and structural weaknesses when diving. Such was the urgency of the programme however that the production line was kept in operation, but a strict embargo was enforced on actual dive bombing by this aircraft. The first D4Ys therefore went to war as reconnaissance machines and not in the role for which they had been designed. Even so only two dozen of this type, the D4Y1-C, had been completed by late spring 1943. It was in March of that year that the wing structural problems were finally resolved and the first *Suisei* (Comet) dive bombers joined the fleet fitted with the Aichi Atsuta 21 engine (Japanese-built version of the German DB601) as the Model 11 Carrier Bomber.

In order to fill the gap the Aichi D3A had to be stretched and this was achieved by fitting the 1,300hp Kinsei 54 engine and larger fuel tanks. A few modifications to the fuselage were also incorporated and the new version began entering service as the D3A2 (or Model 22) in the autumn of 1942, after 478 D3A1s had been completed. Sub-contracted to the Showa company as well, a total of 1,016 Model 22s were produced up to the end of the war.

An even more advanced dive bomber development intended to replace both the 'Val' and the 'Judy' was the Aichi B7A *Ryusei* (Shooting Star), dubbed 'Grace' by the Allies. Another very big bomber by carrier standard, the 'Grace' had a span of 47ft 3in and was powered by a 1,670hp Nakajima Homare 23 engine which gave it a maximum speed of 352mph; and the bomb load was 1,760lb. We will return to the development of this powerful aircraft in a later section.

And so the dive bomber went to war.

A head-on shot of the French Navy Loire-Neuport LN dive bomber shows its twin tail fins, three-bladed prop, spatted undercarriage and inverted gull wing configuration. Little wonder then that during the desperate days of 1940 both friend and foe alike mistook them for marauding Stukas over Northern France.

Fixing one of the small bombs to the under-wing racks of the French Navy's Voughts in France 1940. Beside giving a good view of the bomb crutch arrangement this photo shows the working gear of the French naval ground crews.

14 BLITZKREIG !
The War Years: Germany 1939-40

Germany commenced hostilities against Poland at 0445 on 1 September 1939, but the first dive bomber mission actually preceeded this by some minutes for a kette of three Ju87Bs under Bruno Dilley carried out a surprise assault on the bridges at Dirschau on the River Vistula some time before this. The three aircraft from 3/StG1, were given the task of cutting the detonation leads by which the Poles hoped to destroy the bridges and hold up the German advance. So the first true bombing mission of World War II was a dive bombing one.

The Polish campaign was the first demonstration to the world of the Blitzkrieg technique, with fast, mobile forces, spearheaded by armoured units and dive bombers, blasting their way through the defence works and old-fashioned military units of the enemy, encircling them and destroying them piecemeal. The pattern which developed was to become a familiar one.

The initial strikes were directed at airfields and ships of the Polish Navy. Misty weather conditions, and the dispersal of Polish fighters to hidden airstrips somewhat nullified the first attacks, but soon the dive bomber was striking hard with telling effect. Two *Gruppen* of StG77 under Colonel Schwarzkopf were ready at Neudorf, west of Oppeln and they attacked Lublinitz initially. I/StG76, led by *Hauptmann* Sigel struck Wielun. StG2 struck at a variety of airfield targets, those of I/StG2 under Colonel Dinort were assigned the airfield at Krakow but aborted their mission and instead hit smaller airfields closer to the border, tangling with Polish fighters and losing one dive bomber while destroying one of the enemy in return.

I/StG1 attacked the radio stations of Babice and Lacy but found it difficult to destroy the masts by bombing alone. To deal with the warships of the Polish fleet strikes were mounted for several days against the Bay of Hela and other ports by the naval Stuka unit 4/186 and I and II/StG2, reinforced by IV(Stuka)/LG1. The first success was the sinking of the torpedo boat *Mazur* by *Hauptmann* Kögl at Okswie. The minelayer *Gryf* was hit and burned for two days before sinking. The only casualty was the aircraft of *Oberst* Czuprina which was destroyed, although others were damaged. Next day the *Gdynie* and *Gdansk* were sunk in the Gulf of Danzig by IV/LG1 and on 3 September attacks by 4/186 went in against the destroyer *Wicher* and minesweeper *Mewa* at Hela, and both Karl-Hermann Lion and *Oberleutnant* Rummel scored direct hits on the destroyer. Both vessels sank and they were joined on 6 September by the gunboat *General Haller* while her sister ship, *Kommandant Pilsoski* was badly damaged and had to be scuttled later.

And so it went on, the minesweeper *Czapla* and *Jaskolka* were sunk by Stukas on 14 September and the remaining warships were either forced to flee to England or neutral ports, while others were captured intact. The accuracy and power of the dive bomber, first demonstrated in Spain against ships, was shown to be deadly.

On land the close co-operation between the armoured columns and the dive bombers was also demonstrated. liason officers kept up with the advance and directed Stuka strikes against strong-points, artillery, bridges and troop concentrations, crippling the enemy and restricting his movements. On the first

Bluff called! The original photograph of the Ju87B that was altered by the Germans to re-create an incident when a navalised Stuka jettisoned its undercarriage during the Polish campaign of 1939. The subsequent 'adaption' was used to proclaim the strength and sturdiness of German aircraft and this author was one of those taken in many years later! The claim was true, the incident was true but the photo was pure fake

day of battle I/StG2 found a Polish cavalry unit at Wielun and the thirty Stukas destroyed it. On 2 September StG77 inflicted similar carnage on an infantry column at Radomsko and I/StG2 and 1/StG76 wiped out a disembarking troop train at Piotrkow. LG2 hit Dzialoszyn with similar effect and then the dive bombers were switched with high speed to the southern front where they bombed Polish troops at Tschenstochau.

Some losses were sustained when unescorted Ju87s ran into Polish fighters, for example on 5 September the Polish 114 Fighter Squadron intercepted fifteen Stukas and shot down two of them. By the end of the week this unit had claimed ten Ju87s and similarly III/Dyon was credited with destroying three Stukas on 4 September and three or four others over Torun bridge on the sixth. But the whole campaign only cost a total of thirty-one dive bombers, a minimal loss against the results they achieved.

At the Battle of Ilza on 8-9 September Richthofen sent in 135 Stukas in non-stop attacks on the Polish army trapped there. Repeated assault with 110lb fragmentation bombs and machine-gun fire decimated their ranks and they surrendered on the 13th. A last ditch attempt by the Poles to inflict a defeat on the German armies took place during the battle of Burza between 9 and 12 September. Massed dive bomber attacks were mounted from forward airstrips at Tschenstochau and Kruszyna and the newly formed II/StG51 moved up in support. The Kutno pocket was dive bombed endlessly and the Poles were forced to retreat back across the Vistula in confusion, 170,000 of them laying down their arms by the 19th leaving the way open to Warsaw itself.

By 25 September the city was surrounded and to prevent heavy street fighting some 240 Ju87s were employed in round the clock dive bombing in Operation Seaside, reinforced by Ju52/3m transports dropping incendiaries. The attacks lasted the whole day, by which time Warsaw was in flames. On the 26th its surrender was offered. The garrison at Modlin still held out but the Stukagruppen dropped 318 tons of bombs on the fortress on 26-27 September and the Poles gave up on the 28th.

It had been a remarkable vindication of the dive bomber. For the loss of   113 thirty-one Stukas, eighteen of them to fighter attack, Poland had been brought to her knees in less than a month. The Germans had learnt a lot from the campaign and now planned to put the lessons learned into effect on the Western Front, but bad weather postponed this until the spring of 1940. Meanwhile dive bomber production was substantially increased.

The larger long-range dive bombers, the Ju88s, had also had their baptism of fire. Several dive bombing attacks were conducted against the main British fleet anchorage at Scapa Flow and in the Firth of Forth, during which several cruisers and destroyers were hit and damaged, including the *Norfolk, Edinburgh and Mohawk.*

The next test of these units came with the German invasion of Norway in April 1940. Only one Ju87 unit was involved, I/StG1 under *Hauptman* Hozzel which operated at first from Holtenau near Kiel. Their first mission was to bomb the fortress of Oskarsborg and Akershus which guarded the seaward approaches to Oslo. Twenty-two Ju87s attacked the fortresses, carved out of solid rock in places, and scored many direct hits. The Stukas then moved into Fornebu field itself close to the Norwegian capital and from 9 April were ready to co-operate in the drive north by the German army.

Employing a degree of flexibility the Allies were never able to match, this unit moved up the coast, first to Sola near Stavager and then Vaernes near Trondheim. Again their close-support effect was vital, blasting the stumbling Allied columns in the snow around Namsos, Aandalsnes and finally Narvik. In order to improve their effect they were reinforced by some of the new long-range Ju87Rs which were brought in in May. With their two 66 gallon drop tanks they had a radius of action of 400 miles compared with the 156 of the Ju87Bs and they quickly proved their worth.

Some British Gladiator fighters were hastily flown in and operated from a frozen lake before the Stukas found them and destroyed them, but the Ju87s lost three or four of their number in this action. The main Allied reaction could only come from the sea and the Ju87s and Ju88s quickly found themselves in action with the navies of Great Britain and France off the coast. Ju88s hit and heavily damaged the heavy cruiser *Suffolk* on 19 April after she had bombarded Sola, and many attacks were made on the battleships and carriers of the Home Fleet — the destroyer *Eclipse* was badly damaged.

The greatest impact was made by the dive bombers on the smaller ships which were operating in the restricted fjords and young aces like Hozzel, Grenzel, Möbus and Schaefer all earned the Knights Cross in the attacks on Allied shipping at this time. During the evacuation of Namson on 3 May two large destroyers, the British *Gurkha* and the French *Bison* were sunk by Stukas. Two days later the large Polish liner *Chrobry* was hit amidships by Stukas with a 550lb bomb which started large fires and she had to be sunk. On 30 May the AA sloop *Bittern* had her entire stern blown off by a Stuka bomb and had to be sunk.

Before Norway finally fell completely however the main dive bomber actions were taking place far to the south. For the decisive battle in the West in 1940 the Luftwaffe had a total of 324 Ju87 dive bombers deployed.

The story of the Stuka's role in the Battle of France was a repeat of their success in Poland, for the Allies had learned little, while the Germans had made improvements to their technique which led to even greater efficiency. After the normal pin-point attacks against airfields and fixed fortifications and lines had opened up the Allied front at selected points, the Panzers roared through the gaps. It then became the dive bombers role to keep the enemy paralysed, pulverising his troops and artillery, cutting his supply lines, pounding his reserves and smashing any force which looked like making a stand.

Table 26: Stuka Order of Battle 10 May 1940					
Luftflotte and CO	Army Group and area of ops.	Fliegerkorps and CO	Unit and Type of aircraft		
2 Kesselring	B Belgium and Netherlands	VIII von Richthofen	StG1 StG2 StG77	— — —	Ju87 Ju87 Ju87
		IV Keller	LG1 StG3	— —	Ju88 Ju87
3 Sperrle	A Luxembourg & the Meuse	II Loerzer	II/StG1 IV/St/LG1	— —	Ju87 Ju87

The advanced troops had wireless contact with the Stuka control near HQ and by reference to a map grid any strong point could be neutralised within a short while and then the troops would press forward once more. An additional factor was noticed at this time. The effect of a dive bomber in a steep dive was found to have a numbing effect on unseasoned troops not experienced in being on the receiving end or trained to cope with it. In April 1940 I/StG2 at Cologne-Ostheim airfield fitted makeshift sirens to the legs of their aircraft to enhance this noise and so successful was it that it was adopted official by all Stuka units. The Germans called this device the 'Trombones of Jericho'.

The initial dive bomber attacks were at airfields and fortresses near Liege in Belgium. Fort Eben Emael was taken by shock troops after a Stuka assault and the defences of the River Maas forced. At Moerdijk Stukas struck at defence works and AA positions over the Diep on the 10th through to the 12th. Then they suddenly vanished. They were moved south to support the Panzer thrusts as Sedan.

On 13 May some 700 aircraft were in the air over Sedan, of which 200 were Ju87s. They saturated the French defences flying 200 sorties on that day. Both StG2 and StG77 were involved and they quickly opened up the bridgehead so that Hoth's armoured columns could pour through. Losses were light except for one fierce action when five Curtiss Hawk fighters of the French air force caught a Stuka force dive bombing a motorised column in the Ardennes on the 12th and claimed to have destroyed no less than sixteen of them. This amounted to a quarter of the Stuka losses for the entire campaign. But by the end of the day the German tanks were over the river and racing through hordes of fleeing French soldiers who abandoned their guns and threw away their rifles whenever Stukas appeared.

The short range of the Ju87s made it essential for them to move their forward bases almost daily, but their ground organisation was up to the task. From 15 May the Stukas were constantly on the move across northern France. Allied counter attacks were continually delayed and even when delivered lacked the power to burst through like the German Stuka-tipped wedges. On 17 May the French 4th Armoured Division made one such attempt to cut the long corridor the Panzers were driving. With 150 tanks, de Gaulle thrust north toward Moncornet on the River Serre. They made initial gains and then were bogged down under continual dive bombing. On 19 May they struck out again Laon towards the Serre, now only nine miles away, but were brought to a ginding halt by evening.

It proved difficult to actually destroy individual tanks by bombing but the Henschel 123 came into their own in a classic attack on 22 May near Cambrai. Commanded by *Hauptmann* Weiss II/LG2 attacked a French column of forty tanks and 150 trucks at low level with 100lb bombs and quickly knocked out five tanks. Further attacks stopped the French in their tracks.

When the British attacked south from Arras it was the Stuka attacks which brought them to a standstill in a short time, and by next morning the town was in German hands. As the Allied northern armies withdrew to the Channel ports of Boulogne, Calais and Dunkirk the Stuka units moved up to deliver the coup-de-grace, occupying St Quentin on the 23rd. On 25 May StG1 was in action at Amiens and StG77 operated with good effect against French artillery around their new forward base.

The next phase was the elimination of the fighting garrisons at these ports. On 25 May StG2 mounted heavy attacks on Boulogne which fell that same morning. At Calais the British were fighting hard and StG1 devoted its entire strength to crushing this resistance. Off the coast the destroyers of France and Britain were bombarding advance German units and the dive bombers were called upon to deal with them also. At Boulogne dive bombers had already despatched the French destoryers *L'Adroit* and *Orage* and crippled the *Frondeur*. Stukas operating at the extreme length of their range also sank the tankers *Salome* and *Niger* and the troopship *Pavon*. In the north the Dutch also suffered, losing the destroyer *Jan Van Galen* and gunboat *Johan Maurits Van Nassau* to dive bombers, while the British destroyers *Valentine* and *Whitley* were sunk and *Winchester* and *Westminster* damaged off Holland by the same units.

By 24 May eight Ju87s had been shot down over the coast in attacks on warships, but in return they had damaged the British *Vimiera* and the Polish *Burza* and sunk the *Wessex* off Calais on the same day.

At dawn on 26 May Gen Guderian prepared for his final attack on Calais, held by the stubborn British 20th Division. Over 100 aircraft from StG77 and StG2 attacked in waves throughout the day reducing the old town centre to rubble, and the port surrendered on the same evening.

Next day VIII *Fliegerkorps* containing the bulk of the Ju87s began to direct its full attention to the perimeter of Dunkirk where the British were evacuating their forces. At 0740 the first Stukas arrived over the town and the beaches and sank the French troopship *Cote d'Azur*. Next day the big dive bombers of LG1, Ju88s, sank the largest merchant ship there, the 6,900 ton *Clan MacAlister* and at 1600 a massed Stuka assault was launched on the harbour area. They found many ships crammed with troops alongside the mole and dived to the attack. The paddle steamer *Fenella* was hit by a bomb, while another exploded on the quay alongside riddling her hull and troop-packed superstructure. She listed quickly and went down.

The destroyer *Grenade* took a heavy bomb which penetrated inside before exploding, turning her slender hull into a slaughterhouse. Parting her moorings she swung into the channel with huge fires raging from stem to stern as her ammunition exploded. She managed to get clear before she went down, her few survivors being picked up by a drifter which in turn was hit and sunk almost immediately.

The destroyer *Jaguar* was hit, but not so seriously, and got clear, as did the personnel ship *Canterbury*, also hit by a bomb. The paddle steamer *Crested Eagle* fully laden with survivors from *Fenella* was hit by a Stuka bomb just as she cleared the mole, and was beached and burnt out. Two trawlers were sunk outright, *Polly Johnson* and *Calvi*. The French destroyer *Mistral* caught the full blast of a near miss and her upperworks were completely wrecked. Nor was this all, two Southern Railway ships, *Namannia* and *Lorina* were hit and sunk as was the paddle steamer *Gracie Fields* with 750 troops aboard.

116   Casualties in the Ju87 units that inflicted this carnage amounted to a total loss

of eleven from all sources. British fighters claimed to have destroyed sixty-nine German aircraft this day, a Defiant squadron claiming no less than nineteen Stukas alone, but the true total loss was really only eighteen of all types!

The 30 May brought some respite due to bad weather and although two Stukagruppen got airborne their missions were aborted and the rain closed in. But on 1 June the dive bombers were back over the beaches at 0720. The minesweeper *Skipjack* was hit and sank like a stone, the destroyer *Keith,* with only thirty rounds of ammunition left was attacked again and again. Three near misses brought her to a stop. Another attack saw a Stuka place a bomb straight down her after funnel. Listing and covered in clouds of steam she took another direct hit on her bridge and sank.

In the same attack Ju88s hit the tug *St Abbs* and the tiny vessel disintegrated, while further along a Stuka planted a heavy bomb in the destroyer *Basilisk* damaging her so much she had to be sunk next day. Two further destroyers, *Whitehall* and *Worcester* were damaged, the gunboat *Mosquito* hit, set ablaze and abandoned and the minesweeper *Salamander* hit. The dive bombers hit the destroyer *Ivanhoe* which was towed away and, at 1300, the French destroyer *Foudroyant* was set upon and, according to the French report, 'submerged in a cloud of Stukas'. She was hit by several bombs and went down in an instant. The personnel ship *Scotia* was attacked by twelve Ju87s that afternoon while leaving with 2,000 French troops. Three bombs hit the ship, again one going down a funnel. The troops, panic stricken, rushed the boats and the destroyer *Esk* drove off another attack to pick up the few survivors.

The Stuka attacks continued in mounting fury throughout the afternoon. The paddle minesweeper *Brighton Queen* was hit in the stern and sank with 700 French and Moroccan troops aboard. A small convoy of French auxillaries was set upon at 1600 by eight Ju87s and they quickly despatched the *Denis Papin, Venus* and *Moussaillon.*

Again German losses were only twenty-nine aircraft of all types this day, although the RAF boasted it had shot down seventy-eight! The last dive bomber mission against Dunkirk was on 2 June, and was directed against fortifications and bridges as well as Fort Vallieres, which was destroyed by precision bombing. Eight Stukas attacked two RAF launches off Gravelines at 1530 that afternoon, sinking the *243,* while the railway ships *Paris* and *Worthing* were also sunk.

The final stage of the Battle of France commenced on 5 June and within three weeks it was all over. Britain was now on her own with invasion expected at any time. As if to confirm this the Stukagruppen began to gather on airfields close to the Channel coast. The re-organisation is given in Table 27. Under the newly appointed *Kanalkampfführer* Fink, the Luftwaffe used their dive bombers to clear the English Channel of British shipping while the army and the heavy bombers got ready for the next stage.

The final evacuations from Europe had seen the Ju87s inflict further heavy casualties on shipping. The troopship *Lancastria* was sunk with heavy loss of life off St Nazaire and the destroyer *Bulldog* and personnel ship *Bruges* had been damaged. The British stationed a destroyer flotilla, the 4th, at Dover and continued to run their coastal convoys up the Channel. To draw out the British fighters the Stukas and Ju88s were now despatched against these targets and soon achieved results.

On 10 June nine Ju87s attacked the destroyers *Boadicea* and *Bulldog* operating off the French coast. Each ship was hit by three bombs apiece and heavily damaged. Next target was the big convoy OA168 which two Stukagruppen caught off Portland. Four large merchant ships were sunk (16,000 tons) and nine others damaged severely (40,000 tons), those sunk being the *Britsum, Dallas* 117

Table 27: Organisation of German dive bomber units, July 1940		
Units	Area	Notes
I, II and III/StG1	Angers/St Pol	Incorporated the former III/StG51 and TGr186
I, II and II/StG2	St Malo/St Omer, St Tron and Lannion	
I, II and III/StG77	Caen	Incorporated the former I/StG76
I/StG3	Dinand/Fleurtuit	Stab unit forming
IV(Stuka)/LG1	Tramecourt	
7/StG51		Forming, and later became 4/StG1

City, Deucalion and *Kolga.* The big merchant ship *Aeneas* was also sunk by Ju87s and in attacks on Portland itself the auxillary AA ship *Foylebank,* bristling with guns, was dive bombed and sunk. The whole attack cost StG2 just one aircraft.

Targets now became scarce as the convoys were routed mainly at night, but on 7 July Stukas attacked gun positions on the Isle of Wight; on the 9th they sank the coaster *Kenneth Hawksfield* off Sandwich and on the 10th Ju88s joined in raids on Falmouth and Swansea. On 11th a big effort was mounted by Stukas of StG2 and StG77 in the Portland area, but this was broken up by fighters and they only sank the patrol ship *Warrior II.*

On 13 July they were back in force attacking a convoy off Dover and destroying, and next day IV(Stuka)/LG1 caught another convoy off Eastbourne sinking the coasters *Betswood* and *Bovey Tracey.* On the 18th the Stukas found the Channel clear of shipping and the only ships at sea were patrol vessels. These were duly dive bombed and machined gunned to good effect. The following day Dover harbour was hit and on 20 July the Stukas found convoy 'Bossum' ten miles off the same port. II/StG1, led by Keil, penetrated a fighter screen to sink the collier *Pulborough I* and damage several other ships including the destroyers *Beagle* and *Brazen.*

Dover was hit again on 20 July, but the climax came five days later with the attacks on convoy CW8 which was found off Deal by StG3 and StG1, with thirty Ju88s of KG4 in support. Five ships were sunk outright, *Ajax, Coquetdale, Empire Crusader, Henry Moon* and *Summity* (5,117 tons). Another six were badly damaged for the loss of two dive bomber. Next day the destroyers *Brilliant* and *Boreas* came out of Dover to attack E-boats and were pounced on by Stukas, both taking two direct hits.

On 27 July Ju87s and Ju88s attacked Dover harbour sinking the destroyer *Codrington* outside and damaging the *Walpole,* while Ju87s savaged the 'Bacon' convoy off Swanage, I/StG77 carrying out attacks. Six Staffaln from IV(Stuka) LG1, and II/StG1, forty-eight Ju87s in all, caught the destroyer *Delight* off Portland and sank her. Destroyers had been forbidden to sail by daylight in the Channel by the Admiralty but the local commander thought he knew better and paid the price. They also sank the patrol ship *Gulzar.* Four Stukas were lost.

The last battles fought by the German dive bombers in this phase were between 9 and 11 August, Convoy CW9 was the first victim, when massed Stuka assaults accounted for six ships (70,000 tons) and damage to six more. Waves of Ju87s continued the assault, but for the first time they met strong RAF fighter resistance by Nos 43 and 145 Squadrons. I/StG3 lost three aircraft, I/StG2 and III/StG2 lost one each while the last formation over the target, 2/StG77, was badly knocked about, losing three aircraft shot down and five damaged.

On 12 August IV(Stuka)LG1 under von Brauchitsch attacked a convoy in the Thames estuary, damaging two more ships. Next day *Aldertag* opened in earnest.

The Battle of Britain called for the Stuka units to switch their targets away from the coastal convoys and their tactical role, for which they well designed, to a strategical role, which they were not. The Ju87s were thus mis-used and thrown away in needless sacrifice against top-class fighter opposition. Their hitherto relative immunity received a severe blow as did their reputation in Britain.

The battle commenced officially on 13 August, but weather conditions delayed the big attack until the afternoon when VII *Fliegerkorps* swung into action. II/StG2 mounted a twenty-seven-plane strike against Middle Wallop airfield and StG77 contributed fifty-seven dive bombers to an attack on Warmwell. IV(Stuka)LG1 went to Detling. The results of these attacks were mixed, Maj Eneccerus's formation was jumped by Spitfires over Lyme Bay, losing six aircraft, while StG77, although suffering no losses, failed to locate its target. Detling was hit hard however, and twelve Blenheims and Ansons were destroyed on the ground.

II/StG1 and IV(Stuka)/LG1 participated in the second day's attacks which spread along the south coast, but on 15 August there came a day of disaster for the Stukas. The main targets this day were Hawkinge airfield and Portland harbour. At first they were successful, both Hawkinge and Lympne airfields were badly damaged by heavy and accurate dive bombing and put out of action by II/StG1, Hauptmann Keil and IV(Stuka)/LG1, Hauptmann von Brauchitsch, the latter losing five aircraft, the former none.

The Ju88s of KG30 joined in, dive bombing Driffield, losing six aircraft but destroying twice that number and four hangars. In the afternoon the Stukas put in a second blow, I/StG1 and II/StG2 co-operating with Ju88s of LG1. They were intercepted by RAF fighters, but managed to bomb Worthy Down and Middle Wallop. Fighting reached a new high on 16-18 August. StG2 bombed Tangmere on the first day, losing eight aircraft but causing widespread damage, all the hangars were destroyed, workshops and stores and a pumping station pulverised, while three Blenheims and seven Hurricanes were destroyed on the ground.

Sunday 18 August was a black day for the Stukageschwader. All four were sent out and duly attacked the airfields of Ford, Gosport and Thorney Island, again with good effect, many aircraft being hit on the ground and installations wrecked. But once more the British eight-gun fighters were waiting for them in hordes and they decimated the Stukas before the German fighters could intervene. Hardest hit of all was the hitherto lucky unit, StG77.

Among their targets was Poling radar station. While over Selsey Bill they were intercepted by no less than four fighter squadrons and in the ensuring massacre I/StG77 lost no less than twelve of its twenty-eight aircraft, with six more damaged; among the casualties was Hauptmann Meisel. Four more Stukas from StG77's other units were also lost. Despite the severe damage they inflicted a loss rate of thirty destroyed or damaged was clearly prohibitive.

It was decided to save the Stukas for the proper role, supporting the actual invasion landings themselves. Accordingly they were moved north to the Pas-de-Calais area behind the 16th Army and discussion began with the commanders of the leading infantry and tank units, which were to carry out the landings, on how best to co-ordinate forces on *Der Tag*.

For Operation 'Sealion' it was decided that the Ju87s should concentrate their efforts in supporting the army around Dover, Folkestone and Sandgate, two complete Geschwader being allocated for this. At the same meeting, held on 13

September, a specially equipped Staffel was decided upon to destroy the suspected nest of heavy gun batteries located at Dungeness. Two other Gruppen were allocated for the support of VII Korps, while I/StG3 was to be held in reserve in Brittany for opportune use once the soldiers ashore called for further assistance.

Thus by early September II/StG1 (Pas-de-Calais), II/StG2 (St Omer) and IV(Stuka)/LG1 (Tramecourt) were ready with the other units refitting and retraining. StG77 had suffered such heavy losses that it needed a much longer period of respite to rebuild and at this period was vitually non-operational. But they waited in vain for the word 'go'.

With the final outcome of the aerial battle decided in favour of the RAF and the heavy bombers employed in night attacks on London, the Stukas were dispersed. Many were despatched to Italy and Germany in readiness for the campaigns planned in south-east Europe, but the Ju87s had not completely vanished from the skies over Britain.

Convoys had re-commenced into the Thames and it was decided to up-date the anti-shipping data by mounting a series of selective dive bombing attacks before all the Ju87s moved off to their new combat zones in the spring. III/StG1, under Mahlke, having a large number of ex-navy crews on its strength, and a good record behind it in this form of warfare, was selected to conduct these during November.

Dive bombing attacks took place against these convoys on 1, 8 and 11 November and proved quite successful. No Stukas were lost in the first three attacks and the casualties they inflicted were significant. Being larger ships they proved more difficult to actually sink, but many were damaged.

Table 28: Results of dive bombing anti-shipping offensive November 1940			
Date of attack	Ship bombed	Tonnage	Result
1-11-40	Letchworth	1,317	Sunk
8-11-40	Catford	1,216	Damaged
	Fireglow	1,568	Damaged
	Ewell	1,350	Damaged
11-11-40	Colonel Crompton	1,495	Damaged
	Corduff	2,345	Damaged
	Corsea	2,764	Damaged

The Germans estimated that they had destroyed a far greater tonnage in these attacks than they had, 18,000 tons on 1st, 21,000 tons on 8th and 37,000 tons on the 11th. The final attack took place in 14 November and the RAF met them with a strong force of fighters. Subsequently they claimed to have inflicted wholesale slaughter on the dive bombers, but in fact this was not so. On finding the skies full of fighters the attack on the convoy was called off, so the CO of the German fighter escort diverted the dive bombers to targets in the Dover area. He prudently declined to join them and the Stukas were heavily engaged. Only one Stuka was actually shot down, Oberleutnant Blumers, and three more crash-landed on return to France. Only one Ju87 was undamaged, but most got safely back to their home airfields.

During the winter of 1940-1 the few remaining Ju87s in France conducted a series of pin-prick harassing raids over the Channel on south coast towns. The damage they inflicted was slight and by the new year most had been withdrawn south. A new chapter was to open in the Mediterranean but first let us examine Allied dive bombing attacks, commencing with the destruction of the *Königsberg*.

15 A MUTED RIPOSTE
Sinking of the *Königsberg* and Allied operations 1940

The background to this attack was that a powerful German naval force had penetrated the defences of the Norwegian harbour of Bergen harbour on the 8 April 1940 and landed troops which occupied the town. It was one of a series of such attacks that in one swoop took the major ports of Norway and left the British with the task of ejecting them. Aerial reconnaissance had shown that two of the German cruisers still lay in Bergen harbour and a force of twelve Wellington and twelve Hampden bombers was despatched to sink them. They failed to score a single hit and one of the cruisers returned to Germany. The other, the light cruiser *Königsberg,* which had been slightly damaged by three shells from a Norwegian fort earlier, remained and plans were put in hand to attack her again, but this time with a more effective force.

At the beginning of 1940, following German air raids on Scapa Flow, three squadrons of Hurricanes were based at Wick to defend the fleet anchorage. As their parent aircraft carriers were employed elsewhere this duty had been taken over by two squadrons of Skuas who were based ashore at HMS *Sparrowhawk,* the Naval Air Station at Hatston. These squadrons were No 800, commanded by Capt Richard Thomas Partridge, RM, and No 803, commanded by Lt William Paulet Lucy, RN.

The senior observer of No 800 Squadron, Lt Cdr Geoffrey Hare, RN, had been lent to the RAF Coastal Command squadron employed in watching the Norwegian harbours the Germans had occupied and he had been aboard the plane that had overflown Bergen early on the 9th. It was Hare who had identified the two German cruisers of the *Köln* class then in harbour, and, on his arrival back at Lossiemouth, he lost no time in transferring to a transport which whisked him back to Hatston, Kirkwall, to report to his unit. Already the news of his sighting had led the CO of *Sparrowhawk,* Cdr C.L. Howe, RN, to request permission to use his two Skua squadrons in an attack, and this was granted. Planning commenced at once.

The main problem was the distance to the target, for the limited range of the Skua meant that the fuel situation was bound to be extremely tight. It was essential to have first-class navigation to make precise landfall and Hare, having just been over the target, was obviously an essential part of the mission.

A secondary problem, although it was one that did not seem to enter the heads of the eager young pilots presented with a real target at long last, was the lack of current training in dive bombing. There had been little or no opportunity for the squadrons to carry out any recent practice, a fact commented upon later by the Director of the Naval Air Division. Both risks were willingly accepted and the plan, formulated and pushed forward to top speed, went ahead even though all were rusty.

The departure of the *Köln* had, unknown to the pilots at Hatston, left them with one target ship on which to concentrate their attack, the 6,600 ton light cruiser *Königsberg* commanded by Capt Ruhfus. He was left in an unenviable position after the departure of his senior officer and was eager to follow him back to Germany without further delay. What was keeping him at Bergen was not the three shell hits, which were not serious, but the unreliable machinery of his vessel.

She carried only light armour protection and mounted three triple 5.9in gun turrets, one forward, two aft and twelve torpedo tubes. Her AA defence consisted of six heavy guns, 3.5in and a light automatic weapons battery of eight 37mm guns and four 20mm guns, a battery incidently, far superior to that mounted by equivalent British warships at this time. Her waterline protection was only 2in thick and against air attack her deck armour was a puny $\frac{3}{4}$in maximum, although her turrets and barbettes had $1\frac{1}{4}$in armour. Her weakness made her an ideal dive bomber target.

There was no doubt that ships of light cruiser size and under were vulnerable to bombs of the 500lb SAP type, providing accuracy was achieved. *Königsberg* was 570ft long overall with a maximum beam of 50ft, presenting a reasonable target, more so as she was stationary. This area was cut down for the turret roofs were the most heavily protected part of the ship. This left the bows and quarter-deck as the obvious aiming points, with the clutter of the bridge, funnels and amidships superstructure as secondary ones, for here were concentrated the AA weapons.

However the magazines, ready-to-use ammunition and large machinery spaces below decks gave this amidships portion a high degree of vulnerability if fires could be started by hits or near misses. There was the further advantage that, as she was motionless, no aiming-off was required. Also, as she lay alongside a jetty this would offer firm resistance to her hull if it tried to move away and absorb the water-hammer effect of close misses alongside. Its resistance would increase their effect enormously. The greatest advantage of all however was undoubtedly the surprise they could achieve to keep the flak to a minimum. There was little to fear from fighter defence at this stage, the nearest of which the Germans had were at Sola/Stavenger airfield 150 miles to the south.

Although recognition would present little problem to Navy and Royal Marine flyers Hare noted for the crews that their target would probably have a white band on both forecastle and quarterdeck and a white band with a Swastika, painted on the turret.

Königsberg had in fact moved her anchorage since Hare's first sighting the day before and she lay alongside the Skoltegrund Mole, her starboard side secured, facing east toward the shore.

The plan of attack was a straightforward one, the distance to the target, as related, ruling out anything other than a straight 'in-bash-out' mission. But even so the planning of the best route across the North Sea, up to Bergen to the target without raising the alarm and then out again, called for careful timing. All depended to a great degree on the expertise of the two senior observers, Hare and Lt Michael Hanson, RN. Tribute was later paid to the meticulous work of the Air Staff Officer, Lt Cdr Aubrey St John Edwards, RN, and indeed it cannot be faulted.

Aircraft available for the sortie consisted of eleven Skuas of No 803 and five of No 800 Squadrons. They were to operate in two groups of nine and seven aircraft, but, in the event, one aircraft lost touch during the outward flight and the actual composition of the force was 9-6-1, with the odd aircraft doing its own accurate navigation and carrying out its own separate attack some ten minutes after the others.

Take-off was to be at 0445 on 10 April, to arrive over the target at first light to achieve maximum surprise. The weather conditions on that day put back the actual time of departure to 0515 but this did not, in the end, jeopardise the mission.

The plan called for the two groups to take their departure point from Auskerrey and make a course of 074^0 (true) for Marsten, crossing the Norwegian coast in latitude 60.09 North at a height of 12,000ft. The two groups were at all times to remain in visual contact with each other and, once inside the coastal islands, were advised that a track of 360° would lead them up the fjord. If their landfall was to the southward of this datum it would still lead them to Bergen, but if north to the open sea once more, to westward.

Strict radio silence was to be maintained throughout the outward track and IFF equipment was not carried. The W/T frequency was given as 366 and the silence was only to be broken after the attack to transmit a brief attack report result.

On completion of the attack the fuel situation was to be examined. All aircraft which at that stage had under 50 gallons in their tanks were given permission to land in Norway, but well clear of Bergen itself. Should the aircraft come down in serviceable condition the Norwegian authorities were to be consulted in order that the return flight could be resumed next morning. But if the aircraft was immobilised through damage it was to be destroyed.

The rendezvous point for the re-assembly for the return flight was fixed over the island of Lyson on the coast, some 270 miles from the target area. The crews were told to wait here for 10 minutes only then take track 260° for Sumburgh. Again strict wireless silence was to be maintained on the return leg, only to be broken when 60 miles from Sumburgh when the ETA was to be signalled by either group leaders or single aircraft. Any aircraft arriving over Sumburgh with less than 30 gallons of fuel was to land there as refuelling facilities had been laid on. In the event none of the aircraft needed this emergency service.

A final note of caution was imparted, aircraft were strictly forbidden to land with their 500lb bombs aboard. With their enthusiasm there seemed little likelihood that this would arise, and indeed it did not.

At 0515 on 10 April all sixteen Skuas fully laden with fuel took off from Hatston into the dim, murky half-light and formed up as arranged in two groups before setting off on track 074 for Norway. The weather was good for their mission with 5/10th cloud at 8,000ft to give them protection from the ground and visibility for 20 miles. The wind was north-west, 16 knots.

The Skuas winged east on their course in two groups but for White Leader. Lt Taylor later reported that he could not gain touch with the main party, but he

Table 29: FAA attack on *Königsberg*: Order of Battle	
No 800 Squadron	
Yellow Leader	Capt R.T. Partridge, RM/Lt Cdr G. Hare, RN
Yellow 2	PO Airman H.A. Monk/Ldg Amn L.C. Eccleshall
Yellow 3	PO Amn J. Hadley/Ldg Amn M. Hall
White Leader	Lt E.W.T. Taylour, RN/PO Amn H.G. Cunningham
White 2	Lt J.A. Rooper, RN/PO Amn R.S. Rolph
Spare Section	Lt K.V.V. Spurway, RN/PO Amn C.J.E. Cotterill
Spare 2	Actg PO J.A. Gardner/Nvl Amn First Class A. Todd
No 803 Squadron	
Blue Leader	Lt W.P. Lucy, RN/Lt M.C.E. Hanson, RN
Blue 2	Capt E.D. McIver, RM/Ldg Amn A.A. Barnard
Blue 3	Lt A.B.F. Harris, RN/Ldg Amn G.S. Russell
Green Leader	Lt H.E.R. Torin, RN/Midshipman(A) T.A. McKee
Green 2	Lt L.A. Harris, RM/Nvl Amn First Class D.A. Prime
Green 3	Lt W.C.A. Church, RN/PO Amn B.M. Seymour
Red Leader	Lt B.J. Smeeton, RN/PO Amn B.M. Seymour
Red 2	Lt V.H. Filmer, RN/Nvl Amn First Class F.P. Dooley
Red 3	Actg PO T.F. Riddler/Nvl Amn First Class H.T. Chatterley

nonetheless navigated his way successfully on his own and was the last aircraft in over the target.

The Skuas approached Bergen harbour from the south-east and, after a brief pause to scan the area where the two cruisers were last reported, they identified 'a cruiser of the *Köln* class' at her new berth alongside the mole. At 0720 the sections formed line astern to begin the final phase of the approach dive to clear the thin layer of cloud at 8,000ft. Below it visibility was excellent, at least twenty miles. The German defences moreover were caught flat-footed as the long line of Skuas barrelled in towards them out of the sun.

Most of the aircraft released their bombs at 2,000ft from the final dive point of 6,500ft and the majority went in at a 60⁰ angle of dive, but there were of course variations to this norm. High Dive Bombing was the term most pilots used in their reports, several indeed released at 2,500ft, and two, Rooper and Harris, at 3,000ft. Conversely two others, Hanson and Spurway, pressed in to around 1,500ft before release. Even more cooly Church, having made his vertical dive down to the target, did not release, owing to bad positioning. Not satisfied he pulled up and round and made a second attack from stern-to-bow in a shallow run at 40⁰ and dropped his 500lb bomb from 200ft, clawing away through flak up to 3,000ft and considerable tracer from a now wide-awake flak ship followed him. This highly audacious assault was rewarded for the Skua escaped with nothing more serious than, '. . . one large hole in mainplane close to fuselage'.

Diagram 10: The rough position of the bombs during the *Königsberg* attack 10 April 1940.

N.B. The single hit forward penetrated through her fo'c'sle. The combination of the hit amidships and a near miss closely adjacent probably put her under.

Again the angle of dive varied, 60^0 being the norm, but several aircraft went in at 70^0 and some at 50^0. The final run was bow-to-stern along the full length of the target and the majority of bombs hit the ship aft.

The complete surprise achieved in this attack can be seen by the slowness of the German reaction, about half the aircraft had completed their dives before the first guns opened up, and by the accuracy of the bombing.

Only a single AA gun of large calibre appeared to be manned aboard *Königsberg,* most pilots reporting a solitary gun aft firing shells at five-second intervals that were bursting around the dive bombers. The light weapons opened fire later, both from the target ship itself and from nearby vessels, in particular one ship described, presumably because of the weight of fire, as a 'flak ship'. AA guns ashore were also noted, from a position about a mile south-west of the target vessel, but no crew reported that these in any way affected their approach or aiming.

As the bombs screamed down the cruiser was enveloped in smoke and flame which made aerial observation and confirmation difficult. Two hits were claimed amidships and one on the forecastle, in addition to at least one near-miss. The bombs that hit alongside on the mole, of which there were five, four of them very close, threw up dust and clouds of rubble which increased this difficulty of spotting.

The majority of pilots reported that they could not clearly estimate the damage, although a few seem to have had a better view. Riddler for example stated that his bomb missed the ship altogether and set fire to a building on the jetty. Spurway reported his bomb bursting internally producing clouds of smoke and debris, while Russell reported that Harris's bomb was a hit on the cruiser's forecastle which caused a large black hole from which white smoke and flame extruded.

MacIver scored a direct hit amidships between the two funnels and this was probably the most lethal strike of all. All the bombs were very close indeed, in fact the DNAD report estimated that the Mean Error was approximately 50yd which compared, 'very favourably' with a 1939 practice which averaged 70yd.

The *Königsberg* soon started sinking by the bows with flames leaping 100ft into the sky as she sank deeper and deeper. Her stern cocked up exposing her screws and some 50 minutes after the attack she rolled over and capsized.

Petty Officer Gardner, the last pilot over the target, reported that the target appeared to have been hit badly, but her final end was witnessed by an American captain aboard the *Flying Fish,* also in harbour.

The striking demonstration of the power of the dive bomber made a deep impression, but unfortunately the next attack caried out by the FAA Skuas lacked all the essential requisites for such a mission. They were sent in against a target they could not possibly have sunk, the German battle cruiser *Scharnhorst,* and without the vital element of surprise. The result was a disaster.

Aerial reconnaissance had revealed the presence of the German fleet, *Scharnhorst, Admiral Hipper* and four destroyers, in Trondheim Roads on 12 June 1940 and plans were at once made to strike at them with the dive bombers embarked aboard the carrier *Ark Royal.* A feature of the planning was the provision for a pre-emptive strike which was to be mounted by RAF Beauforts against the fighter airfield at Vaernes, to take place not earlier than 0200 on the 13th. Long-range Blenheim fighter escort for the attack and return flight was also supposed to be laid on by the RAF, but this latter failed to materialise at all. The Beaufort attack did in fact take place, but it had exactly the opposite effect to that intended, for, far from destroying enemy fighters on the ground and prematurely bringing them up too early, it merely stirred up the hornets nest too late and resulted in German fighters being airborne ready and waiting when the Skuas arrived over this target area.

The German flak defences were also similarly warned in time to be effective, in fact, by this strike, the Fleet Air Arm's major asset, surprise, was thrown away by the RAF. As it was 20 minutes flight from the head of the fjord to the target it is possible that German coastal observers would have had the same effect anyway. Be that as it may, they were not caught napping this time but were fully prepared. Under such circumstances the DNAD later considered that the FAA Skua attack had a right to expect only one hit and a 25 per cent chance of a second, with 30 per cent casualties from flak and up to a further 30 per cent from fighters. His figures proved to be only too accurate.

Ark Royal arrived at her flying off position undetected and prepared a strike force of fifteen dive bombers, six from No 800 Squadron and nine from No 803 Squadron. This number was governed by the following considerations:

1 Of the Skua pilots available only these fifteen had previous experience of dive bombing with the Skua.
2 The standing air patrol over the fleet limited the number available for the strike.
3 With the light winds then prevailing fifteen was the maximum number that could be flown off with a full bomb load in one range.

The force flew off the carrier at 002 on 13 June, each armed with a 500lb SAP bomb and were led by Lt Cdr Casson, RN and Capt 'Birdy' Partridge, RM. They crossed the Norwegian coast at 0123 and split into two formations in readiness for their attack. They found the weather clear and the fighters and flak waiting. No 800 Squadron made shallow dive bombing runs in line astern down to 8,000ft from the north being met by heavy anti-aircraft fire. No 803 Squadron attacked from south to north, bow to stern of the battle cruiser, save for the last section.

As the Skuas boared in the German fighters closed with them, Me109s and Me110s tangling with the dive bombers early on and others waiting for them to complete their runs. Despite the inferno into which they flew the survivors pressed on down and were rewarded with two direct hits and several near misses according to contemporary reports, although the Germans only admit to one, and tragically, this bomb was a dud which failed to explode.

But they paid a very heavy price for this minimal damage inflicted, no less than eight of the fifteen Skuas were destroyed and the few survivors only managed to escape by hugging the deck in the mist. The RAF fighters which were supposed to protect them only appeared after it was all over and they were on their way back to the *Ark Royal.*

Scharnhorst duly sailed for Germany with her efficiency unimpaired. The RAF launched a series of attacks on her while she was off the coast on 21 June, when Bristol Beauforts carried out shallow dive bombing attacks at 200mph from a height of 1,500ft. But although these attacks were most gallantly pressed home only GP bombs were carried, virtually useless against the deck armour of the battle cruiser, which was $4\frac{1}{4}$in thick in places. This showed a complete misunderstanding of the problems involved in attacking large warships and airscrews were sent out to their deaths on an impossible mission with no chance of success. This fuzziness was a hang-over from the pre-war days when dive bombing had been scorned by the RAF and early war experience had taken time to seep through. That the performance of the German Stuka in Poland had influenced the RAF's thinking a little is shown by correspondence in February and March 1940, just before the Norwegian campaign broke. Here we see the first hints of concern with regard their attitude. SASO wrote to Group Capt Training as follows:

> . . . in the order of priority of training in methods of bombing dive bombing is placed in a low order. In view of the increased importance of the role of the Battle squadrons in support of the Army, and in view of the likelihood of Battles being employed in operations against military road movements, I think that the order of priority of dive bombing of the type envisaged in our Command Tactical Memorandum No 8 should be placed in high order.

Meanwhile a Secret Memo from ACAS to SASO, Bomber Command, revealed that DGRD was of the opinion that no concessions could be made on the speed limitations. 'He is of the opinion that the figures laid down in the Pilots' Handbook represent the extreme concessions which the technical experts are prepared to make without further investigations'. Further trials had been arranged 'as a matter of urgency', and were in progress.

The report on these trials was duly submitted in March 1940. The types of dive bombing investigated were to commence between 7,000 and 8,000ft with bomb release at between 4,000ft, emerging from the dive between 3,000 and 4,000ft. Owing to adverse weather conditions these trials were limited to single aircraft. Seven pilots carried out attacks, dropping fifty-six bombs. Moreover as there were no observation quadrants at Perpignan where the trials were conducted, no accurate assessment of the results was possible! 'It appeared, however, that the average bombing error from the experimental heights was double that from normal heights.' The CO of the Advanced Air Striking Force summed up the attitude to these small-scale experiments, which only seemed to confirm the RAF's already deeply-held opinions on the matter thus: 'It cannot be said that these trials provide sufficient data on which to base any final conclusions. It is regretted that training requirements of a more urgent nature prevent further trials being carried out on high dive bombing in the near future.'

And that, for the time being anyway, was that as far as the RAF was concerned. The Norwegian campaign produced another flurry. A Secret Memo dated 5 May stated: 'The dive bombing successes obtained in Norway by the Skuas and Junkers have raised in the minds of the Air Staff the suspicion that perhaps the pre-war policy of neglecting the dive bomber was not entirely sound', and that, '. . . probably the dive bomber will be put forward as a future Air Staff requirement.' But further reflection was that 'The problem of making our existing bombers do steep dive bombing is a formidable one, and is probably insoluble as a short-range project. I am therefore reluctant to embark on it until we have enough evidence to show that it will be worth while.'

With the Blitkrieg in France and the Low Countries such attitudes were shown to be bankrupted. The low level methods utilised by the RAF proved fatal and battle losses were ghastly. If the RAF had no dive bombers then the French had a few, though pitifully low in numbers compared with the Germans. They did what they could. Only fifty-two Vought V-156Fs were on hand in May, and twelve of these were destroyed on the ground in a single attack at Boulogne-Alprech airfield. The replacement aircraft for this unfortunate unit, AB-3, did not arrive until 23 May, by then far too late. AB-2 survived a similar attack with only slight damage. AB-4 equipped with the Loire dive bomber had been the last to equip, and they moved to Berck on the evening of 17 May.

Missions with both Voughts and LNs took place from 15 May onward with the *Aerononvale* dive bombers operating against targets at Walcheren Island with some success on the following three days, with few losses. On 19 May word came in that French troops were encircled in the forest of Marmal and AB-2 and

AB-4 were sent in to help them, fielding eleven and nine dive bombers respectively. At 1800 they made their approach in vics of three.

Unfortunately the promised fighter cover failed to show up, nonetheless the Loires deployed to the attack as instructed, diving from 6,000ft to 1,000ft before releasing their bombs. They were met by very heavy flak and no less than ten of the LNs were shot down over the target. The survivors, six from AB-2 and four from AB-4, returned to base at 2030. Of these only three remained airworthy, having been holed by flak and by their own bomb splinters. They had, however, caused some damage to the German armour and, considering that they had received no training in this type of targeting, did wonders. They were now no longer operational as a fighting unit and were out of the action for two days refitting.

In a desperate gamble to stem the flood of German armour across the River Oise every available dive bomber was despatched against the Origny-Ste-Benoite bridge on 20 May, Capt Mesny leading in eleven Voughts of AB-1, with one Loire of AB-2 and two of AB-4. RAF Hurricanes failed to provide the cover promised and they were jumped by Me109s some distance from the target. Five Voughts were destroyed and the others failed to attack accurately. The three LNs managed to slip through, and although one was shot down by flak, PO Hautin scored a direct hit with a 330lb bomb which destroyed the bridge.

Their ranks thus decimated, only token strikes could now be mounted by the French Navy dive bombers. It is to their lasting credit that they fought on to the end. On 21 May the only two surviving Loires went out again against enemy targets on the River Aisne, from which only one came back. Meanwhile the five serviceable Voughts of AB-1 were evacuated from Boulogne the day before it was overrun and flew to Dunkirk. All its ground staff and damaged aircraft were captured by the Germans. AB-2 and AB-4 likewise moved out of Calais as the Panzers surrounded it and flew to Cherbourg. They had four aircraft left fit for operations, and one of these from the total of thirteen dive bombers, was shot down over Rouen. The Dunkirk aircraft were also joined to the others at Cherbourg on 22 May, carrying out an attack on enemy tanks near Abbeville *en route*.

The French Navy was re-equipping with the export version of the American Chance Vought Vindicator during early 1940 but deliveries had not been turned into full combat squadrons before the Blitzkreig broke over them and most were lost in the heavy fighting of May and June. Here an immaculate V156F of AB-1 is given a final check on its home base.

A very rare photograph indeed. Very few of the French Navy Voughts were camouflaged, and very little is known of the scheme used. Squadron markings on fuselage side were overpainted and replaced by a small diameter cocarde.

With the Germans attacking the perimeters of the Boulogne defences the remaining Voughts of AB-1 were again thrown in to bomb the German-held Fort de la Crache that afternoon. They made two attacks and lost another plane to flak. For the second attack the four V-156s were joined by three more from a maintenance unit, all seven got back safely but one crashed on landing.

By now all northern French airfields were in danger of being over-run and AB-1 pulled its six Voughts out of Cherbourg to Britain, landing at Tangmere. On 1 June these French dive bombers took off from this British airfield to strike at German forces near Furnes. This mission was carried out without loss but they became dispersed, four landing at Cherbourg, one back at Tangmere and one at Hawkinge.

With the arrival of reserve aircraft AB-1 was built up to six Voughts and these were despatched against targets at Gravelines. They missed the rendezvous with their fighter escort and the mission was aborted forthwith, the aircraft landing at Cherbourg still bombed up.

By now the end was very near. On 3 June AB-2, AB-3 and AB-4 began to move their equipment out and shifted their base far south to Hyeres once more on the Cote d'Azur. Some ten Voughts and fifteen LNs survived to carry out this operation, but during the transfer they lost one LN-401 to an attack by a Polish fighter pilot in a Morane 406 who thought it was a Stuka. Of the five Voughts left on strength of AB-1 at Cherbourg yet further sacrifice was asked. On 9 June they attacked a German column at Rouen successfully, losing one aircraft to flak damage and a crash landing. On 23 June they joined the remaining French dive bombers in the south, for by this time Italy had joined in the war against the Allies. With the fall of Cherbourg imminent the squadron had operated briefly from Brest with four Voughts and when Brest in turn went under on the 19th they shifted to Hourtin near Bordeaux. They carried out their last mission on the 21st destroying a bridge over the Loire without loss.

Italy entered the war on 10 June and the three *Escadrilles,* freshly equipped, took the war to the new enemy. On 13 June four Voughts of AB-3 attacked an Italian submarine off Albenga, dropping five bombs and inflicting some damage, but that same afternoon one Vought was destroyed by Italian fighters. Further losses were suffered when six Voughts of AB-3 were destroyed on the ground at Cuers-Pierrefeu. Further decimation followed with an attack mounted on the night of 18-19 June against Imperia and Novi-Ligure by thirteen Loires of AB-2 and AB-4. Two were hit by flak over the target, two more were lost in bad weather over the Alps and one crash-landed.

With the Armistice Capt Mesny set out with four Voughts for the south, as related, but two turned back due to bad weather and only two arrived. The remaining aircraft of AB-2 and AB-4 were evacuated to Corsica and were there made unserviceable. Thus passed the French dive bombers for the time being. Reports that captured Voughts were put into service by the Luftwaffe for testing, and even used operationally in attacks on Dover Harbour in July 1940, have not been confirmed or otherwise, despite efforts by this author.

Meanwhile the pre-war reputation of the RAF's light attack bombers having vanished, together with the bulk of the Fairey Battles in futile sorties and severe losses, British counter-attacks were no more effective than those of the French Army Air Force in restoring the situation. The rapid progress of the German armies was watched and monitored as they pounded across France, but little in the way of effective opposition could be offered after the first four days.

Not having a dive bomber of its own the RAF was forced to call on any type of aircraft it could lay its hands on to perform this function and the true cost of its pre-war stand against dive bombing was made apparent by the pressing into service of such antiques as FAA Swordfish and obsolete Hawker Hector biplanes to perform this function as the crisis rose.

Eleven Swordfish from No 812 Squadron were sent on a dive bombing mission against German troops at Gravelines on 26 May, armed with 250lb bombs. They claimed the destruction of three tanks for the loss of one Swordfish. The RAF continued this dive bombing support for the Calais garrison throughout the 27th, not knowing for certain that it had surrendered. A large variety of aircraft were utilised in this role, six Westland Lysander's being despatched on the 25th, dive bombing a German battery without observing results. On the 26th six Hectors of No 613 Squadron dive bombed the same battery, led by Sqdn Ldr A.F. Anderson. They went back next day with six Hectors and nine Swordfish and one Hector failed to return.

The Skuas of the FAA saw a great deal of action at this period over France. No 801 Squadron flew into RAF Detling during the second half of May, just in time to start helping to cover the collapse of France and during the German thrust into Belgium. As well as some reconnaissance work over the channel ports they attacked bridges and barges as well as land targets. They found themselves targets for both the Luftwaffe and the RAF fighters, and had to fight their way both to and from their targets. They attacked German batteries at Cape Gris Nez as well, but, working under RAF Coastal Command, they found little appreciation of dive bombing work, targets or problems, among their new masters.

Working from the *Ark Royal* during the Dakar fiasco in September 1940, FAA Skuas and Swordfish conducted dive bombing attacks against the Vichy battleship *Richelieu*. This was an even more futile exercise than the attacks on *Scharnhorst* in June, for the French giant's armour was of even greater thickness and she was completely unscathed.

16 DEATH FROM THE SKY
Axis re-organisation and Mediterranean operations, 1940-42

We have seen how the early Italian experiments had resulted in the production of the SM85 and the prototype of the SM86, neither aircraft performing very well. Nonetheless, with the Italian entry into the war in June 1940, these were the only available dive bombers on hand for the Regia Aeronautica to carry out Mussolini's demands to sweep the Mediterranean Sea clean of the Royal Navy!

Thus on 29 May the 96⁰ *Gruppo Bombardamento a Tuffo* was formed, the first and only Italian-built and manned dive bomber unit. It consisted of eighteen SM85s and the solitary SM86, under the command of Capt E. Ercolani, with 236 and 237 *Squadriglia* led by Ten E. Marcozzi and Ten F. Malvezzi respectively. Named the *Gruppo Autonomo* this unit was transferred from Rome's Ciampino airfield down to the island of Pantelleria in the middle of the Sicilian Channel, close to Malta, in readiness for its chance of a contest with the ships of Adm A.B. Cunningham's Mediterranean Fleet, this transfer being completed by 5 June 1940.

Their opportunity soon arose for on 19 July was fought the naval battle of Calabria, when the British fleet chased the Italian fleet back within sight of its home ports before losing contact. Here, with an enemy fleet within biscuit toss of the Italian airfields, were plum targets for the asking, three battleships and an aircraft carrier with no fighters aboard. But unfortunately for their hopes the new Gruppo never even made contact, let alone carried out any dive bombing attacks.

The damp, humid conditions at Pantelleria were just too much for the wooden structure of the 'Flying Banana'. During the whole of June and July the SM85s managed only two recce sorties from the whole Gruppo and then they were retired to Rome once more with a zero war efficiency rating. Although refurbished and based for a while at Comiso in Sicily, all these dive bombers were soon broken up.

The solitary SM86, still being flown by test pilot Scarpini for the makers, *did* make one solitary combat flight against Malta (in company with some Ju87s) on 15 September, during which it dropped its single 500kg bomb on Hal Far airfield. But the Regia Aeronautica was not impressed and had by this time, as in so many other things, turned to its Axis partner for the solution to its dive bomber problems, although many experiments continued to be conducted to find a suitable Italian-built dive bomber in the years which followed.

A special mission was despatched to Germany by the Chief of the Italian Air Staff, Generale Pricolo after he had studied reports of the SM85 failure. Generale Urbani and Col Teucci, Air Attache in Berlin held talks with Reichsmarschall Goering which resulted in the purchase of batches of Ju87Bs and Rs, while provision was made for the training of pilots at the *Stukaschule 2* at Graz in Austria, the first fifteen pilots starting in July with fifteen more in August. The Stukas purchased by Italy were tropicalised by having sand filters fitted and desert survival equipment added for use by the new *Gruppi Tuffatori*. Despite repeated rumours that the Italians built Ju87s under licence in Italy, the fact remains that this is not the case, all were brought in.

The first Stukas arrived in Sicily on 21 August where they formed 96⁰ *Gruppo*   131 under Capt Ercolani with thirteen aircraft of 236 and 237 *Squadriglia,* led by Ten Malvezzi and Ten G. Santinoni at Comiso airfield.

Similar arrangements were also made to equip dive bomber units of Germany's other allies. The *Magyar Királyi Légierö* of Hungary formed the dive bomber group *I Onálló Zuhanöbombazö Osztály* with two squadrons of Ju87B2s and these were replaced by Ju87Ds two years later when it finally became fully operational. The Rumanian air force formed *Grupul 6 Picaj* with Bs, having three nine-plane squadrons ready by 1941 in time for the invasion of Russia. Bulgaria took small batches of Ju87B2s and later Ds during the same period, as did the Slovakian air force.

The only home-built dive bomber to serve with the Bulgarian Air Force during the war was the DAR10F, which was a modified version of the DAR10 fighter bomber with structural strengthening. The dive bomber modification was influenced by events in France in 1940 and first flew early in 1941. Only a limited number of DAR10s were so modified for front-line service however before they were replaced by Ju87D5s supplied by Germany. However the DAR10Fs still surviving by that time found some useful combat service in the anti-guerilla operations in Yugoslavia until late in the war.

The DAR10F was a low-wing monoplane, with fixed spatted undercarriage and a crew of two. It was powered by a 960hp Fiat A74 RG38 engine which gave it a top speed of 282mph at 16,400ft and a range of 870 miles. This little bomber had a wing span of 41½ft, a length of 32¼ft and was armed with two fixed 7.92mm MG17 machine guns and two 20mm MG FF cannon in the wings, with a flexible MG15 in the rear cockpit.

The Rumanian IAR81 and 81A was a modified version of the IAR80 and 80A fighter respectively, featuring an increased wing span of 34ft 5¼in, a length of 29ft 2½in and a height of 11ft 10in. The fitting of bomb racks under the wings for four 110lb bombs and under the fuselage for one 551lb bomb was supplemented by four 7.92mm cannon in the 81A. It was powered by a single 1,025hp IAR (Gnome-Rhone) 14 K115 engine, which gave it a top speed of 317mph at 13,120ft and a range of 584 miles. This single-seater adaption was further supplemented in the dive bomber field by the 81C, a fighter/dive bomber version which featured two 20mm MG151 cannon which could also carry bombs. A total of 260 were built of the A and C series, along with the B which had no dive bombing potential, and were used on the Eastern Front.

More potent for the Mediterranean theatre of operations was the transferring of StG2 with over one hundred aircraft as part of *Fliegerkorps X* to airfields in Sicily. Here they were to pose a great threat to Malta, Egypt and the Royal Navy. Their first, and most spectacular attack, took place on 19 January 1941. I/StG1 led by Maj Enneccerus and II/StG2 led by *Hauptmann* Hozzel attacked the British fleet in the Sicilian Channel. They scored one hit on the battleship *Warspite,* in return for the loss of one Stuka shot down by the battleship *Valiant,* but their target was the aircraft carrier *Illustrious* and in a precision assault they hit her with no less than six heavy bombs while three more were near misses. Heavily damaged the only thing which saved the ship was her armoured deck. Next day another attack sank the cruiser *Southampton* and damaged the *Gloucester,* and not for more than eighteen months did heavy ships attempt to dispute these waters again.

Repeated attacks were made on Malta, with both the dockyards and airfields being the targets, and in these the German Ju87s were joined by the growing numbers of Italian dive bombers. Further units moved into desert air strips to support the Axis attacks through Libya and into Egypt and took a major part in the subsequent campaigns in the years 1941-2 as the tide of war flowed up and

Italian Stuka. A Junkers Ju87R-2 of 101º Gruppo B.aT, this one is from 208º Squadriglia on patrol over Greece in 1941. The long-range fuel tanks can be clearly seen in this photograph.

down the North African coast. Other targets for both German and Italian Stukas and also of Ju88 units, were the convoys from Gibraltar and Alexandria which attempted to lift the seige of Malta during the same period. It is no mean boast by the Ju87 crews that they inflicted more damage on the Royal Navy in this period than the entire Italian Navy and Air Force combined. During the evacuation of Greece and the Battle of Crete in April and May 1941, the Ju87s took on the Mediterranean Fleet in earnest and inflicted heavy casualties, while further losses of smaller warships became a regular feature of operations off Tobruk and other North African ports. The successes of the Stukas against warship targets in the Mediterranean theatre during this period are summarised in Table 30.

It will be recalled that the first Italian dive bomber unit to re-equip with the Ju87 arrived at Comiso, Sicily, in August 1940. Their first mission took place on

A splendid portrait of a formation of Junkers Ju87R-2s of 208º Squadriglia, 101º Gruppo of 5º Stormo Tuffatori returning to their airfield at Trapani Milo in Sicily after an attack on Malta. To the left can be seen the distinctive Monte Erice.

Table 30: RN warships sunk or damaged by Ju87s in Mediterranean 1941			
Date	Ship	Type	Result
10-1-41	*Illustrious*	Aircraft Carrier	Heavily damaged
10-1-41	*Warspite*	Battleship	Slightly damaged
11-1-41	*Southampton*	Cruiser	Sunk
11-1-41	*Gloucester*	Cruiser	Damaged
16-1-41	*Perth*	Cruiser	Damaged
16-1-41	*Illustrious*	Aircraft Carrier	Damaged
19-1-41	*Illustrious*	Aircraft Carrier	Damaged
22-2-41	*Terror*	Monitor	Sunk
24-2-41	*Dainty*	Destroyer	Sunk
27-4-41	*Diamond*	Destroyer	Sunk
27-4-41	*Wryneck*	Destroyer	Sunk
21-5-41	*Ajax*	Cruiser	Damaged
22-5-41	*Greyhound*	Destroyer	Sunk
22-5-41	*Gloucester*	Cruiser	Sunk
22-5-41	*Fiji*	Cruiser	Sunk
22-5-41	*Carlisle*	Cruiser	Damaged
22-5-41	*Naiad*	Cruiser	Damaged
23-5-41	*Kelly*	Destroyer	Sunk
23-5-41	*Kashmir*	Destroyer	Sunk
26-5-41	*Formidable*	Aircraft Carrier	Damaged
26-5-41	*Nubian*	Destroyer	Damaged
28-5-41	*Ajax*	Cruiser	Damaged
28-5-41	*Imperial*	Destroyer	Damaged (sunk later)
29-5-41	*Hereward*	Destroyer	Sunk
29-5-41	*Decoy*	Destroyer	Damaged
29-5-41	*Dido*	Cruiser	Damaged
29-5-41	*Orion*	Cruiser	Damaged
31-5-41	*Napier*	Destroyer	Damaged
1-6-41	*Calcutta*	Cruiser	Sunk
24-6-41	*Auckland*	Sloop	Sunk
29-6-41	*Waterhen*	Destroyer	Sunk
11-7-41	*Defender*	Destroyer	Sunk
12-7-41	*Flamingo*	Sloop	Damaged
12-7-41	*Cricket*	Gunboat	Damaged

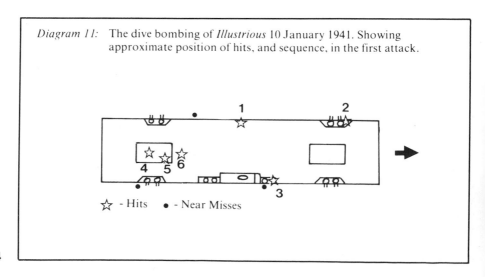

Diagram 11: The dive bombing of *Illustrious* 10 January 1941. Showing approximate position of hits, and sequence, in the first attack.

☆ - Hits   • - Near Misses

2 September with an abortive search for a reported convoy near Malta. It was finally located the next day, and at 1425, five Ju87s of 96⁰ *Gruppo* went into action against it with an escort of six Macchi 200 fighters. Although they subsequently claimed to have hit a cruiser, no hits were in fact made. A second raid with four Stukas made the same claim and a third attack added another cruiser plus a carrier damaged, but again this was over-confidence and no hits had in fact been scored on any vessel. On 5 September five Italian Stukas dive bombed Malta.

Further attacks followed and on 17 September the *Gruppo* suffered its first loss when twelve Stukas attacked Mikabba airfield in a dive. They were intercepted by Hurricanes of No 261 Squadron and lost Sgt Catani from 237 *Squadriglia* who became a POW. On 27 September the Italian Stukas transferred to Lecce airfield in readiness for the invasion of Greece, but eight of these aircraft subsequently returned to Comiso on 11 November to form the nucleus of the second Italian unit.

The first actions of 96⁰ *Gruppo* over Greece took place with attacks on Janina, Presba and Florina airfields on 5, 14 and 16 November 1940 and on 7 December they were joined at Lecce by 97⁰ Gruppo. 96⁰ was brought back for a period in January 1941 to take part in the *Illustrious* action, but they aborted their mission. Both units continued to support the hard-pressed Italian troops on the Albanian front into the New Year, with some successes and a few losses. On 5 March a third Stuka *Gruppo* was formed, 101⁰.

Both these units were joined by the other four *Squadriglia* at Lecce, 208 during 7-8 March and 209 on 17 March. The Italians were taking a bad beating from the Greeks at this time and were hard-pressed to hold Valona itself, so great demands were made on the dive bomber crews, and, as a result of bad weather conditions in the mountains during the winter and the poor state of the landing grounds, the attrition rate was high.

In February 1941, the first Italian Stukas joined the Germans in North Africa, 96⁰ *Gruppo* transferring to Benghazi airport in stages from the 1st of that month as they were replaced by 101⁰ *Gruppo* in the Balkans. 236 *Squadriglia* under Capt E. Malvezzi was the first and was joined by five Ju87s of 237 *Squadriglia* under Capt G. Santioni later, and these were soon in action over Tobruk.

The solitary SM86 prototype was attached to 96⁰ *Gruppo* to prove itself in combat being flown by Scarpini and making an attack on Hal Far with a single 500kg bomb. When 96⁰ moved to Lecce-Galatina for the Greek operation a dive bombing attack was made by Scarpini in this aircraft on Greek positions at Giannina. However, on 21 December, Scarpini was shot down while flying a Ju87 and the SM86 was relegated to a hangar at Galatina and forgotten about.

In the summer of 1941 this aircraft was dismantled, but a second prototype (MM398) fitted with two IF Gamma RC351 engines, was tested at Vergiate by Cdr Guido Nobili. The initial flight took place on 7 August and trials continued until December, but nothing much ever came of it.

For their own training the Italians modified three Caproni Bergamasca API which had a fixed landing gear. These had been built for Paraguay, but were never paid for, so the *Regia Aeronautica* took them over and the *Nucleo Addestramento* of Lonate Pozzolo (Varese) modified them as dive bomber trainers. They were fitted with Junkers-style dive brakes made of wood under the wings, and stripped of non-essential gear. As such these three API were used sparsely during 1941-2 but were not a success, and, in June 1942, they were scrapped.

In North Africa StG3 moved into Castel Benito, Sirte and Arco Philernorum airfields in January 1941, and were joined a month later by I/StG1 and both units provided the spearhead of the newly formed Afrika Korps. The first German Stuka lost was shot down over Agheila on 6 February 1941. By April 1941 III/StG1 had moved over from Sicily also. Those that remained continued to pound Malta non-stop, being reinforced by the larger long-range Ju88s, and yet another *Gruppe* was moved out of France to reinforce them during the same month, leaving only sixty Ju87s in that country.

In order to remove the threat of British bombers operating against his vital Rumanian oil fields from Greek bases, Hitler determined to get Mussolini out of the mess he was in in Greece and throw the Allies out of Europe for good. He tried diplomatic means first, but when Yugoslavia threw out her Government, German plans were hastily re-cast. The Stuka units already earmarked for the invasion of Russia, operation 'Barbarossa' in May, were quickly moved into forward bases in the south of Austria and Rumania instead for another Blitzkrieg demonstration. I and III/StG77, now refitted and refurbished, moved into Rumanian bases, I and III/StG2, I/StG3 and the crack II(Schlacht)/LG2, moved into ready-use strips on the Bulgarian border as part of *Fliegerkorps VIII,* and II/StG77 lay ready in Austria, with the Italian units outflanking them at Albania. The Axis forces jumped off on 6 April 1941 and achieved complete surprise.

Once more the combination of Stuka and Panzer were irresistible as Hitler had predicted. II(Schlacht)/LG2 wiped out the tiny air base of Prilep on the first day, then swung into their classic role of breaking up troop columns. The Yugoslav army was on par with the Polish army of two years before in bravery, but also in obsolescence and the effects on it were just as devastating. StG77 co-operated in the massive attack that gave Belgrade the Warsaw treatment, while Stab/StG3 and II/StG77 blasted their way into the northern part of the stunned country. II(Schlacht)/LG2, moving at breakneck speed, put in heavy attacks around Skopje, Servia and over into Greece itself. Yogoslavia sued for terms on the 14th but the Panzers had thrust on into Greece without stopping and within a few days had done what Mussolini's legions had failed all winter to do, thrown the Greek Army into hasty retreat along with its British allies. Athens capitulated on 27 April and German paratroops crossed the Corinth canal, turning the last defence line left to the Allies.

In an effort to bolster the Italians in their fight against the British Mediterranean Fleet in 1940 and in attacks on Egypt and Malta, the Luftwaffe moved powerful forces into the area, including two Geschwader of Stukas and some Junkers Ju88s. This picture shows Italian airmen clustering round to examine one of the first Ju88s in transit down Italy to bases in Sicily in early 1941.

Almost incidently the Luftwaffe turned on the ports and harbours of Greece, sinking, among others, the old battleship *Kilkis* in dock, the destroyer *Hydra*, nine lesser warships and forty-three merchantmen totally 63,975 tons, the Ju87s contributing in full measure to these losses. Heavy toll was taken of shipping evacuating the British forces and in addition to the warships the transports *Hellas, Pennland, Costa Rica* and *Slamat* were sunk with heavy loss of life among the troops aboard. The long range dive bombers, Ju88s, also struck across the water to Suda Bay, Crete, hitting the already damaged heavy cruiser *York* and finishing her off.

The surviving Allied troops reached Crete and began methodical preparations against the attack they daily expected against that now isolated island. Over in the western Mediterranean at this time Stuka operations, both German and Italian, were more limited, the main mission was that undertaken against the 'Tiger' convoy bringing tanks and troops through from the UK via Gibraltar and Malta. An attack on 8 May by Ju87s was frustrated by Fulmar fighters from *Ark Royal* and heavy cloud cover and no ships were hit.

Dive bombing operations were stepped up on Malta, a heavy raid being mounted on 14 April with both Ju87s and Ju88s. The bulk of the fighting however lay in the eastern basin as the Axis armies swept east along the North African coast and isolated the port of Tobruk, and 5/StG1 under *Hauptmann* Joachim Rieger, an anti-shipping expert, was kept busy attacking the warships keeping the port provided.

Meanwhile the Stuka units had been re-grouping in readiness for the assault on Crete itself, 'Merkur' Operation. For the first three weeks in May they were busy preparing forward airfields in southern Greece and the south-east Peloponnese islands for the dive bombers and troop transporting Ju52s, and into the newly created airstrips at Melos, Lulaoi and Scarpanto flew the Stukas. They now had the range to cover all the seaward approaches to Crete. StG2 had its *Gruppen* placed in readiness by 20 May, with two at Molai and Mycene and a third at Scarpanto. At Eleusis the longer ranging Ju88s of I and II/LG2 settled in under *Hauptleute* Hoffmann and Kollewe.

They were eager to face the British fleet, but their first task was to soften up the islands' defences to pave the way for the airborne troops. In order to increase the killing power of their bomb loads, which tended to explode upward on contact with the rocky surface, new fusing systems were adopted by the Stuka crews themselves to give a more lethal lateral spread against concentrations of troops. This involved fitting a metal rod with a 8cm (3in) diameter disc at the end to the bombs, the bomb was thus detonated some 30cm (12in) above the ground giving a high scatter effect. It was named *Zünderabstandstäbe* or *Dinortstäbe* after Dinort whose unit was the first to use them.

The battle for Crete opened on 20 May 1941 and initial dive bomber targets ashore were the defences around Maleme and Canea airfields, especially the AA batteries. An hour after these attacks started the first gliders arrived over these fields and at the Akrotiri Peninsula overlooking the main harbour area of Suda Bay, and strong and continuous dive bomber sorties were flown all day in support.

The Mediterranean Fleet was at sea in strength to deal with the expected seaborne landings and during the days which followed they were subjected to an unprecedented scale of air attack by the Stuka units. Although on the 21st the dive bombers were still mainly preoccupied with supporting the troops ashore one *Gruppe* was allocated to deal with the British warships at daybreak. Attacks were made at first light and the cruiser *Ajax* was hit and damaged. Just as important was the scale of expenditure of the warship's AA ammunition, and after one day's non-stop dive bombing the fleet found itself dangerously depleted in this respect for the next day's combat.

On 21 May the destroyer *Janus* was sunk in a combined attack by Italian Cant bombers and the Stukas of III/StG2 under *Hauptmann* Brücker, which hit her at 1239 with three bombs. The first two struck aft, wrecking her boiler room and engine rooms, while the third exploded her after magazine. A photograph taken by the Italian Stuka unit, 210⁰ *Squadriglia,* which also attacked, shows her blowing up.

The pattern was repeated during the following days, the Ju87s more and more being switched to take on the warships. At 0630 on 22nd the cruisers *Fiji* and *Gloucester* were both near-missed without serious damage. Attacks by LG1 damaged the cruisers *Carlisle* and *Naiad.* At 1320 the destroyer *Greyhound* was detached from the fleet to sink a solitary caique between Pori and Antikithera islands and she was set upon by eight Ju87s, which hit her at 1351. A 550lb bomb fell directly on her solitary 3in AA gun and the two 110lb bombs were also hits. *Greyhound* sank in four minutes with heavy loss of life. This was bad enough, but the error was compounded by the detachment of two more destroyers to pick up her survivors, with the *Gloucester* and *Fiji* in support. These ships steamed away from the protection of the battleship's AA fire and into the arms of the Stukas. By the time they were recalled it was too late. Already low on ammunition *Gloucester* was soon reduced to firing practice shells at the waves of dive bombers that pounced on the squadron.

Having survived numerous attacks by Ju87s and Ju88s *Gloucester* was hit at 1527 by at least two bombs. The first exploded in the gunroom flat damaging a boiler room and extinguishing all lights, the second hit the after AA director and demolished the main topmast. A further attack resulted in several near misses and then another hit was received on her port torpedo tubes, and yet a fourth detonated on her port pom-pom mounting. Heavily on fire the cruiser slid to a standstill and still the bombs rained down. Three more explosions rent her hull at 1545, she listed over to port and finally sank at 1715, her death throes being recorded on film by the victorious airmen.

Fiji did not long outlast her. Continuously near-missed during the afternoon, her AA armament all but depleted, she was finished off by a single direct hit after a Me109 *Jabo* of 1/LG1 had brought her to a halt earlier with a 550lb bomb that blew in her plating amidships. After a second hit she rolled over at 2015.

During the course of the day the battleships *Warspite* and *Valiant* were both hit, as were, again, the cruisers *Carlisle* and *Naiad.* During the following night the same errors were repeated and three destroyers were detached to bombard Maleme airfield. At dawn on the 23rd they were located while withdrawing by I/StG2 under *Hauptmann* Hitschold. The *Kashmir* was hit first and quickly sank. Then the *Kelly,* turning hard under full helm at high speed, was struck by a heavy bomb which capsized her. This was at 0800. Survivors from these two ships were picked up by the *Kipling,* which herself survived several heavy attacks that left her trailing oil, but she reached port.

In attempts to limit the scale of Stuka attacks ashore, where the fighting had reached a critical stage, it was decided, in the lack of any RAF contribution, to launch a carrier attack on Scarpanto airfield from the *Formidable.* This was done on the night of the 25-6 May, but, although some slight damage was done to a few aircraft, the losses inflicted were negligable and the price paid was exhorbitant. Although the fleet withdrew beyond normal Stuka range quickly, they overlooked the fact that Stukas were still operating from Libya also. Thus they were caught by II/StG2 under Maj Enneccerus at 1320. The twenty Ju87Rs were operating at the extreme edge of their range when they picked up the fleet and they made their attacks immediately. Penetrating the barrage the Ju87Rs scored two direct hits on the carrier, damaging one of the 4.5in turrets and hitting the carrier also on the starboard side aft, blowing out the ship's bulkheads and starting large fires. Eight Stukas had attacked *Formidable,* while the others turned their attentions to her consorts. The destroyer *Nubian* was hit by a bomb which blew her stern off, but she managed to limp home. Subsequent attacks by the Ju88s of LG1 scored one hit on the 'Y' turret of the battleship *Barham.* On the same day the evacuation of Crete began.

At 1700 on 28 May a force of three cruisers and six destroyers heading to embark soldiers was located about 90 miles from Scarpanto and subjected to non-stop dive bombing until nightfall. The destroyer *Imperial* was near missed, as was the cruiser *Ajax,* which had to be sent back damaged. By 0255 the remainder had finished loading and again stood out to sea with 4,000 troops aboard. At 0345 the rudder of the *Imperial* jammed and she had to be sunk by another destroyer. By 0600, while clearing the Kaso Strait, the force was located and the dive bombing commenced. *Hotspur* was attacked by six Ju87s but survived. Not so fortunate was the *Hereward.* Attacked at 0625 she was hit close by her fore funnel by a Stuka which dived below 1,500ft in a determined attack. She was crippled, left behind and later finished off.

Next to be damaged was the destroyer *Decoy,* her engine room taking splinters from a near-miss which fractured her turbine feet and reduced her speed to 25 knots. This was at 0645. The promised fighter cover never materialised and at 0735 Stukas machine-gunned the cruiser *Orion,* wounding her captain. A near-miss reduced her speed to 21 knots. At 0815 the Ju87s planted a direct hit on the cruiser *Dido.* It is thought that this one hit, on 'B' turrey, killed twenty-seven sailors and eleven soldiers, with many more wounded. Eight close misses were counted around her at this time.

The ordeal continued. At 0900 the *Orion* was also hit, on 'A' turret, by a Ju87 that onlookers mistook for a suicide attack, so low did the aircraft dive before release. The Stuka failed to recover and crashed into the sea just off the bows of *Dido.* It is likely that the pilot was badly wounded and determined to sell his life dearly. The whole armoured casing of the ship's turret was torn away and the guns destroyed, while 'B' turret, next to it, was also heavily damaged.

At 0930 *Orion* was near missed and at 1045 eleven Stukas delivered another concentrated attack on her about one hundred miles south of Kaso Strait. She was immersed in the spray of near missed too numerous to count and one bomb hit her hard. It passed straight through her bridge and sick-bay and exploded deep inside her, demolishing the stokers' messdeck which was packed solid with troops. This single bomb killed 107 sailors and 155 soldiers, wounding 300 more. The scene below defied description.

A similar ordeal awaited a second squadron of warships on the 30th when the cruiser *Perth* was hit behind her bridge by a bomb that penetrated to her foremost boiler room at 0930. She was also near-missed in a later attack as was the destroyer *Jaguar.* Some fighter cover appeared after this which drove off one heavy attack by Ju87s and Ju88s and no ships were actually sunk.

During the same day the destroyer *Kelvin* was so damaged by three Ju88s that she had to be sent back and next morning twelve Ju88s damaged the destroyer *Napier.* The transport *Glengyle* escorted by three cruisers and six destroyers embarked 6,029 soldiers that night without loss, but the final drama of the Crete campaign took place the next day. The anti-aircraft cruiser *Calcutta* was sent to help escort her in but was herself caught by surprise by two Ju88s diving out of the sun at 0917, despite radar warning. The second aircraft straddled *Calcutta* with a perfect stick, two bombs striking the old vessel which sank rapidly within a few minutes. Thus ended the Battle of Crete, perhaps the Stukas greatest victory at sea.

Although the bulk of the Stuka units were almost immediately transferred back north in readiness for the postponed assault on Russia, a number of units remained in the Mediterranean, and these, in co-operation with the Italian Stukas, were instrumental in giving the British army more bitter lessons. By now the Italians had built their strength up to four units as shown in Table 31.

Table 31: First four Italian Stuka units operational 1940-1					
Gruppo	Commander	Strength	Squadriglia	Commanders	Date
96^0	Capt Ercolani	13	236 237	*Ten* Malvezzi *Ten* Santinoni	August 1940
97^0	Col Moscatelli	14	238 239	*Ten* Bertuzzi *Ten* Genni	November 1940
101^0	*Magg* Donadio	16	208 209	Capt Bertuzzi Capt Romanese	March 1941
102^0	Capt Genni	20	209	Capt Stringa *Ten* Bigoni	May 1941

The dive bombers that remained were fully committed to supporting Rommel's thrust east to the Egyptian border which left Tobruk cut off. The supplying of this garrison gave the depleted Mediterranean Fleet a further chore, and one in which the dive bombers were able to take good advantage of. Heavy attacks were also made on Tobruk itself.

The German units employed in 1941 in North Africa were I/StG1, II/StG2 and I/StG3. The main assault had broken earlier, in April, but the garrison had withstood it well. During the quick German advance the dive bombers had performed well in their textbook drill of army co-operation. One observer noted: 'On 7 April the GAF struck in considerable strength at the Derna defiles, which were chock-full of retreating vehicles. inflicting much damage and seriously delaying the withdrawal.'

Between 11 April and 24 June 1941, no less than forty-six Stuka missions were made on Tobruk and its harbour, many of the attacks being directed at AA positions, the heaviest assaults being on 14 April (40 Ju87s), 29 May (60 Ju87s) and 2 June (60 Ju87s). Out of 959 aircraft missions made the defences claimed the destruction of fifty-four Stukas by the heavy and light AA batteries of the garrison, proving that well-trained gunners could inflict damage on dive bombers if they stood their ground. At sea losses were heavy.

On 25 May 239 *Squadriaglia* led by Commandante Genni, attacked warships off Tobruk at 1720, sinking the merchantman *Helka* (3,741 tons) and her escort, the sloop *Grimsby*. On 24 June Stukas sank the sloop *Auckland* and so it went on. Between 12 April and 9 December the Royal Navy lost twenty-six naval vessels, including the brand-new minelayer *Latona,* which was sunk in a night dive bombing attack. Six merchant ships were also sunk and many others damaged.

As 1941 turned into 1942 the dive bomber was making an impressive mark on the North African desert campaign, but the Allied response was weak or non-existant. Let us turn to Britain and see why this was so.

17 WAR IN WHITEHALL
British limited operations and disagreements, 1940-42

The massive and decisive defeat of France and the conquest of the whole of Western Europe in the same manner as the over-running of Poland the year before rammed home the lesson of the power and effectiveness of the dive bomber, both as a battle-winner and economical force. With Great Britain penned into her home islands and daily expecting an invasion, a hasty re-examination of the hardware with which they might expect to repel such an invasion emphasised the complete lack of any type of dive bomber in the RAF for army co-operation work. This caused much adverse comment from Winston Churchill down and the new Minister for Aircraft Production, Beaverbrook, quickly set to work to try and rectify the situation.

The RAF, having set their faces against the type for many years, and with no quick way of obtaining a dive bomber from home factories, countered with the oft-repeated paper arguments which varied from time to time but remained always, in essence, firmly opposed to the dive bomber and more and more deeply committed to the long range heavy bomber. It was not the German armies they wished to destroy but the German cities, and this they felt would be all that was required to win the war anyway.

Gen Ironside had been one of the senior Army officers who had foreseen the need for close air-support in the same manner as the German Army had been served by the Stukas. He had strongly advocated an Army Air Arm long before the war, much to the distaste of the Air Marshals. He maintained that for such a job specialised aircraft and aircrew were needed, both attuned to the require-ments of land warfare. The Air Chief's would have none of this, maintaining their faith in general purpose light bombers to carry out the tasks, the only specialised role for which they catered was the provision of spotter aircraft in the form of the Lysander, which was totally unsuitable for the type of mechanised warfare which had broken over Ironside's troops in May 1940. As his biographer subsequently noted: 'The opening stages of World War II, with German dive bombers preparing the way for armoured columns, now proved Ironside right.'

No less an impact had been made on his successor, Gen Brooke, at Dunkirk he noted, 'After seeing yesterday the ease with which a dive bomber can sink a destroyer it is an unpleasant feeling.' His biographer noted that, 'A subject to which Brooke devoted almost as much time was air co-operation with ground troops. His experience in France had made him fanatical about this.' But he was not to get much further than his predecessor in convincing others for the need for this.

An American historian noted that, 'The RAF and French Air Force also began the war with little in the way of an effective, trained air arm for close co-operation with ground forces. In the 1940 crisis in France this cost them dearly.' Too late, the French acknowledged the truth of this: 'Even though the Stukas had already shown their worth in Spain, and though General Vuillemin, at General Milch's invitation in 1938, had watched an impressive display of dive bombing, our High Command, both air and army, did not see fit to adopt this type of warfare.'

Even Churchill himself, a staunch defender throughout the war of the RAF   141 line in Parliament and public, from time to time allowed himself to vent his frustration at the lack of British dive bombers and the will to produce one. The RAF view was upheld in the many debates that followed by Sir Archibald Sinclair, Air Minister. Beaverbrook was convinced of the need for dive bombers even if the Air Staff was not and a bitter conflict of priorities was to feature large over the year between the two rival ministries, who failed to see eye-to-eye over many topics, not least, the dive bomber. Being a Canadian Beaverbrook took a broader trans-Atlantic view. He saw the untapped resources of the USA as a safe base upon which the immediate needs of Britain in the air could be built up, and although the British Purchasing Commission had already been established in the wake of the original Anglo-French team, he went right over their heads through Maurice Wilson of the Royal Bank of Canada to get the aircraft he considered necessary.

In April 1940, the French had ordered 192 of the Brewster 340 dive bombers through the Anglo-French Agreement, this being a modification of the US Navy Buccaneer dive bomber, prepared by the Corporation. With the collapse of France this contract was taken over by the British Government under the terms of the Purvis Block-Laine agreement. The contract, as had been placed by the French, contained an option to order a further 150 aircraft, and this option was exercised by the BPC on 27 July 1940.

At that date Brewster offered a further option of 100 aircraft, and this option was also exercised by the BPC on 1 November, 1940, bringing the total number of Bermudas (as the RAF re-named them) dive bombers on order to 450. On 2 November a *new* contract was placed covering the supply of a further 300 aircraft of this type, of which delivery was to be made of the total 750 commencing in January 1941 and completing by March 1942.

But between the taking over of the original French order in July and the placing of the November orders a great deal other things had happened, for, with the formation of the MAP, yet further orders were placed in the USA that cut across these arrangements. On 16 June 1940, Sir Henry Self sent a telegram to the MAP which contained an offer of 200 Vultee Vengeance dive bombers, a decision having to be made by 21 June. Beaverbrook consulted with Anthony Eden and the details were shown to the Air Ministry, who approved the order. On 28 June Eden wrote to Sinclair confirming the order of 200 Vengeance aircraft and suggesting that the General and the Air Staffs should consider the organisation of units together. This Sinclair agreed to do.

Meanwhile the subject of dive bombers had been raised by Moore-Brabazon in a private capacity. His idea was to build dive bombers under licence in new factories in Canada. The availability of American types with promise of early delivery, over-rode this idea and further orders were placed in the USA instead. As Lord Beaverbrook wrote to Sinclair later, 'We ordered in the USA as you know because prior to July 1940 no one at the Air Ministry had included dive bombers in their requisitions, nor had anyone even ordered a prototype. So we had none on home stocks and the quickest way to get them was in the USA.'

A.J.P. Taylor recorded the outshot of the July order thus: 'In July 1940, he placed a large order for dive bombers in Canada and the United States. Eden, then Secretary for War, was enthusiastic. The Air Ministry protested and refused to supply or train pilots.'

On 2 August a meeting took place between the Air Staff and the General Staff, with the threat of invasion looming large over them. The Air Ministry viewpoint prevailed although the final salient features agreed on for a new 'Close-Support' aircraft were as follows: 'A single engined dive bomber (light or medium type) with a crew of two primarily for operating by day; in consequence it must be adequately armed and protected against air and ground opposition. In this respect it should be armoured underneath while the majority of its gun armament should be in self-defence against fight attack mainly from above.' With a suggested bomb load of 700lb, 'In addition to the normal qualities of a dive bomber the aircraft should be suitable for flying at a very low altitude to achieve surprise.' An optimum top speed of about 300mph was required and a maximum range of 700 miles, constructed with a view of ease of maintenance and be robust. All well and good, but the Air Ministry had the last word: 'The technical specifications of an aircraft to meet these requirements is a matter for the Air Staff to decide.' Just what this meant was revealed later. 'While a steep dive bomber was *not essential,* the aircraft should have as steep an angle of dive as possible without prejudice to other essential requirements.' This proved to be the 'out' they required to ensure the plane would not be a true dive bomber. The RAF was not talking about a dive bomber at all, but the allocation of the Blenheim to the close-support role. Meanwhile further orders were placed by the MAP for American built dive bombers, but the heady promises of the builders soon fell short and deliveries were more and more delayed as teething and shop

Table 32: Revised Delivery Forecasts for US Built Dive Bombers for RAF, May 1941

Type	Date	Number	Type	Date	Number
Bermuda	June	1	Vengeance	June	1
Bermuda	July	12	Vengeance	July	1
Bermuda	August	41	Vengeance	August	2
Bermuda	September	70	Vengeance	September	9
Bermuda	October	86	Vengeance	October	20
Bermuda	November	90	Vengeance	November	32
Bermuda	December	90	Vengeance	December	44
Total		390	Total		109

floor problems delayed the programme month upon month. By May 1941 a revised estimate of delivery dates for the Vengeance and Bermuda was submitted.

Beaverbrook again raised the question of dive bombers with Sinclair in February 1941 and was duly informed that no further orders for this type of aircraft were going to be placed. In despair at this attitude Beaverbrook tried another tack and approached Margesson at the War Office direct. The reply he got left no doubt that the War Office had been weaned away from their original stated specifications of the previous summer. 'While we were deeply impressed with the capabilities of aircraft used in this manner, we are not convinced that the so-called "dive bomber" is the most suitable aircraft to use. Hence we have abandoned the use of the term "dive bomber" and have spoken of a "close-support" bomber.'

As a further step the priority given to existing orders was further downgraded, a memo of 25 February reduced the dive bomber in priority from third to bottom place, behind the heavy and medium bombers, fighters and army support types. The Air Ministry went further after a meeting with US Gen Arnold on 23 April. On 26 April the Air Ministry notified MAP that: '... the Air Ministry confirm that the additional orders for dive bombers are not wanted unless such orders are necessary to enable the Brewster, Northrop and Vultee plants to be switched later on to types which are needed. If there is no such need or intention, the Air Ministry suggests that the expenditure of labour and materials on these order is wholly unjustified.'

Despite such statements further orders were placed by the MAP, for 300

Vengeance on 9 April and another 300 on 17 June under the Lease-Lend Agreement; this was in addition to the 200 ordered on 25 February, *pre*-Lease-Lend. When Churchill enquired why no dive bombers had yet entered service in the RAF, despite the pressing need for them, he was told: 'A dive bomber, which of necessity would be inadequate for any other role, was a luxury which we could not afford.' So, two years after the Ju87s had shown what could be done Britain was still arguing about the need for such aircraft, with France, Norway, Greece and North Africa behind them. In September 1941 a total of 1,400 Vengeance and Bermuda dive bombers were on order. It was then stated that it was hoped to equip ten squadrons with Bermudas starting in February 1942. The Vengeance dive bombers were to equip squadrons in the Far East, Australia, India and Canada!

In May 1942, a further review revealed that no Bermuda aircraft had yet become available from production, deliveries were now expected to start in July, only one Vengeance had been delivered in March and twenty-three more in April; of these, five were being shipped to Australia. Total aircraft accepted on 12 May 1942, were nineteen from Vultee, fifty-one from Northrop, sub-contracting. The fact that the latter were ahead in supply was due to the fact that they had concentrated on the Vengeance, whereas Vultee were still working on modifications to the basic design, as a result the planes from the two plants were virtually different types. The Northrop version lacked fittings for the F24 camera, fixed gun heating, long-range fuel tanks and other extras.

The RAF had insisted on a number of improvements following initial trials, the chief of which were strengthening the undercarriage, re-designed elevators, change of propeller blade and fuel system modifications. It was planned to equip nine squadrons in Australia, two in Canada, six in India and one in South Africa. Earlier offers of Dauntless dive bombers from the USA had been rejected out of hand by the RAF, as the SBD was considered obsolete.

Camouflaged Skua II with Bristol Perseus XII engine L2928 over England. After Dunkirk, Skuas, operating under RAF Coastal Command who understood little about dive bombing, if anything, carried out many hazardous missions dive bombing German shipping and installations across the Channel, often having to fight their way out from Britain and back in again after facing the enemy across the water.

Meanwhile the last Skua dive bombers of the Royal Navy had been disbanded, most of them being replaced by Fulmar fighters and the new Fairey Barracuda, which combined a principal role as torpedo bomber with strong dive bomber potential, had been delayed by replacement of the power-plant. The last operational dive bomber unit with the British forces, other than experimental units, was No 810 Squadron, still operating under Coastal Command direction, though sometimes embarking aboard carriers to conduct strikes against coastal shipping and land installations off Norway with the fleet. This was now a hard-flying, tough unit who had developed a sturdy independence and pioneered many new dive bombing innovations off their own backs. They still came up against a wall of ignorance as to how their aircraft could be properly employed and suffered much frustration, being given missions and tasks impossible to carry out in safety. Their end came abruptly when the Luftwaffe attacked their base at St Eval and destroyed many Skuas parked near the control tower. It is on record that many of the crews openly cheered and applauded this destruction of their aircraft, so bitterly did they feel they had been mishandled by their new masters. A sad end to what could have been a potentially invaluable unit.

In contrast to the British abandonment of dive bombing and the continued expansion of Axis uses of it, it is interesting to see the developments taken to fruitition by one small neutral state in the European Theatre during this period to see what conclusions they had reached. Because Sweden was not involved in the war her independant train of development is of considerable interest as it was free of any bias. It will be recalled that the first batch of CFM licence-built Harts, B4s, were delivered from July 1936 onward. These deliveries continued from July 1938 to May 1939 with the balance of the CVM and ASJA contracted B4s, a total of forty-five in all, until May 1939. The three original Hawker Harts, S7s, were kept in service for a number of years, being phased out of service between 1940 and 1947, one with 1,284 flying hours on the clock. All the B4s built in Sweden served through the 1930s until 1940-1, some continuing until 1946-7 clocking up 1,100-1,235 flying hours.

Meanwhile anti-shipping tactics had been developed by the Swedish dive bomber groups, the basic attack plan being based on the nine-plane squadron attack. By 1939 the Swedish dive bombers had been organised with F4 Jamtlands at Frösön (near Ostersund in Northern Sweden and F6 Västgöta at Karlsborg) west of central Lake Vättern. With F4 the Harts served operationally from January 1938 until October 1940 being replaced at that time although a couple of Harts were in use after that date for minor duties until December 1943. The F6 Wing received its first Harts in February 1940 and the type served operationally until November 1941. From 1940-1 the Light Bomber units were re-equipped but during the Winter War of 1939-40 between Soviet Russia and Finland, a few Swedish Harts saw limited combat when in early 1940 three (and later four) B4As served with the Swedish Volunteer Flight F19, a mixed squadron of fighters and light bombers sent to aid the Finns in the north. Losses in this brief campaign consisted of two Harts which collided on 12 January over Märkäjärvi-Salla, and a third was shot down by Soviet fighters soon afterward.

During 1940-1 their replacements arrived. These were SAAB B5s, a licence-built version of the American Northrop 8A-1 light attack bomber. Powered by a single Bristol/SFA Mk XXIV 980hp engine, the B5 was a great step forward. It had a top speed of 330kph (205mph) and a range of 1,700km (1,056 miles) with a 500kg (1,100lb) bombload. Even so this was only an interim type and in 1942-3 the introduction of the SAAB B17 began.

Dive bombing in Sweden, as in other nations, was meant to utilise the element of surprise and attacks were usually mounted from 1,500-2,000m (4,900-6,500ft)

145

Northrop in Swedish guise. This Northrop 8 A-1 dive bomber was purchased by the Royal Swedish Air Force to replace its ageing Harts and entered squadron service during 1941-2.

using cloud cover if available. 'The pilot must localise his target with the utmost rapidity and at once like a thunderbolt from a clear sky, dive down onto it', read one account. 'When starting the dive the flying speed is usually less than 200km/h, in the almost vertical plunge it accelerates quickly to about 400km/h.'

Meanwhile the main Luftwaffe effort from mid-1941 was directed against the Soviet Union, but limited and renewed use of the dive bomber continued to dominate their war effort in the Mediterranean theatre as 1941 gave way to 1942. Long-range dive bombers, Ju88s, of LG1 for example, carried out a mission against Suez itself from their bases in Crete on 14 July 1941, during which they hit the liner *Georgic* (27,751 tons), set her afire and she became a total loss.

A B17 on patrol over the Swedish forests in 1943. The first Swedish built, Swedish engined dive bombers were the SAAB L10s, designated as the B17 dive bomber. They began to enter service in 1943 and formed the basis of two Wings placed on full war alert towards the end of World War II.

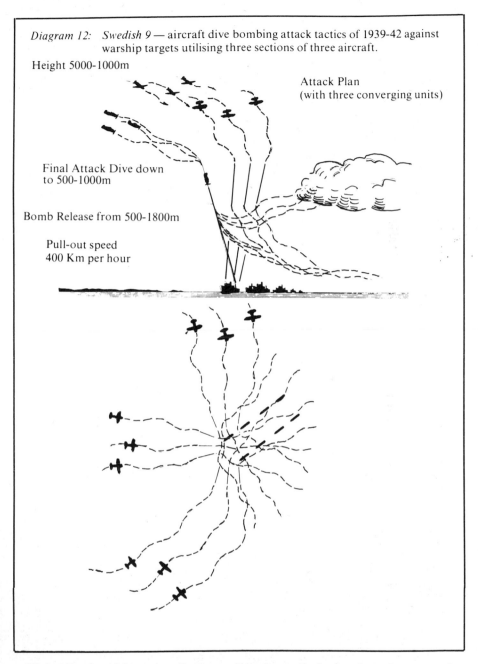

Diagram 12: *Swedish 9* — aircraft dive bombing attack tactics of 1939-42 against warship targets utilising three sections of three aircraft.

Height 5000-1000m

Attack Plan
(with three converging units)

Final Attack Dive down
to 500-1000m

Bomb Release from 500-1800m

Pull-out speed
400 Km per hour

Night dive bombing operations continued on a limited scale and some took place over Britain in the autumn of 1941. Although only training units remained in Northern France the experienced gained led to a series of small-scale night 'tip-and-run' raids which were launched against south coast towns to gain further combat experience. Operating from Pas-de-Calais airfield some thirty or so Ju87s were used and attacks were made on Margate and Ramsgate (7-8 September) and Dover (1-2 October and 2-3 October), resulting in some civilian casualties.

Back in the Mediterranean the arrival of *Luftflotte 2* in Sicily in November 147

During the intensive Blitz on Malta in the spring of 1942 Luftwaffe and Regia Aeronautica dive bombers joined forces to drive the Royal Navy out. Here is a Ju88A-4 of Kampfgeschwader 77 over Sicily enroute to Malta.

1941, heralded a renewal in German intentions to force the issue over Malta. Although many of the Stuka units allocated initially, had to be retained in the Russian theatre to hold the Soviet winter offensive, Ju87D strength reached its peak in the Mediterranean in 1942.

With the arrival in Sicily of *Erganzungs Gruppe* of StG1 in December 1941, the attacks were renewed on Malta. Their aims then were two-fold. To reduce the island as a base for offensive operations by the Royal Navy and to soften it up in preparation for its invasion and occupation, 'Operation Hercules', planned for the summer of 1942. The success of the first part, conversely, led to the abandonment of the second prematurely and Malta was to survive.

I/StG3 was already in the area and the two new units were re-organised in March 1942, to form a complete *Geschwader* with I/StG1 becoming II/StG3 and II/StG2 re-designated as III/StG3. With more than seventy Ju87D/*Trop* Stukas and the long-range Ju88s of LG1 operating from Crete after undergoing an intensive anti-shipping course, the stage was set. Co-operating were the Italian 209⁰ and 239⁰ *Squadriglia* of 102⁰ *Gruppo*. Capt Giuseppe Tamborra of the latter unit being killed over Malta on 30 May, his replacement Ten Fulvio Papalia in turn being shot down by a Spitfire on 12 July. These units operated from Gela from May 1942 onward. III/StG3 converted to Doras at Biscari-San-Pietro in March.

The assault which broke over Malta during the first four months of 1942 was the heaviest concentration of bombing to date and enormous damage was done to the dockyards and airfields. But in the interim the island's defences had been improved with numerous heavy and light AA batteries and the establishment of strong forces of Spitfires with better facilities. Constant reinforcing of these fighters was carried out by aircraft carriers of the Royal Navy, with the USS *Wasp* also making two such ferry trips as well. Thus the battle was much more evenly joined than before and dive bomber losses were severe. They retained their effectiveness however and the warships based at Malta took such heavy losses they had to withdraw.

On 9 February 1942, Stukas operating from the desert badly damaged the destroyer *Farndale* off Mersa Matruh during a convoy operation, and in the aftermath of another convoy Ju88s destroyed the supply ships *Clan Campbell, Pampas* and *Talabot* and the Naval Auxillary *Breconshire,* between 23 and 26 March. During the same period Ju88s also hit the destroyer *Legion* south of Malta. She joined the destroyer *Kingston* in dry-dock and there both were subjected to violent Ju87 attacks, *Legion* being finished off on 26 March.

In April dive bomber assault on the harbour grew to a high intensity. On 9 April the destroyer *Lance* was wrecked in dock and on the 11th *Kingston* and the already damaged destroyer *Gallant* were hit and wrecked. The light cruiser *Penelope* was damaged but escaped to Gibraltar despite several attacks by Ju88s *en route*. Among other ships sunk by the dive bombers in this period were the submarines *Glavkos, Pandora* and *P36*, the tanker *Plumleaf* and minesweeper *Abingdon* on 5th. South of Crete the Ju88s of LG1 caught the destroyers *Jackal, Kipling* and *Lively* on 11 May and sank them all.

Attacks on relief convoys continued unabated. In June a double operation was mounted by the Royal Navy, 'Harpoon' from the west and 'Vigorous' from the east. In the narrows the Axis dive bombers attacked the former on 14 June without success, but next day Stukas sank the *Chant* (5,601 tons) and *Burdwan* (5,600 tons) and disabled the tanker *Kentucky,* which was later abandoned. 'Vigorous' fared even worse, as Stukas operating from Crete and the desert air fields were switched to this target. This saved the retreating troops of the 8th Army but decimated the ships.

On 12 June Maj Walter Linke led a Ju87 attack that so damaged the transport *City of Calcutta* that she had to turn back to Tobruk. The Dutch freighter *Aagterkerk* developed engine trouble and was also sent there, but an attack by forty Ju87s outside the harbour sank her on the 14th and damaged the corvette *Primula.* LG1s Ju88s under Capt Helbig attacked the same afternoon, sinking the *Bhutan* (6,104 tons) and damaging the *Potaro* (5,410 tons). Next day StG3 mounted a saturation attack, sinking the destroyers *Airedale* and *Nestor* and damaging the cruiser *Birmingham* before the convoy turned back to Alexandria.

In August the biggest Malta convoy was mounted 'Operation Pedestal', via Gibraltar. It was given the protection of three aircraft carriers, two battleships and a host of smaller warships. On the evening of 11th Ju88s near-missed the carrier *Victorious,* and on the 12th Ju88s of I/KG54 (Gerbini), KGr606 and KGr806 (Catania), II and III/KG77 (Comiso and Gerbini) and LG1 (flown in from Crete to Gerbini), mounted a succession of heavy attacks. A heavier assault by thirty-seven Ju88s at midday damaged the freighter *Deucalion* (7,516 tons). By 0635 next day the convoy was in Stuka range and a combined attack by twenty Ju87s of StG3 from Trapani and nine Italian Stukas from 239 *Squadriglia* broke through the defences. Near misses were scored on several ships, including the battleship *Rodney,* while the carrier *Indomitable* was hit by two heavy bombs and near-missed by three others. She had to withdraw badly damaged and heavily on fire.

On the evening of the 12th a strong attacks by thirty Ju88s sank the *Empire Hope* (12,628 tons), and *Glenorchy* (8,982 tons). Next day twelve Ju88s sank the *Waimarama* (12,843 tons), Italian Ju87s hit the *Dorset* while German and Italian attacks hit this ship again and the *Port Chalmers* and the tanker *Ohio.* Then Stukas hit the *Rochester Castle,* while *Dorset* (10,624 tons) was finished off by Ju87s, fourteen of which concentrated on her that evening and another Stuka crashed into the *Ohio.*

In June StG3 conducted heavy dive bombing attacks which crushed the defence line held by the Free French at Bir Hacheim and soon afterwards heavy Stuka assault led to the fall of Tobruk itself. This further success led to a Motion of Censure on the Government, in which to defend himself Churchill had to defend the anti-dive bomber policy of the RAF. But in truth such were the delays to the promised US built Vengeance and Bermuda types that even if the Air Marshals had somehow been forced to admit that they had been as wrong in 1942, as they were in 1940, 1935 and 1918, they would have been unable to do much to rectify matters.

Not only in the Mediterranean had the dive bomber achieved a lasting mark on events in 1942. By now the war was world wide and in Russia and the wastes of the Pacific and Indian Oceans other nations dive bombers were dictating the course of events.

18 CLASH OF GIANTS
The Eastern Front 1941-2, German and Soviet developments

While everyone was busily writing off the Ju87 on paper in Britain the Germans were developing a new mark of this aircraft incorporating many wartime lessons. This was the D (*Dora*) series, the most widespread mark to be built. In essence the *Dora* was a cleaned-up *Bertha* with a re-designed cockpit and improved armour protection for the crew. The defensive armament was modernised with the fitting of the twin MG17 initially and then by the MG81 gun. The power-plant was the new Jumo 211J-1 engine developing 1,400hp for take-off. After initial teething troubles with this engine had been surmounted, causing delays in production, the *Doras* soon began to leave the assembly lines. Bomb load was a much improved 4,000lb. Thus the new 2,205lb SC-1000 GP bomb or the armour-piercing 3,086lb PC 1400 bomb were both to feature in their operations. As time went by the outer wing racks, capable of carrying an assortment of 110lb, 550lb or 1,100lb bomb loads, were also adapted to carry a wide variety of specialised weapons packs,like the *Waffenbehälter WB81* with six 7.9mm MG81s for ground-strafing troop concentrations, or the paired 20mm MG FF cannon for tank busting. Although designed initially as an interim aircraft, its continued handiness and the lack of a successor with its all-round abilities and utility, meant that in fact, the Stuka continued in production on a large scale throughout 1941-3, production totals being 476 and 917 respectively for the first two years.

The experimental Ju87 V-21 and V-22 first flew in February 1941, being joined by two more prototypes in May and June. The fifth, Ju87 V-25, was a tropicalised version. Production at the Bremen-Lemwerder factory was well in hand with orders for over one thousand D1s when the Russian campaign got underway, but re-equipping the units took time and the first *Dora* did not make its debut until January 1942, with I/StG2 in northern Russia. Another varient, the Ju87D-2, was identical except that it featured a strengthened rear fuselage and tailwheel and carried a towing hook for ferrying cargo gliders.

Meanwhile the bulk of the Ju87 dive bombers which took part in the opening stages of 'Barbarossa' remained the *Berthas* with some *Richards,* which had been secretly transferred to their eastern airstrips in record time after their victories in the Balkans in May 1941.

Preparations for the long-cherished annihilation of the hated Soviet empire had been taking place with painstaking care ever since October 1940, when the blitz was still in full swing against London. Under the *Ostbauprogramm* German construction units and material had been steadily moved into Poland and throughout the winter of 1940-1 airfields and support facilities steadily mushroomed along the uneasy Eastern frontier. This programme was greatly increased in the spring of 1941 and the first flak units moved in to take up positions. During the Balkan campaign the first active steps were taken for the speedy reception of the squadrons themselves, but the actual movement of the units was delayed as long as possible to avoid detection. Training schools were set up openly in areas then secretly moved west and replaced by the administration train of the operational units. Even so, the move, when it did come in the wake of the hard-fought Crete campaign, was a masterpiece of organisation, especially for the Stuka spearhead of *Fliegerkorps VIII* under von Richthofen. They had to move at the greatest speed from their forward airstrips in the Greek islands and Crete itself, northward across the primitive terrain and poor communications network of the Balkans, into Germany and then, after a short period of refurbishing, into their newly-prepared airfields.

All this was done with complete success and absolute surprise was achieved. By 1 June the first units were entraining in Rumania for Germany, while their ground staff flew north direct to Poland in Ju52/3m transports. Other units were also moving in from France and, in less than three weeks, 2,500 aircraft were established on their jump-off fields in readiness.

Table 33: German dive bomber dispositions 22 June 1941			
Luftflotte	Fliegerkorps or location	Stuka units allocated	Number of aircraft
2	*Fliegerkorps VIII*	II & III/StG1	87
		I & III/StG2	83
	Fliegerkorps II	I, II & III/StG77	122
5	Kirkenes, Norway	IV(Stuka)/LG1	42

On the opposite side of the border we have seen how almost the entire Soviet Air Force interest in army support roles had been concentrated on their very efficient *Shturmovik* units and, despite their interest in early German dive bomber trials pre-war, they had not followed this line of development themselves. It was not until the Spanish Civil War awoke them to the potential of the dive bomber that they began to cast around for a suitable aircraft for themselves.

The brilliant designer Vladimir Mikhaikovich Petlyakov had been in the forefront of a high-altitude bomber concept and had produced a sleek machine in answer to that requirement, the *Vysotnyi Istrebitel,* VI100, which was adapted to bomber requirements as a three-seater.

With the instruction to change its specification yet again, to produce a dive bomber, Petlyakov's design team kept the main features of the VI100, including the twin M105R engines, all-metal construction and retractable undercarriage, and made modifications including the fitting of slatted dive brakes. The result was the *Pikiruyuschii Bombardivrovshchik,* the PB100, the first prototype of which flew for the first time on 22 December 1939, with test pilot P. M. Stefanovskii. Tests continued through to June 1940 and by that time it had proven itself an ideal dive bomber. It is to be noted how the Russians thus, with little or no previous experience in dive bomber design, produced a first-rate aircraft of this type first time round.

Apart from its high landing speed, and a tendency to spin, coupled with a famed landing characteristic of bouncing on heavy touchdowns, the PB100 was an extremely advanced aircraft for its day. It had a span of 56ft 3½in and a length of 41ft 6½in making it a large aircraft for a dive bomber, but its performance was superb. Its engines gave it a top speed of 335mph, thus overcoming the main limitation of all other foreign dive bombers, for it could outpace most fighters! The fact that it could attain such high speed and still dive bomb perfectly should give pause for though, and one finds it hard to understand why twenty years of pre-war study in Britain should have concluded that such a combination was impossible!

It was a three-seater and had an armament of two fixed forward-firing machine guns when it was put into production as the Pe2 in 1940. The rear

In the Soviet Union A.N. Tupolev started design work on a high speed bomber with dive bombing as one of its functions. The SB-2 was still under test in 1941 but some two hundred were completed with the M-105R engine and dive brakes as three-seat dive bombers. They were given the designation SB-RK, and were commonly known as the Archangelsky Ar-2, seeing combat in 1941-2.

defensive armament was a flexible 12.7mm gun and a non-retractable central gun of the same calibre was fired by means of a periscope gunsight. Heavy protective armour was installed from 6-9mm in thickness, and other refinements included a fully automatic dive recovery system as in the German Junkers Ju88. It had a range of 932 miles and could carry a bomb load on underwing racks of up to 2,200lb, although 1,320lb was a normal combat loading.

All-in-all it was an impressive aircraft by any standard, it brought enthusiastic comment by RAF Sqdn Ldr Lapraik when he tested it in 1942, but the RAF ignored this. Unfortunately for the Soviets, in June 1941, although production had been underway for some time, few of these dive bombers had reached front-line service when the Germans opened their attack all along the 1,000-mile front.

One other Soviet dive bomber *was* in limited service at this time. This aircraft was an adaption to dive bombing profile of the Tupolev SB2 bomber, a three-seater, with a span of 66ft 8½in and a length of 40ft 3¼in, and designated the SB-RK or Ar-2. The Ar-2 was powered by two 1,100hp supercharged M-105R engines, and featured a reduced wing area over the SB2bis from which it was modified. Only some 200 dive bomber versions were built.

The requirement for the Samolet-103 bomber which A.N. Tupolev began designing in 1938 called for a high speed bomber with the speed of a fighter, capable of horizontal and dive bombing, but prototypes were still under test at the outbreak of the war with Germany.

The SB2 however, powered by two M-100 in-line engines behind frontal radiators, went into mass-production in 1936. It was a three-seat monoplane and could carry a bomb load of 1,320lb. Each M100 was of 860hp giving the aircraft a maximum speed of 263mph at 13,120ft, with a range of 608 miles. Some 200 were completed as dive bombers with the M-105 engine, and wing brakes under the designation SB-RK or Ar-2, and these saw combat in 1941-2.

The German assault on Russia opened in dramatic style with huge losses being inflicted on the Russian air strength and gains of hundreds of miles being made within a short while. Whole armies were surrounded and surrendered.

Of the initial air strikes more than 4,000 Soviet aircraft were destroyed for the loss of only 150 German aircraft of which a mere twelve were Ju87s. On the combination of Stuka and Panzer much has been written. Close co-operation reached new stages of perfection with liason officers actually riding in tanks and calling up the Stukas to break the strong-points. The further they penetrated into the vast Soviet hinterland the worse communications became, but the Luftwaffe was a leader in this field and managed to keep the Stukas supplied as they leap-frogged ever further east, until they were within 65 miles of Moscow itself.

Further north Leningrad was beseiged and the vast Soviet fleet lying at Kronstadt was the objective of an all-out assault by the Ju87s of I and II/StG2, brought up in haste from the central front to their new base of Tyrkowo. Unfortunately the new heavy armour piercing bombs did not arrive at first but the attacks, launched with some panache between 21 and 24 September 1941, achieved great success. Led by Dinort again repeated dive bombing resulted in the sinking of the battleship *Marat* by Hans-Ulrich Rudel and the damage of the cruiser *Kirov* by the death dive of Hpt Steen, commander of III/StG2. A second battleship, *Oktyabrskaya Revolutsiya,* received slight damage from six bomb hits and the destroyer *Steregushci* was hit and capsized. Other ships damaged included the destroyers *Gordy, Grozyashchi* and *Silny,* the depot ship *Smilny* and the submarine *Shch306.* On 23 September the cruiser *Kirov* was hit and damaged again as was the cruiser *Maksim Gorki* and destroyer *Grozyashchi.* The destroyer *Minsk* was hit and sunk along with the patrol vessel *Taifun* and the submarine *Shch302* damaged before the attacks were called off owing to the pressure of the land battles developing again in the south.

The German armies were switched from the Moscow front towards Kiev and the Stukas operated from the Konotop region in support of the 4th Panzer Army in this offensive, resulting in another great victory. But now the Russian winter was setting in and the resumed offensive against Moscow, 'Operation Typhoon', was brought to a halt just short of its target and the Russians counter-attacked in strength. Serviceability among the Stuka units fell to an all-time low in the severe conditions. Many units were pulled out to refurbish, others were switched south to the Mediterranean theatre. Attacks in the south on the Crimea against the fortress of Sebastopol on 17 December, and in the north, at Litsa against the vital Murmansk rail link, both supported by dive bomber forces, ended the same way. Brought to a dead stop by the combination of the Russian weather and their extended lines of communications the Germans were almost overwhelmed by the massive counter-attacks with fresh Siberian troops in the winter months. Only heroic fighting by the troops on the ground and the firm orders of Hitler to stand fast and not panic, saved the day.

The Stukas did much to help by attacking Soviet tank forces whenever they broke through, and they often had to fight for their own advanced airstrips as the marauding T34 tanks threatened to over-run them as was the case at Kalinin with II/LG2 and I/StG2. Meanwhile IV(Stuka)/LG1 was re-designated I/StG5 under Hans-Karl Stepp and this unit was moved south for a while to co-ordinate attacks with StG1 led by Walter Hagen on the Leningrad Front. They began to re-equip with *Doras,* as did StG77 with the same aircraft at Böblingen.

When the spring thaw came preparations were put in hand for a renewal of the German offensive, which for 1942 were to be mainly directed towards the south. At first though preoccupations with the northern areas saw the Ju87s fully extended. At exactly the same time as their compatriots were pounding the warships of the Royal Navy in their base at Malta, the Ju87Ds on the Eastern Front were opening up further heavy assaults on the Russian fleet at Kronstadt, with a view to immobilising it before the thaw was completed. Sixty-two Stukas of StG1 under Hagen spearheaded this attack, supplemented by I and II/StG2 and the thirty-three Ju88s of KG1, commanded by Angerstein. Walter Hagen had been the original leader of the *Flugzeugträger Gruppe* I/186 and had a first-class anti-shipping record behind him (210,000 BRT sunk). A total of 596 sorties were made during 'Operation Eisstoss' during which the battleship *Oktyabrskaya Revolutsiya* was hit four times, the cruiser *Maksim Gorki* seven times and the cruisers *Kirov* and *Petropavlovsk* and destroyer *Silny* seriously damaged, while the minelayer *Marti,* the destroyer *Grozyashchy* and the training ship *Svir* were also damaged.

In May *VIII Fliegerkorps* was moved from the central front to new airfields in the Crimea after the forcing of the Kerch Peninsular had left the massive fortress of Sebastopol isolated the previous month. In readiness for the German assault a larger number of dive bomber sorties were flown against the many strong forts and gun positions in the area. Into this attack the whole of StG77 was thrown in a round-the-clock offensive.

Between 2 and 6 June 1942, StG77 flew some 600 sorties per day against Sebastopol, delivering pin-point attacks on such defensive positions and among other prime targets destroyed by the Ju87s were the giant 'Maxim Gorki' guns, 30.5cm (12in) monsters. Only direct hits could damage such dug-in weapons, but StG77 managed to put them out of action. Other targets calling for the greatest precision were pumping stations and power stations of the garrison's water supply, as well as the endless lines of field works and gun-pits. The Ju87s and Ju88s also carried out numerous sorties against the port and shipping bringing reinforcements to the fortress across the Black Sea. On 10 June Ju88s sank the transport *Abkhaziya* (4,727 tons) and the minesweepers *Svobodny* and *T413* in the harbour and the next day the transport *Gruziya* (4,857 tons) was also sunk there. On the 18th the destroyer *Kharkov* was hit and damaged and on the 26th the destroyer *Bezuprechny* was sunk. The destroyer *Tashkent* was sunk with many casualties among her wounded evacuees on the 27th.

StG1, StG2 and StG77 were all fully committed in the classic role as the final Blitzkreig got under way in July 1942, and the field-grey soldiers and Panzers moved over the endless dusty steppe through Voronezh, across the Rivers Tim and Don, ever eastward, smashing south past Rostov towards the Caucasus and the distant oilfields of the Caspian Sea.

This advance finally ran out of steam on the foothills of the Caucasus and in the rubble of the city of Stalingrad on the River Volga. Here determined Soviet troops clung to their strongpoints among the ruins of factories and rail yards and for some reason the German army under Paulus became immersed in a vicious and intense street fight, from house to house, floor to floor, instead of merely by-passing the city in the hitherto efficient German manner. The Ju87s of StG2 became adept at attacking targets a mere block or less from their own front-line troops, whose positions among the debris could only be made out by flying with map in hand.

Despite the utmost efforts of the dive bomber pilots, forbidden to release their bombs until certain of their targets, the small eastern part of the city held out against all attacks and the German divisions were fed in and ground down piecemeal. Then, on 19 November, fresh Soviet armies massed on their flanks, broke through north and south of the city, crushing the Italian and Rumanian armies holding those sections and encasing the German 6th Army in gigantic claws. Attacks by StG2 from Karpovka failed to stop them and at Oblivskay the Stukas were hard-put to prevent their own airfield being over-run. The German offensive was over.

Meanwhile, up on the edge of the Arctic circle I/StG5 based at Kirkenes, under Maj Hans-Karl Stepp, was operating in bad conditions supporting the further attempts to cut the Belomorsk-Murmansk railway. They made frequent
attacks on lines and rolling-stock, but it proved impossible for the German

troops under Gen Dietl to advance across the tundra and take the major supply port of Murmansk itself. The dive bombers' efforts were therefore turned toward attacking that base and the ships and convoys from Britain approaching it with vital American war supplies. The Ju87s lacked the range to attack the Arctic convoys for anything but the last few miles of their long journeys, but I/StG5 did achieve much success in anti-shipping sorties around the Kola Inlet area.

On 15 May 1942, they dive bombed Murmansk harbour badly damaging the Soviet submarine *Shch403* and the American freighter *Yaka* (6,187 tons). On 1 June Ju87s sank the British freighter *Empire Starlight* (6,850 tons), and on 25 June caught a flotilla of British minesweepers in the Kola Inlet and sank the *Gossamer*. Their other achievements included a dive bombing attack on a convoy that had just reached Murmansk, on 27 and 28 February 1943, during which they scored direct hits on three freighters totalling 11,341 tons, and again on 6 and 13 March 1943, when they sank one merchant ship and damaged another.

The main dive bombing attacks on the convoys of Allied merchantmen carrying tanks, aircraft and munitions to north Russia, were carried out by the Junkers Ju88 units based at Banak and Bardufoss, the three *Gruppen* of KG30 being the most notable in these operations, especially III/KG30 under Hpt Klaus Nocken. On 28 March 1942, a storm scattered convoy PQ15 and the dive bombers of III/KG30 were able to attack isolated merchant ships with ease, sinking the *Raceland* (4,815 tons) and *Empire Ranger* (7,007 tons). On 11 April the same unit attacked and sank the *Empire Cowper* (7,164 tons) from the homeward bound convoy QP10 and the *Harpalion* (5,486 tons). A greater victory came on 14 May when III/KG30 dive bombed a British cruiser squadron in the Barents Sea and scored hits on the cruiser *Trinidad,* which so damaged her that she had to be sunk.

Against the convoy PQ16 III/KG30 mounted an attack with six aircraft on 25 May, damaging the freighter *Carlton* (5,127 tons), while on the 27th 111 sorties were flown which resulted in the sinking of the *Alamar, Mormacsul, Empire Lawrence* and *Empire Purcell.* Four other freighters were damaged, one of which, the *City of Joliet,* later sank. Against the ill-fated PQ17 convoy even greater slaughter was executed. Again the ships were left without escorts after the convoy scattered. This left easy pickings for the Ju88 crews and they sank, or in some cases finished off ships crippled by U-boats, the freighters *Washington* (5,564 tons), *Bolton Castle* (5,203 tons), *Pankraft* (5,644 tons), *Peter Kerr* (6,476 tons) and *Fairfield City* (5,685 tons), as well as the rescue ship *Zaafaran.* They also hit and damaged the freighters *Paulus Potter, Earlston, Empire Byron* and the fleet tanker *Aldersdale,* all of which were finished off by U-boats later. Hunting down the few survivors later the three *Gruppen* under Kahl, Stoffregen and Herrmann sank the *Pan Atlantik* (5,411 tons) on 6 July.

Against the better protected PQ18 convoy in September 1942, they fared less well. It had the escort carrier *Avenger* in company and most of the dive bombing attacks were directed against her rather than the convoy. Despite many near-misses she survived. KG30's only successes were the blowing up of the ammunition ship *Mary Luckenbach* (5,049 tons) on the 14th and the *Troubador* (6,458 tons) on the 18th.

On 4 November attacks against independently-routed ships by I/KG30 sank the Soviet *Dekabrist* (7,363 tons), while II/KG30 scored a hit on another two, one of which, *William Clark* (7,176 tons) was finished off by U-boats later, on the 4th, while the other, *Chumleigh* (5,445 tons) was similarly disposed of on the 16th.

The last major battle in the East in which the Ju87 participated in large

Table 34: Battle of Kursk, 1943	
Stukagruppen and Commanders	
Gruppen	Commanding Officer
StG1	Obst Gustav Pressler
StG2	Obst Dr Ernst Kupfer
StG77	Obst Helmut Bruck

numbers in their dive bombing role, after the holding actions of 1942-3, was 'Operation Zitadelle' against the Kursk salient. This was also the last great German offensive of the war on the Eastern Front. The above units took part, supplemented by the Hungarian Stuka unit, 102/1:

The decline of the Ju87 took place after this battle and an indication of the future role of the aircraft was given by the inclusion in one *Staffel* of each of the first two *Gruppen* of the 'Kanonvogel' Stukas, each equipped with a tank-busting Flak 18 37mm cannon under each wing. This interesting development however falls outside the scope of this study, but had been described in depth elsewhere. Conversely as the dive bomber declined in the Luftwaffe it increased in usage and value in the Soviet Air Force. The Petlyakov Pe2 increased in stature with the development of new techniques. Some 460 had been ready as early as June 1941, but their pilots lacked expertise in the dive bombing technique. A.G. Fedorov of 9th Bomber Air Regiment conducted a detail survey on the Pe2 in 1942 analysing its combat record. Meanwhile the famous Col I.S. Polbin of the 150th Bomber Air Group was developing his own techniques for attacks in this aircraft after early experience at the Battle of Smolensk in July 1941. Another leading pilot flying the Pe2 was Col V.E. Nestertsev of the 23rd Bomber Air Division which featured in the winter fighting of 1941-2.

It was Polbin who evolved the classic dive bombing technique known as the 'Dipping Wheel' or *Vertushka* which he used during the Stalingrad counter-offensive and had perfected by the time of Kursk, and on 7 July Soviet dive bombers inflicted heavy casualties on the Panzers with these methods. With full and complete pre-knowledge of the German plan of attack betrayed to them the Soviets were not only able to hold the German thrusts but, within days, had launched their own counter-offensive at Orel on 11 July. Before this onslaught the Germans in many places were forced back. Non-stop dive bomber missions by the Ju87s was once more to stabilise the front in many places and this setback was not the disaster that Stalingrad had been, nonetheless it was a massive defeat and the turning point on the Eastern Front. From now on it was the Soviet Pe2 that dominated the dive bomber scene in this vast area while the Germans switched over more and more to dive bombing by high performance fighter aircraft, Jabo units, equipped with the FW190 aircraft.

The increasing vulnerability of the ageing Ju87 was now recognised and although production continued it was more as a specialised tank buster and night bomber that it was used in this theatre. This change was emphasised with the change of title of the dive bomber units from *Stukagruppen* to *Schlachtgruppen* which now took place. It was a transition to be reflected also among the Allied air forces at this time.

Table 35: Transition from *Stukagruppen* to *Schlachtgruppen*, October 1943		
Original designation	New designation	Area of Operations
StG1	SG1	Eastern Front
StG2	SG2	Eastern Front
StG3	SG3	Balkans
StG5	SG5	Norway
StG77	SG77	Eastern Front

19 DIVE BOMBER ARENA
The Pacific War 1941-42, American and Japanese operations

War between the United States and Japan, long simmering, broke out with the attack on Pearl Harbor on 7 December 1941. The strike was made with carrier-based dive bombers and torpedo aircraft and was directed against the fleet in harbour and the military airfields. The planes took off from the six big carriers of the Nagumo strike force and achieved considerable surprise. The first wave included fifty-one Aichi D3A1 'Vals' led by Lt Akira Sakamoto and their target was the two main American fighter bases. Sakamoto himself led twenty-five 'Vals' in a dive bombing attack on Wheeler Field, dropping the first bomb on the Pacific War at 0755. A second group of twenty-six 'Vals' under Lt Kakuichi Takahashi hit Hickham Field and the seaplane base on Ford Island. To their regret their original targets, the American carriers, had been reported as missing. Each 'Val' in the first wave carried 250lb fragmentation bombs to destroy parked aircraft.

A second wave followed and consisted of seventy-nine D3A1s led by Lt Cdr Takashige Egusa, the pre-war dive bomber ace. Their target had been the carriers, but in their absence they turned their wrath upon the battleships which had survived earlier attacks. In return for the loss of one 'Val' from the first wave and fourteen from the second the Japanese dive bombers hit the battleships *Nevada,* heavily damaged, and *Pennsylvania,* damaged, and hit and wrecked the destroyers *Cassin* and *Downes* in dock, and *Shaw,* whose magazines exploded. Some ninety-two Navy and ninety-six Army aircraft were destroyed on the ground.

On their way back to Japan after this strike forty-two 'Vals' were despatched against Wake Island and on 21 September eighteen of them were despatched, but thick cloud aborted their mission. A second strike led by Lt Hijiro Abe, also of eighteen dive bombers, went in next day and on the 23rd December the 'Vals' covered the landing which took this island.

After a brief respite in Japan, Nagumo's remaining four carriers were despatched to the southern area of operations to assist in crushing any opposition to the invasion forces that were swarming all over that area. After refuelling at Truk they launched a ninety-plane strike at Rabaul on 20 January, but found little in the way of opposition and fewer worthwhile targets, the 'Vals' sinking a solitary merchant ship in the harbour.

On 21 January a strike was mounted against Kavieng, Lae and Salamuaua on the eastern coast of New Guinea, with similar results. Rabaul was again dive bombed on 22nd before the force returned to Truk. Here two Japanese carriers were detached to patrol off Japan following the US carrier strikes against the Gilbert and Marshall islands, but they failed to locate the American force.

Meanwhile the *Hiryu* and *Soryu* had also come south and their dive bombers launched attacks on the naval base of Ambon in the Celebes on 24 and 25 January 1942. On 4 February the 'Vals' of this force, operating from the airfield at Kendari, attacked an allied naval squadron south of Kangeon Island, badly damaging the American light cruiser *Marblehead* and hitting the heavy cruiser *Houston* on one of the after 8in turrets, putting it out of action, to the north of Bali.

Terror of the Allies in the Pacific in 1942, the classic profile of the Aichi 'Val' dive bomber, part of a squadron ship-hunting in the Pacific. The Aichi D3A was the standard Imperial Japanese Navy dive bomber from Pearl Harbor to Guadalcanal and swept all before it in air-sea warfare in those dramatic months.

Thus far it had been the Japanese dive bombers which had made most of the running, but in January and February two small Task Groups built around the carriers *Enterprise* and *Yorktown* made tip-and-run raids on Wotje, Maloelap and Kwajalein on 1 February and on Jaluit, Mili and Makin.

Although the Dauntless had received its blooding at Pearl Harbor, when several *Enterprise* planes had been destroyed, the strike launched from the same ships by SBDs against Roi at 0445 on 1 February was its debut as a dive bomber. Unfortunately surprise was not achieved and Cdr Hopping's Scouting 6 was met by heavy flak and fighters. Thirty-six SBDs took part in this raid, which at 0700, dropped the first bombs of the war to hit Japanese soil, but Hopping himself was shot down. A further dive bombing attack on shipping in Kwajalein harbour resulted in the loss of five more SBDs with scant results, one transport claimed sunk and nine damaged. A later raid on the airfield destroyed hangars and several bombers for the loss of another Dauntless.

Further missions were launched, *Lexington* flew Dauntless raids against Rabaul, now in Japanese hands, on 20 February and *Enterprise* hit Wake on 24th and Marcus Island on 4 March. Attacks by dive bombers from *Lexington* and *Yorktown* on Lae and Salamaua claiming the sinking of a minesweeper and two transports.

If the results of the US Navy Dauntless strikes in early 1942 were disappointing then the activities of the A24 units of the USAAF in the same area were more so and confirmed the Army's long-held conviction that dive bombers and dive bombing were a pointless and costly exercise.

At the time of Pearl Harbor it will be recalled, the US Army had on order a large number of the A24 Banshee and had placed further contracts for the A25A, the Army equivalent of the Curtiss SB22 Helldiver. Not content with this, immediately after the outbreak of the Pacific War the US Army, seeking a faster way to supplement their strength, cast their eyes on the British dive bombers being built in America and, as a result, some 492 of these were appropriated by the USAAF in January 1942: 300 Vengeance aircraft and 192 Bermudas (the US Navy's Buccaneer). Beaverbrook wrote to Sinclair that: 'The Arnold/Portal agreement increased the number of these which we surrendered, and sanctions the seizure from our orders of 300 Vengeance dive bombers, 158 of these were ex-contracts for which we had paid in full hard cash and 142 were from Lease-Lend.'

However in actual combat conditions those dive bombers the US Army

The US Army Air Force equivalent of the Dauntless was the Douglas A-24. It was offered to Great Britain in 1940 but rejected by the RAF. Used by the USAAF in the south-west Pacific in 1942 lack of expertise failed to produce the same results as those of the US Navy flyers.

already had proved a disappointment to them. Operations by the 91st Bombardment Squadron in the Dutch East Indies achieved little or nothing, while the 8th Bombardment Group based in northern Australia were no more successful. The Army pilots verdict was that the Dauntless was too slow, unmanoeuvrable and obsolete. The principal action in which they participated was an attack by the 27th Bomb Group (Light) with seven A24s on a Japanese naval squadron off Java on 29 February 1942, in which they claimed, falsely, several hits on a cruiser. Two dive bombers were lost.

Further dive bombing missions were undertaken in April 1942, against Laue and Salamaua, but the next operation was a complete disaster, for in a raid on Buna on 29 July, six out of seven A24s were lost, and thereafter the Army withdrew them from combat.

Although the bulk of the Aichi D3A1s were operating from carriers during this period, land-based dive bomber units were set up by the Japanese on 1 February to assist the Army operations during the conquest of the Philippines and Celebes.

Sixty-eight 'Vals' were in reserve in Japan on the outbreak of war and from these the 31st NAC was formed and undertook dive bombing missions during the final drive on the fortresses of Bataan and Corregidor. Similarly the 33rd NAC was set up at Saeki and transferred to Macassor on 2 March from where it participated in the conquest of Java.

The Nagumo force reformed round the carriers *Akagi, Kaga, Hiryu* and *Soryu* at Palau in mid-February 1942 to strike at the only major port and supply base in Australia capable of reinforcing the hard-pressed Allied troops in the southern zone. On 19 February, from a position in the Banda Sea these aircraft carriers flew off a strong strike force of 188 aircraft, reinforced by fifty-four land-based planes, and this mass hit Port Darwin without warning.

Seventy-one 'Vals' were included in this formation. Only eight defending fighters managed to get into the air and these were quickly overwhelmed, fifteen more were destroyed on the ground. The 'Vals' were then turned loose on the mass of shipping in the harbour with good effect, meeting hardly any opposition. In the precise dive bombing which followed seven transports were sunk (43,429 tons), including one spectacular hit on an ammunition ship which ignited its cargo of 200 depth charges and caused widespread destruction. Also sunk was the American destroyer *Peary* while among the many ships damaged in varying degrees were the American aircraft tender *William B. Preston,* the Australian 159 sloop *Swan* and six other freighters. Numerous small auxillary craft were destroyed and the whole port rendered unusable for weeks.

A similar raid was launched against Tjilatjap on 3 March, sinking two freighters and damaging fifteen more which were later scuttled when the port was evacuated.

Next the Nagumo force, with five carriers, four battleships, three cruisers and nine destroyers sailed from Staring Bay in the South Celebes on 26 March to launch air strikes at the known naval bases of Colombo and Trincomalee in Ceylon (Sri Lanka), in the hope of catching the new British fleet under Adm Somerville. Having been sighted earlier the Japanese launched a strike force at Colombo on 5 April, which included thirty-six Aichi D3A1s, but they found the harbour empty of shipping. In the ensuring air combat twenty-five RAF and FAA aircraft were destroyed for the loss of seven Japanese. The 'Vals' scored hits on the armed merchant cruiser *Hector* (11,198 tons) and the old destroyer *Tenedos,* the latter having her stern blown off, and both were sunk.

Meanwhile two British heavy cruisers, *Cornwall* and *Dorsetshire,* which had been detached from the main fleet in an error reminding one of Norway and Crete, were located by the Japanese steaming south to rejoin it. Soon after midday a powerful force of eighty 'Vals' under Lt Cdr Egusa were despatched to attack them. At 1330 this force had found the two ships and 10min later they commenced their attack dives, splitting themselves equally between the two targets. Their accuracy was phenomenal despite the violent twisting and turning of the cruisers and the barrage from their combined AA armaments of sixteen 4in guns and many smaller weapons. The *Cornwall* took fifteen bombs in 7 minutes and sank. The *Dorsetshire* was pulverised in the same manner, one bomb penetrating her magazine which exploded and within eight minutes she too had gone.

Having failed to find the main British fleet at Colombo, Nagumo turned next to Trincomalee. On 9 April another strike force was despatched which included thirty-six 'Vals'. They were met by Hurricane fighters from No 261 Squadron and Fulmars from the FAA No 273 Squadron, who claimed to have inflicted a smashing defeat on the Japanese. In truth the Japanese only lost nine aircraft in all, while British lost nine Hurricanes and one Fulmar destroyed.

The dive bombers continued in and found few worthwhile targets, so contented themselves with hitting the monitor *Erebus* and sinking the transport *Sagaing.* All the other ships had been cleared from the port and sent south without any protection at all. They were soon sighted by the Japanese and their position radioed to Nagumo. On receipt of this news Egusa was launched with his eighty D2A1s to deal with them, and, at about 1300 they located their prey steering frantically towards the coast and broadcasting plaintive appeals for fighter cover. It never came! Instead came the redoubtable Egusa with the 'Vals' deploying in their classical style and commencing their dives.

Their targets were the aircraft carrier *Hermes,* without planes embarked, the Australian destroyer *Vampire,* the corvette *Hollyhock,* the naval auxillary *Atherstone,* the tanker *British Sergeant.* Naturally the carrier was the prime target.

At her maximum speed of 23 knots the *Hermes* sought to evade her fate, opening fire with her pitiful AA armament, two 4in guns and some Oerlikons, but in the first pass by ten dive bombers most of these weapons were wiped out by hits, one of the 4in guns being blown over the side with its entire crew. The forward lift was hit and blown 20ft into the air before falling back into the hangar well killing all those inside. Hit followed hit and after less than fifteen minutes of this the carrier was a gutted wreck on fire from bow to stern and

Scratch one flat-top! The first aircraft carrier to be sunk by carrier dive bombers was the British Hermes *in 1942 off Ceylon. Caught flat-footed by Vals of the Nagumo Task Force without air cover or planes of her own she quickly went to the bottom of the sea after a large number of direct hits had been made on her.*

sinking fast. An attempt was made to beach her in shallow water but she sank so quickly this could not be done.

The destroyer *Vampire* was hit just as hard and followed the *Hermes* soon after. The dive bombers took as alternative targets those other ships still afloat and they were also rapidly despatched within minutes. So many hits did Egusa and his pilots score that they were unable to count them all.

Events in the Indian Ocean caused the Admiralty to withdraw Somerville's fleet from the chance of any further confrontation with an enemy so powerful as the Nagumo Force, but the Japanese had never meant their foray to be anything more than a sharp reminder that the Royal Navy, without dive bombers of their own, no longer ruled the waves, and they soon withdrew after inflicting these humiliating defeats on the baffled admiral. The next Japanese drives were north against the Alleutians, south to take Port Moresby in New Guinea, south-east along the Solomon Islands to isolate Australia and out eastward across the central Pacific to Midway Island to extend their defensive perimeter and draw out the American carriers and destroy them in combat. In enlarging their already considerable commitments thus they badly over-reached themselves and were checked at each pause with heavy losses. The tide of war in the east began to turn in 1942. In all the resulting major actions, both American and Japanese, it was the dive bomber which played the overwhelmingly decisive role.

A Japanese invasion convoy bound for Port Moresby was escorted by the light carrier *Shoho* and given distant cover by the *Shokaku* and *Zuikaku,* each of the latter having twenty-one D3A1 'Vals' embarked, under Vice Adm Takeo Takagi. They were intercepted by a Task Force commanded by Rear Adm Frank Fletcher with the carriers *Lexington* and *Yorktown.* The resulting battle, Battle of the Coral Sea, in May 1942, was the first to be fought by opposing carrier air groups without the combat warships sighting each other at all. It was, as a result, a highly confusing battle.

161

At 0610 on 7 May the Japanese got in the first blow, flying off a strike force against the American carriers which included thirty-six 'Vals', but these aircraft instead located and attacked an oiling group, completely overwhelming the destroyer *Sims* and the tanker *Neosho* and sending both to the bottom. Meanwhile a heavy force of US aircraft from their carriers also came into action at 1100 when they found the *Shoho*. In all there were twenty-eight SBDs from *Lexington* and twenty-five from *Yorktown* as dive bombers, and these, along with torpedo bombers and fighters, all concentrated their attentions on this one small carrier. Not surprisingly, she was smothered in hits and near misses and sank at 1135, the first Japanese carrier to be destroyed. Lt Cdr Bob Dixon's excited radio signal to *Lexington* heralded a new era in sea warfare: 'Scratch one flattop. Dixon to carrier. Scratch one flattop!'

The coming of darkness aborted a second Japanese strike but hostilities re-commenced at dawn, the two air striking forces passing each other *en-route* to their respective targets. In both cases it was the main carriers which were engaged this time instead of the secondary targets of 7 May. Thirty-three 'Vals' dive bombed the two American carriers scoring a hit on *Yorktown* that penetrated four decks and killed sixty-six of her crew, but although badly damaged she was still capable of operating aircraft. The *Lexington* was hit by two torpedoes and sank later, taking fourteen of her SBDs to the bottom with her.

The American strike included twenty-two Dauntless dive bombers from *Lexington* (with three stray SBDs from *Yorktown*) and twenty-four more from *Yorktown* herself, the units involved being VB5, VS5, VB2 and VS2. They arrived over the Japanese ships at 1050 but the *Zuikaku* evaded attack by steaming into a rain squall and the bulk of the dive bombers struck at *Shokaku*. The *Yorktown* strike was intercepted by Zero fighters and VB5 only scored one hit. They were followed down by Lt John Powers in the last plane and he held his attack dive, even though hit by AA fire time and time again, finally dropping his bomb at 300ft before smashing into the sea alongside his target. His bomb carved through the carrier's wooden deck inflicting heavy damage. *Lexington's* VB2 under Cdr William B. Ault led by Lt Cdr Weldon Hamilton made the final attack and scored a third direct hit. However, like *Yorktown* the *Shokaku,* although heavily damaged, did not sink and lived to fight another day.

The loss of one large US carrier and damage to a second, was matched by the loss of one small Japanese carrier, damage to a larger one, but the sinking of the tanker and destroyer made Coral Sea tactically a Japanese victory. The invasion fleet however, turned back unnecessarily, enabling the US to claim a strategical victory.

The most famous carrier-to-carrier battle in history was the Battle of Midway which followed in June 1942. Although the actual occupation of this tiny attoll was desirable to the Japanese, their main plan all along was to lure the remaining US carriers out in its defence and overwhelm them with superior numbers. However faulty dispositions of their powerful fleets left the Japanese ships dispersed instead of concentrated and therefore unable to support each other at the vital time. Of the eight Japanese carriers included, four were wasted on secondary tasks, and the outcome of the battle was therefore decided between four Japanese ships, *Akagi, Kaga, Kiryu* and *Soryu,* against three American, *Enterprise, Hornet* and the patched-up *Yorktown*. The influence of the nine Japanese battleships present, which should have been decisive, was thrown away by Yamamoto because he kept them too far astern of the carriers to be able to intervene.

The initial air strike launched by Nagumo against Midway Island itself on 4

June included thirty-six D3A1s led by Lt Takehiko Chihaya of *Akagi* and Lt

Masaharu Ogawa of *Kaga.* Each Japanese carrier had twenty-one D3A1s embarked, but this battle also marked the operational debut of the D4Y 'Judy' too, for a pair were embarked in *Soryu,* but only as reconnaissance planes, the aircraft were still not passed as suitable for dive bombing. This strike hit Midway at 0620, but all the US aircraft based there had been scrambled away and little lasting damage was done.

Return strikes from the island base included sixteen Dauntless of VMSB241 led by Maj Lofton R. Henderson and eleven SB2U-3 Vindicators led by Maj Benjamin W. Norris. Henderson was a veteran dive bomber pilot who had served in Nicaragua. These two formations attacked at 0755 and suffered heavy losses from flak and fighters, in all eight SBDs and two Vindicators were lost without achieving much in reply. One pilot who made it back counted 259 hits on his aircraft.

Further attacks by shore-based level bombers, torpedo bombers and heavy bombers also failed to score any hits, despite ludicrous claims by the USAAF to the contrary. The real climax of the battle came at 1027. Nagumo had hesitated in sending off his second strike at Midway, and when word came in of US carriers he had to re-arm his bombers. This had just been completed when the first US dive bombers arrived overhead unmolested and commenced their dives on the four Japanese carriers.

Thirty-six SBDs of VB-6 and VS-6, led by Lt Richard H. Best and Lt Wilmer Earl Gallaher were launched from *Enterprise,* with thirty-five SBDs of VB-8 and VS-8 under Cdr Stanhope C. Ring from *Hornet,* but they missed their target and landed later at Midway without sighting the enemy. Lt Cdr C.W. McClusky from *Enterprise* fared better than these. Due to the need to recover scouting aircraft sent out by *Yorktown,* seventeen SBDs of VB-3 commanded by Lt Cdr Maxwell F. Leslie, took a more direct route to catch up and was able to join the *Enterprise* dive bombers in their assault. The Japanese were taken by surprise and suffered heavily.

Kaga was struck by at least four direct hits which turned her hull into an inferno. She finally sank some nine hours later. Lt Best led the *Enterprise* planes down on *Akagi* with similar results to Leslie's, two hits plunging through her decks into her packed hangars. Racked by a series of internal explosions she was abandoned and drifted throughout the night before being despatched by Japanese destroyers the following morning. The third victim of this classic dive bombing attack was the *Soryu,* attacked by Gallaher's section. They hit her three times, her packed aircraft ignited and she was swept by fires and further explosions, finally sinking at 1913. With the three Japanese carriers went their entire air groups and scores of highly-trained navy dive bomber crews.

Only the *Hiryu* remained to launch a counter-blow against the three remaining US carriers. This she did at 1100, but eighteen 'Vals' commanded by Lt Michio Kobayashi, with six Zeros, was all they could send in the first wave. Only four fighters were left to guard them against the hordes of Wildcat fighters that pounced on them when they reached the *Yorktown* later, and ten Japanese dive bombers were destroyed before they could commence their runs. The others attacked two more being shot out of the sky by escorting cruisers. Another 'Val', shot through and through, scored a direct hit on the starboard side of the flight deck before crashing into the sea alongside, leaving one wing aboard the carrier. Another bomb penetrated the port side of the *Yorktown's* flight deck and exploded in her funnel uptakes, while a third hit her to starboard, penetrating four decks and starting fires close to the ship's magazines. Only five 'Vals' returned having survived this gallant attack against all odds, and landed back on *Hiryu.* But despite her damage the *Yorktown* stayed afloat at this time.   163

At 1331 the *Hiryu* got off a second strike, this time of ten torpedo bombers, and they scored two direct hits. This was the end of the *Yorktown,* or almost, but it was also the last gasp of the *Hiryu* for at 1703, twenty-four SBDs from *Enterprise* and sixteen from *Hornet* found her and attacked out of the setting sun. Four devastating hits punched into the Japanese ship, enormous fires broke out and she was abandoned, finally being sunk at 0510 next morning.

The destruction of these four carriers was the greatest victory scored by the Dauntless. The Japanese called off their invasion plans and retired. Even so they took further casualties. A heavy cruiser squadron had been sent ahead to bombard Midway's defences, but before it could do so it was recalled. A collision took place during the night turn damaging two of these ships and slowing them down. They were still well within striking range of the island next day and were also subjected to prolonged dive bombing attacks from the US carriers.

At 0805 six Vindicators and six Dauntless from Midway made the first strike. The Vindicator of Capt Fleming was heavily hit and crashed onto the rear turrets of the *Mikuma,* cremating its crews. *Enterprise* and *Hornet* launched strong dive bomber attacks on the main Japanese fleet that same afternoon but they found nothing except a solitary Japanese destroyer, the *Tanikaze* and she survived the attentions of thirty-eight SBDs.

On the 6th the same two carriers launched attacks on the crippled Japanese cruisers: at 0800 with twenty-six SBDs from *Hornet;* at 1045 with thirty-one SBDs from *Enterprise;* and then two dozen more SBDs from *Hornet* once more. The cruiser *Mogami* was hit several times and wrecked, but she managed to crawl to safety. The *Mikuma* was also struck by many bombs and finally sank in flames with few survivors. Although the *Yorktown* was later sunk, along with an escorting destroyer, by a Japanese submarine, the results of the Battle of Midway were as decisive as any naval battle could be.

A minor part of the Midway operation called for the invasion of some of the Aleutian islands in the far north of the Pacific. 'Vals' from the carriers *Junyo* and *Ryuko* participated, making an abortive raid on 3 June when twelve D3A1s from the former ship were weathered out, and on the 4th when eleven from *Ryujo* dive bombed Dutch Harbour. In the absence of ships or aircraft targets Lt Yoshio Shiga attacked the radio station and oil tanks at 0407. Subsequently an attack launched against reported American destroyers was also weathered out.

The final stages of the Japanese thrusts for 1942, the drive down the Solomon Islands chain, was halted, and then reversed, when the US marines landed at Tulagi on 7 August and also Guadalcanal Island across the 'Slot', quickly occupying the almost complete Japanese airstrip, which they duly dubbed Henderson Field. The Japanese reacted strongly and for the next five months a series of violent sea, air and land battled raged around the island to gain or hold this one airfield.

A total of 103 SBDs were embarked in the carriers *Enterprise, Saratoga* and *Wasp* which covered the initial landings, but after limited operations Fletcher withdrew on the 9th. The Marines therefore flew in Marine Air Group (MAG) twenty-three to operate from Henderson Field, and for a while the SBDs of VMSB-231 and VMSB-232, with the Mark 3 Dauntlesses, held the ring under Lt Col Richard C. Mangrum, 232 flying in off the escort carrier *Long Island* on 20 August.

Opposing them was the Japanese land-based Air Fleet at Rabaul some 550 nautical miles away in New Britain, just beyond the operational range of the 'Val'. One Japanese historian later wrote how: 'Our "Val" dive bombers, however, were despatched on missions in which their crews despaired of survival. Simply stated, the aircraft could not carry sufficient fuel to make the

Two more immortal names. Dauntless SBDs operating from Henderson Field on Guadalcanal. In 1942 the Navy and Marine Corps SBDs operating from this small jungle airstrip sank a huge number of Japanese ships attempting to recapture this strategic base and finally turned the tide of the Pacific War.

round-trip flight from Rabaul to Guadalcanal and return. Within two days of the American invasion we lost eighteen "Val" bombers but not one fell to the enemy's guns. Their fuel ran out as they struggled to reach Rabaul, and all these bombers crashed.'

An interim air strip was constructed at Buin which eased this problem. In an attack on 7 August 'Vals' dive bombed and damaged the destroyer *Mugford* with sixteen aircraft, while, during a later strike by 'Vals', one D2A1 was hit by AA fire and crashed into the transport *George F. Elliott* (8,378 tons) which burnt out and later sank.

The Japanese Combined Fleet sortied out to cover a troop convoy attempting to land 1,500 soldiers on Guadalcanal on 23 August. Nagumo had the carriers *Shokaku* and *Zuikaku* on hand with the light carrier *Ryujo* stationed some distance ahead as a lure. The American Task Force 61 under Fletcher had the carriers *Enterprise, Saratoga* and *Wasp*. On location off the convoy *Saratoga* flew off a strike force which included thirty-one SBDs, but they lost their target in a squall and had to land at Henderson Field.

On the 24th the *Ryujo* group was located and at 1030 *Enterprise* flew off a strike which included fifteen SBDs. Meanwhile Cdr Don Felt had landed back aboard the *Saratoga* with his group, and, after refuelling, his twenty-eight SBDs were launched at 1435. The *Enterprise* planes attacked the *Ryujo* at 1500, dive bombing from 11,000ft out of the sun but only scoring near-misses. Two others from the same ship made a surprise attack on the *Shokaku* at 1545, claiming to have damaged her, but she continued operating.

The *Saratoga* group hit *Ryujo* at 1620, bracketing her with near misses before Felt himself scored a direct hit on her flight deck, '. . . slight port and aft of dead centre . . . .' Seven SBDs from VB-3 followed him down from 15,000ft and blasted the little carrier to the seabed with three more hits and four close misses.

In the interim the two Japanese carriers had got their own air strikes away, some thirty-three 'Vals' being included in the first wave at 1505, which were followed by eighteen more in the second wave launched an hour later. While the latter failed to find their target at all, the first group sighted *Enterprise* at 1625 and commenced their attack dives. Astern of their target was the new battleship *North Carolina,* her myriad of long-range 5in and close-range automatic cannon winking and flaming, putting up a huge barrage over the carrier in front. 'Val' after 'Val' was shot out of the sky by this new battleship, but a few survivors scored three direct hits. The first of these struck the *Enterprise* on the after lift and penetrated three decks before exploding, causing a 20^0 list and heavy casualties. The second hit close by, within 15ft of the first, destroying all the AA guns on the starboard quarter and killing thirty-nine of their crews as the ammunition exploded. The last bomb hit the flight deck just behind the island and blew a hole in the deck. It was faulty and caused little other damage, so the stricken *Enterprise* remained afloat despite this pounding.

In a further counter-strike two *Saratoga* Dauntless aircraft attacked and hit the old seaplane tender *Chitose,* destroying her port engine room with a hit that tore her side open. With a 30^0 list she trailed back to Truk. This ended the operation as the Japanese again withdrew from the field of battle.

At Henderson Field the Marine SBDs were joined by the Dauntless orphans from the damaged US carrier on the 24th, eight from VS-5 and three from VB-6. These were commended by Lt Turner F. Caldwell and for the next few weeks this group, Flight 300, became an integral part of the Dauntless team that inflicted heavy casualties on the transports and destroyers of the 'Tokyo Express' endeavouring to land Japanese troop reinforcements on the island.

These shore-based dive bombers survived bombardments by Japanese battleships, heavy cruisers and destroyers as well as numerous air attacks. Their achievements were so many that we can only summarise them. They were finally reinforced on 30 August by the twelve SBDs of VMSB-231 under Maj Leo Smith.

On 25 August they attacked and sank the destroyer *Mutsuki* and the transport *Kinryu Maru,* they also damaged the light cruiser *Jintsu* with a direct hit between her two forward gun turrets. On 28th they sank the destroyer *Asagiri* and damaged the destroyers *Shirakumo* and *Yugiri* badly and the *Amagiri* slightly. On 24 September the destroyers *Kawakaze* and *Umikaze* were damaged by dive bombing and on 5 October they also hit the destroyers *Minegumo* and *Murasame.*

On 15 October Dauntless attacks so damaged the transports *Azumasan Maru, Kyushu Maru,* and *Sasago Maru* that they had to beach themselves and were destroyed, while the destroyer *Samidare* was also hit. In return blows the dive bombing of 'Vals' from the carrier *Zuikaku* sank the American destroyer *Meredith* and the tug *Vireo* the same day. But on 19 October the Japanese destroyer *Ayanami* was damaged by the SBDs.

The last carrier-to-carrier duel in this period took place on 26 October 1942, when Nagumo returned to the fray with the *Shokaku, Zuiko* and *Zuikaku* and his full battleship strength. The light carrier *Junyo* was with Adm Kondo's Advance Force. Facing this array was the *Enterprise* with TF16 and the *Hornet* with TF17 along with the new battleships *South Dakota* and *Washington.* The resulting battle was known as the Battle of Santa Cruz.

On the 26th the Japanese sighted the American fleet and launched strong air attacks which included twenty-two D3A1s in the first wave and twenty in the second. At 0655 the first wave, led by Lt Cdr Mamoru Seki, found the US ships and attacked on their own. Their target was the *Hornet* and the battleships escorting her put up a terrific wall of fire. Nonetheless the 'Vals' attacked and plunged into it, led by Seki. Although very heavily damaged his dive bomber continued its plunge straight into the heart of the carriers hull, its exploding bombload wrecking the ship's boilers. Three more direct hits were made, one aft to starboard, another exploded on impact with the flight deck, while a fourth gouged its way down to the fourth deck of the carrier before detonation. The *Hornet* slewed round and came to a halt, listing and disabled, and was then hit by two torpedoes as the Japanese torpedo bombers joined in the assault.

The second wave of 'Vals', led by Lt Sadomu Takahashi, was waylaid by US
carrier fighters and decimated. Takahashi himself having to ditch along with

others, but enough got through to plant two direct hits and two near misses around the *Enterprise* while other 'Vals' dashed themselves against the defences of the battleship *South Dakota,* flanked as she was by the AA cruiser *San Juan* and the light cruiser *Portland.* Against this huge array of AA firepower all their attacks broke with heavy losses among the dive bombers involved. One 'Val' hit the battleship with a heavy bomb on 'A' turret, but failed to inflict damage to such a heavily armoured target. Another 'Val' scored a direct hit on *San Juan* and her flimsy decks offered little resistance, the bomb penetrating almost through to the ship's keel before exploding deep inside and jamming her rudder. A torpedo bomber crashed into the destroyer *Smith* wiping out her bridge, but she stayed afloat.

The return strike from the American ships found the Japanese carriers at 0840, two SBDs making a surprise dive and hitting *Zuiho* aft with two bombs, these planes being piloted by Lt Birney Strong and Ensg Charles Irvine of *Enterprise*'s VS-10. Meantime *Hornet* had launched fifteen SBDs at the same time as *Enterprise* got away another three from VB-10. *Hornet* followed up with a further Dauntless contribution of nine aircraft at 0920. Fifteen dive bombers found their targets and dived down, four being lost to defending fighters on the way down. The remaining eleven scored at least three direct hits on the *Shokaku.* The *Enterprise* group attacked a heavy cruiser, the *Chikuma,* demolishing her bridge with two bombs while a third penetrated her vitals badly damaging her. In all a total of twenty SBDs were lost in this battle, but the D3A1s were almost all wiped out. The crippled *Hornet* was again attacked by the *Junyo's* last six 'Vals' led by the senior surviving dive bomber pilot, Sub-Lt Shunko Kato, and they hit *Hornet* yet again. Having taken an enormous amount of punishment, including further torpedo hits, *Hornet* was finally abandoned and sent to the bottom by a Japanese destroyer at 0135 on the 27th.

Despite getting marginally the better of these two set-piece battles the Japanese carriers withdrew, as did the Americans. The surface ships then took over the struggle and a series of titanic pitch battles involving warships were fought in the 'Slot' — from battleships blasting each other at point-blank range, down to destroyers and torpedo boats fighting high speed duels in the inky blackness. But most of these great clashes took place by night — in the morning after it was left to the dive bombers from Henderson Field to mop up the cripples and hunt for survivors of the previous night's actions.

On 7 November, the destroyers *Naganami* and *Takanami* of the 'Tokyo Express' were hit by SBDs and damaged. 'Vals' from the light carrier *Hiyo* returned the compliment attacking an American troop convoy on 11 November and damaging the transport *Zeilin* badly, as well as hitting two others, but losing nine out of twelve of their number in so doing. On the 13th Dauntless strikes assisted those from *Enterprise* in pounding the drifting hulk of the Japanese battleship *Hiei* wrecked in action the night before. The two groups co-operated again on the 14th when SBDs from both units attacked a convoy and its escorting cruiser force withdrawing after another night encounter. The heavy cruiser *Kinugasa* was sunk while the cruisers *Chokai, Isuzu* and *Maya,* and destroyer *Michishio* were all dive bombed and severely hit. From the convoy Dauntless attacks sank the transport *Canberra Maru* and *Nagara Maru,* while the *Sado Maru* was damaged. Further SBD strikes the same day sank the *Brisbane Maru, Arizona Maru* and *Nako Maru,* drowning some 400 soldiers.

On the 24th the SBDs sank the destroyer *Hayashio* and on 8 December the *Nowake* was hit and abandoned. Finally, on the last day of 1942 the Japanese decided to admit defeat and Guadalcanal was finally secured by the Americans, due in no small measure to the efforts of the Dauntless dive bomber.

20. FULL CIRCLE
New developments and the return of the fighter dive bomber

While the various factions in Britain argued and debated, a war was being conducted in the Pacific which centred almost entirely around the dive bomber. Throughout 1942 the Dauntless and the 'Val' had fought this war on their own, although both were regarded as obsolete designs. But at the end of 1943, at long last, their replacements began to appear on the battlefield in increasing numbers. The change-over from a peacetime footing to war production had not only affected the production of the Bermuda and Vengeance, but had not helped the Helldiver either. In Japan the development of the 'Judy' matched the long delays of its American counterpart but, finally, both appeared at the front.

The problem of wing-flutter was not finally solved in the D4Y1 *Suisei* (Comet), code-named 'Judy', until the spring of 1943 and was overcome by strengthening. With this problem solved the aircraft could thus, in theory, be fully used in its proper role and not just for reconnaissance as hitherto. Full-scale production was got underway by the Aichi company, almost 600 being turned out in the first year. In combat the Comet did not live up to expectations and the Atsuta in-line engine was therefore replaced by a large radial, the 1,560hp Mitsubishi MK80 Kinsei 62. This involved structural alterations forward to fit it to the existing airframe and this version became the Model 33, the D4Y3. A 3a variant was fitted with a 13mm rear gun. The more powerful radial engine increased the maximum speed of this modification to 357mph.

Meanwhile as a stop-gap measure the 'Val' had been improved by re-engining with the 1,300hp Kinsei 54 and extra fuel bunkerage was added. The cockpit was streamlined and a propeller spinner fitted to become the Model 22, 1,016 of

When the floodtide of Japanese conquests swept across the Pacific there was an obvious need for floatplanes to give the far-flung island bases local protection. One answer to this problem was the Aichi E16A Zuiun, a reconnaissance floatplane, code-named Paul by the Allies. The AM-22 prototype first flew in May 1942, when Japanese conquests were at their peak. By August 1943, a dive bomber version specially strengthened was under production as the E16A1, but after service in the Philippines it proved out of its element and many were expended as Kamikazes in 1945.

which were produced by the Aichi and Showa plants to the end of the war, compared with a total of 470 Model 11s.

Gone were the days when numerous models could be tried and tested, the need was for combat-fit aircraft in the maximum numbers. Thus one Navy-designed dive bomber which fell by the wayside was the Nakajima D3N1, a small carrier-based aircraft featuring a retractable landing-gear. One very late development in the dive bomber field was initiated by the Army however.

This was the 'Experimental Attacker' aircraft, the Kawasaki Ki119. It was a radial-engined version of the 'Tony' fighter, but larger in size due to the fitting of the 2,000hp Ha104 engine. It had a combat radius of 375 miles, which special drop tanks could increase to 750 miles. It had a wingspan of 45ft 9in, a length of 38ft 10in and a height of 14ft 9in, with an all-up weight of 8,766lb.

It was the Japanese who came up with the most novel form of dive bomber, nothing less than a floatplane dive bomber! This was the Aichi E16A Zuiun, designed by Matsuo and Ozawa, the first model of which was completed in May 1942. It was designed to operate over the wastes of the Pacific from remote island bases and was built from the outset with dive bomber capability. It thus featured hydraulically-operated dive brakes mounted on the front leg of the N-struts, but the original design caused severe buffeting and had to be modified. With fully perforated dive brakes the aircraft went into service in late 1943 as the E16A2 Navy Reconnaissance Seaplane.

It was a single-engined twin-float seaplane of all-metal construction with stressed skin covering, wooden wingtips which folded and control surfaces which were fabric covered. It was a two seater powered by the Mitsubishi MK8D Kinsei 54 radial engine of 1,560hp, which gave it a top speed of 273mph at 18,045ft. It was armed with two 7.7mm type 97 machine guns in the wings and a flexible type 92 of similar calibre in the rear cockpit. It had a span of 42ft and a length of 35ft 6½in. Some 256 were built and served with the 301st, 634th and Yokosuka Kokutais. Known to the Allies as the 'Paul', it was severely mauled during the Philippines campaign of 1944 where it was completely out of its element. In common with most other types of Japanese aircraft, the survivors ended their days in flaming pyres off the Okinawa beach-head as Kamikazes.

The Army Ki119 did not even get that far. Although emphasis was laid on both the ease of maintenance, avoiding as far as possible the inclusion of wrought-metal plates of which there was a bottleneck, production was slow. It was designed to attack US Task Forces far out from Japan's shoreline in the face of overwhelming fighter defences, itself with fighter-like manoeuverability. Plans were made to mass-produce the Ki119 in underground workshops, but it all came far too late. Work did not commence until March 1945, and full-scale production was hoped-for by September 1945!

In America the non-appearance of a replacement led to further improvements to the basic type as an interim measure. For the US Navy this involved the fitting of the SBD Dauntless with the improved R-1820-60 engine of 1,200hp and increasing the range by extra tankage to 370gal. The resulting SBD5 began production in February 1943 and proved by far the largest mark, no less than 2,900 or so being built before production ceased in April 1944. Comparison with the 'Val' production figures show just how wide the gap was in the respective capacity of the US and Japanese War Plants, and just how hopeless the conflict had now become for the Japanese as early as 1943.

The US Army's indecision was reflected in their own Dauntless version, the A24. Although a failure in combat to date, they nonetheless ordered 170 A24A-DEs (the equivalent of the SBD4) and 615 A24B-DTs (equivalent to the SBD5) which were to be constructed at a new Douglas plant set up at Tulsa. However in 169 the interim another change of heart had taken place and again, of all these aircraft, only a handful ever saw service. This time there was some considerable success, for 531st Fighter Bomber Squadron operated dive bombing missions with the A24B from airstrips in the Makin Islands during December 1943.

The Curtiss SB2C1 actually joined the fleet comparatively early, despite the many problems surrounding it, embarking with VS9 in the new carrier *Essex* in December 1942, but, once afloat it became clear that its problems were only just beginning! Numerous faults were discovered in this period including tailwheel and hook failures that led to them being relegated to VB17 aboard the escort carrier *Santee* and ashore with test units. Consequently the initial batch of 200 Helldivers had to be modified again before they could be passed fit for combat.

In a similar manner those thus modified, when embarked with VB4 and VB6 aboard the new *Yorktown*, second ship of the name, in May 1943, also fell down badly, so much so that the ship's captain, Capt J.J. Clark, recommended the entire Helldiver programme be scrapped! His squadrons were re-equipped with the faithful Dauntless and went off to war. The SB2Cs were dumped ashore and there underwent yet a third modification, involving considerable strengthening, fitting of self-sealing fuel tanks and non-retractable tailwheels, a .30in machine gun mounting replaced by a .50in at the same time.

They tried again, VB17 embarking in the *Bunker Hill* in July 1943, for further sea trials, and, when the third modification was completed she took these Helldivers, some thirty-six in all, out to battle. Meanwhile the fitting of the 20mm cannon in wings and hydraulic flaps to production line models resulted in the SB2C-1C in August. The second fleet carrier to embark the modified Helldiver in a fit state to use was the *Intrepid*.

The Army, meantime, experienced further similar problems with its own versions, the A25A. Under the same expansion scheme that they adopted with the A24, the USAAF placed orders to obtain 100 SB2Cs from the Navy quota in 1940, and confirmed this on the last day of that year. After Pearl Harbor this modest start was supplemented by orders totalling an additional 3,000 dive bombers of this type, which was beyond the capacity of the parent company to produce as well as its Navy orders. Therefore a plant was set up at St Louis to sub-contract the Army specification, this version being named the Curtiss S84 *Shrike.*

The first Shrike took to the air on 29 September 1942, and still had Navy-type folding wings, but so many modifications were required to fit Army requirements that it soon became a different airplane. Only ten were built by March 1943, before the folding wing was dropped, different radio sets fitted and larger wheels adopted, and the contract was transferred to the Army as attempts at standardisation were merely delaying production of both models.

All this took place during another shift in USAAF policy, which finally rejected the whole dive bomber concept anyway and the completed aircraft, again re-designated as the RA-25A Helldiver, were employed on target-towing duties, a seemingly inevitable fate for unwanted dive bombers the world over!

A further twist in the complicated story was the allocation of 150 of these A25As to Australia, only ten of which were finally delivered due to delays. In the final event, these, and 270 surplus Army machines, were to be modified and transferred to the Marines as land-based dive bombers, after production stopped when 900 Army types had been completed. All this required yet further alterations and by the time they arrived at the end of 1944, they were of no value to the US Marines either and served in a secondary role as trainers.

In Europe in 1943 the development of the fighter dive bomber was gradually taking hold and this spread to the Pacific as we shall see. There gradually emerged a blending of the concepts of the dive bomber and the fighter bomber, even in those Allied airforces most opposed to specialised dive bombers, the RAF and the USAAF. Even they could not remain blind to the advantages of dive bombing and although they steadfastly refused to admit they had been wrong hitherto in public, more and more dive bombing was conducted by them as time went by. Happily the lifting power of the new generation of fighters enabled them to carry equivalent bomb loads to the old type dive bombers and, with the final acceptance of dive bombing when carried out by such machines, the operational use expanded. But it was a very gradual process in the RAF and the traditional dive bomber indeed soldiered on in all air arms save the British, as 1942 gave way to 1943 and 1944.

The high-tide of Axis success in North Africa was reached in September 1942, when Rommel swept across the Egyptian frontier and for a time looked like taking Cairo and the Suez Canal. There was widespread panic behind the British lines at HQ but the Germans were at the end of their tether, lacking the necessary supplies and reinforcements for this last push. Rommel had always been heavily outnumbered by the British, despite his successes, now with the crisis in Russia leaving him unsupported, the scales tilted still further against him.

Operating from airfields at Daba and Fuka Ju87s of StG3 were heavily committed and began again to take severe losses from RAF fighters now operating freely in large numbers from the pre-war airfields of Egypt. In one such encounter on 3 July 1942, two squadrons of British fighters caught fifteen Stukas over El Alamein and claimed to have shot down thirteen of them! A great victory was announced and tales were spread of Stukas crashing all over the desert, but despite this the Ju87s continued to be heavily engaged in the subsequent land fighting to the discomforture of the British troops although their numbers dwindled as the crisis after Stalingrad drew more and more of them to more important areas. Attacks by RAF bombers concentrated on Stuka airfields on 5 July, which gives a indication of how the RAF really felt about them, and nine were destroyed on the ground. Despite these desperate attempts to pre-empt the Stukas the Ju87s were again prominent in the German attacks of 31 August and 1 September 1942, formations of up to forty of these dive bombers again spearheading German armour thrusts. But the Afrika Korps was held by extensive minefields and the offensive ground to a halt.

Throughout October heavy rain made the forward airstrips unserviceable and the bulk of the Stuka forces were pulled back to Sidi Haneish and with the opening of the British offensive they were in short supply and unable to contain the overwhelming advance of the 8th Army, operating as it was under an enormous fighter umbrella. On 11 November fifteen Stukas of I/StG3 operating from Gambut under Oberst Martin Mossdorf were intercepted by strong fighter forces which brushed aside their slender screen and destroyed eleven of them in continuous attacks. By November 1942, StG3 had pulled back all the way to Tunisia and began transferring units to airfields in the Balkans.

Nonetheless the Ju87 was again much in evidence in the battles of March 1943, which saw the Americans badly mauled by Rommel and the British attacks blunted and brought to a standstill for a time. In fact the position of the previous October was reversed with the Stukas able to operate extensively from the runways of the Vichy bases, while the airstrips of the Allies were washed out. Never exceeding a total strength of fifty to sixty Ju87s the Stukas, based in both Tunisia and Sardinia, gave the allies several bloody noses before Tunis finally fell in May 1943. This unexpected re-emergence of the Stuka yet again, after the RAF had written it off in the press so many times before, again caused some unrest in Parliament.

In Germany the Ju87's replacement was having no more luck than similar aircraft in America and Japan. This aircraft was the Me210. The original specification dated back to 1938 and at that time called for an improved twin-engined fighter destroyer to replace the Me110. The second and fourth prototypes (V2 and V4) had however been fitted with dive brakes and in 1940 dive bombing trials were held before they were removed. Despite this dive bombing testing with the Me210 continued with the V12 and the early production models, Me210-AOs, were built with dive bombing as one of their main functions, two 1,100lb bombs being the maximum bomb load carried in this profile. But the Germans did not take the idea much further. The Me210 *was* used as a dive bomber in combat, but by the Hungarians, who used licence-built Me210Cs with their 102 Group as dive bombers in 1944.

Meanwhile the first American built dive bombers had entered squadron service with the RAF and to their embarassment, proved highly successful. No 45 Squadron was the first RAF Vengeance unit to see combat. The first mission took place on 27 November 1942, in support of the Arakan offensive. During a brief period of operations the Vengeance carried out five offensive dive bombing operations. The targets attacked on four of these missions were enemy occupied villages, and the fifth was an enemy defended position and the target was indicated by smoke. On each mission six Vengeance aircraft took part flying in a box of two Vics of three.

With the monsoon season further operations were curtailed and an intensive period of training was undertaken as the Vengeance allocation enabled the RAF and Indian Air Forces to build up to full Wing strength in preparation for the next big push. In India, in 1942, there was no doubt at all about the efficiency of the dive bomber and every confidence in its future.

As allocations of Vengeance aircraft suffered the delays mentioned earlier, the RAAF had to make use of anything available in New Guinea and among the first dive bomber operations they carried out were those conducted by No 4 Army Co-Operation Squadron in late 1942. This unit was equipped with the Commonwealth Wirraway, a two-seater, low-wing monoplane designed for close-support and aerial reconnaissance. Equipped with two 250lb bombs on underwing racks they operated in the winter of 1942-3 in the Papuan Campaign.

The first Vengeance squadron was formed in Australia in the spring of 1943 and made attacks on Timor with some success, being joined by a second squadron in September.

During 1942-3 the development of the fighter dive bomber was steadily increasing in favour, on the Eastern Front, in the Mediterranean and later in the Pacific, with the British, Germans, Americans and Italians, all producing viable ideas on this same theme. But before the Junkers Ju87 vanished from the daytime skies over Europe, its role as a dive bomber being eclipsed by this full-circle return to its origins, the Stuka was to score one last spectacular victory over its old adversary, the Royal Navy.

We have seen how their earlier unhappy experiences with the A24 had put off the development of the dive bomber proper in the USAAF, despite massive, unfulfilled orders for their own adaptations of various US Navy and RAF types being built in America. Failure of these adaptations to arrive in squadron service in time, due to production difficulties, further worsened the situation when the Army variants of the Helldiver and the Buccaneer failed to materialise, in particular the XA32. Then the Vengeance (A35A) also failed to show up on time and so it went on. This led the USAAF to adapt the versatile and long-range fighter, the North American Mustang, built in the US to a combined Anglo-US design, and include for it a new dive bombing role to fill the gap. Surprisingly, it

Among the earliest Allied fighter aircraft adapted for dive bombing was the North American Mustang. The USAAF operated their adaptations in dive bombing missions over France in 1943 and the RAF eventually followed suit. The Mustang could carry two 500-lb bombs as a dive bomber.

was at once successful in this role and it followed the German Fw190 as a dive bomber adapted from a front-line fighter.

In fact the USAAF development could be said to have preceded the German for it was in August 1942, that the dive bombing version of the Mustang, the A36A, was ordered and deliveries followed off the production line almost at once, no less than six squadrons being so equipped by early 1943. These conversions from the normal P51 were fitted with dive brakes and could carry a handy bombload of two 500lb bombs, one under each wing, in special racks. Powered by a 1,325hp Allison V-1710-87 engine, the A36A could attain a top speed of 356mph which made it ideal, when coupled with its high endurance.

By early 1943 the first of these units were moving into the Mediterranean theatre and their first combat sorties took place on 6 June 1943, over Sicily, prior to the Allied invasion of that island, 'Operation Husky', with the 27th Fighter-Bomber Group. They also dive bombed the island of Pantelleria in July, just before the main assault on Sicily proper. For both operations the 27th and 86th Groups were employed as dive bombers. Although proving very effective the A36A took some heavy losses from the superior German flak defences, both groups losing twenty aircraft from this cause between them. But they proved the effectiveness of dive bombing against armour by stopping enemy formations at Salerno during German counter-attacks on the Allied beach-head there in September 1943, and later gave invaluable assistance during the drive on Rome itself.

However production was limited, while losses and wear-and-tear steadily reduced the numbers of A36As operating towards the end of that year. All such aircraft were therefore concentrated in the 27th Group when the 33rd switched to India and finally, in 1944, even these were replaced by the P47 Thunderbolt.

Specialised dive bomber research work in the USAAF had been finally dropped at this time, the final attempt to produce a viable product for that service being the abortive Vultee XA41. This was a very large aircraft which could carry up to 7,000lb of bombs and was armed with four 37mm cannon plus four .5in Browning machine-guns. All-up weight was a colossal 23,000lb and it was powered by a single 3,000hp engine. However by the time it was put forward all Army interest in such highly-specialised dive bombers was dead and it was never ordered.

Before the final collapse in North Africa the Italians had already withdrawn their Stuka units, 102⁰ *Gruppo* being located at Lonate Pozzolo in Northern Italy

Throughout the reverses of 1943 the Regia Aeronautica continued to find useful employment for its Ju87 dive bombers. This Ju87D-3 of 216 Squadriglia of 121⁰ Gruppo Autonomo Bombardamento a Tuffo is seen taxiing along the runway of Capua airport near Naples in August 1943.

at this time. Their worn-out Ju87B2s and R2s were then replaced by new batches of Doras and a new formation, 103⁰ *Gruppo,* was set up on 1 February 1943.

This unit transferred to Siena Ampugnano in Central Italy in March, command of 237 being taken over by Capt Leo Vacellio. In May it was switched to airfields in Sardinia in readiness for operations in the Western Mediterranean, but in heavy attacks by USAAF bombers on their bases it was almost wiped out on the ground before seeing combat.

During the defence of Sicily a few Italian Ju87Ds operated from Boccadifalco airfield near Palermo and carried out an attack on Allied shipping at Licatabia on 11 July 1943, in which they claimed to have scored some hits. Only four Stukas, led by Capt Cesare Zanazzo took part, all returning to Sardinia with damage. Meanwhile another Stuka unit, 121⁰ *Gruppo,* had been hastily formed with the few remaining R5s. When the attack on Sicily developed these were rushed into Gioia del Colle airfield in the south of Italy, with 237 *Squadriglia* on 11 July, and on the same day seven of these Stukas, with an escort of Macchi 202s, attacked shipping off the beach-heads, claiming two hits. They were intercepted by Spitfires and lost two of their number. The same story continued throughout the brief campaign and by the end of it the Italian Stuka formations were again at a very low ebb and took very little part in any subsequent fighting in the mainland campaigns.

Table 36: Final Italian Stuka units Operational 1942-3				
Gruppo	Commander	Nbr aircraft	*Squadriglia*	Commander
103⁰	*Ten Col* Savarino	25 Ju87D	207	*Capt* C. Zanazzo *Capt* V. Marcoccia
121⁰	*Magg* L. Orlandini	12 Ju87R	206 216	*Capt* Zucca *Capt* Pergoli

Meanwhile the development of the fighter dive bomber had also taken place in the *Regia Aeronautica.* Several types were under development at this time, as follows. The Avia LM02 was a special glider dive bomber, developed especially to attack Allied shipping at Gibraltar, a somewhat ambitious project. It was all-wooden construction and fitted with Junkers dive brakes. The idea was that this aircraft, fitted with a pair of 820kg bombs, should be towed across the Mediterranean by a SM79 bomber to about twenty to thirty miles of the Rock, whereupon it would be released, carry out its dive bombing attack at about 530kmp (330mph), and then make a water landing off Algerciras with the pilot being picked up by submarines. This whole concept was the brainchild of Pieraldo Mortara, an engineer, and backed by E. Lombardi, owner of the AVIA company.

It was to have been a glider of great strength. The dive brakes were to be held by elastic ribbon and, in the dive, when the speed had built up to about 450kph (280mph) holes in the wings would force the air through, thus extending the brakes. Tested by Nello Raimondo at Vercelli at the end of 1942, the further development was retarded at this time, for the use of radar made the value of its silent approach to a heavily defended target useless anyway. Although AVIA built parts of this strange dive bomber concept for structural tests and began to assemble a second prototype, all work stopped in 1943 and it became merely another curiosity of the war.

More realistic and worthwhile was the adaptation of the Reggiane Re2002 fighter, with a Piaggio PIXIX RC45 engine of 1,185hp. It could be used for bombing at angles of 45^0 with light bombs of 100 or 250kg under the wings and was thus tested and allocated to 101^0 and 102^0 *Squadriaglia* based at Lonate Pozzolo in December 1942.

After some teething troubles these two groups moved to Tarquinia. On 10 July 1943, with twenty and twelve aircraft respectively, they moved into Crotonone-Isola Capo Rizzuto, making their first dive bombing attacks on ships off Reggio and Augusta. Four Re2002s were lost in this attack including *Stormo* leader Guido Nobili. By 24 September these units had only two dozen serviceable aircraft left between them, thirty-two being destroyed, and among the casualties were Gino Pricolo (on 19 July) and *Magg* Cenni (on 4 September), the two most outstanding Italian dive bomber pilots of the war.

The successes they claimed was a hit on the battleship *Nelson* (not confirmed by British records) and the sinking of the troopships *Talamba* on 11 July, *Fort Pelly* on 20 July and *Fishpool* on 26 July which caused numerous casualties. Training in dive bombing continued at Lonate Pozzolo, where 50^0 *Stormo* had ten Re2002s on hand until 8 September, when all such operations ceased on the Italian surrender. Some captured Re2002s were reputedly used by the Luftwaffe later in France, while 5^0 *Stormo* used its dive bombers against their former ally in Greece, Yugoslavia and Albania until the end of hostilities.

During this period also the ninety IMAM Ro57bis aircraft ordered in 1942 joined squadron service with 97^0 *Gruppo*. On 9 July 1943, this unit, led by Raoul Zucconi, had just fifteen aircraft fit for operations, but ten of these were destroyed in Allied air attacks on the 13th. 97^0 *Gruppo* moved the few remaining Ro57s to Tarquinia, but they never saw extensive combat.

Back in Britain ordinary fighter-bomber exploits with Kittyhawks and Hurribombers had wrongly been reported by the press, who knew no better, as being dive bombing. When the USAAF Mustangs carried out actual true dive bombings, with their dive brakes wired shut incidently, the whole question of why the RAF was still the only major service out of step was raised. The continued delay also of the re-introduction of the dive bomber into the FAA was reported to Churchill. The reason for the delay to the Barracuda, it was said, was due to the replacement of its power plant by a less efficient one. As for the US-built dive bombers, although the Vengeance was entering service in India it received little or no publicity in case it embarrassed the RAF, who had steadily carried out a policy of scorning the dive bomber in press and Parliament. So the Vengeance successes in the Arakan were hushed up. What of the Bermuda situation?. In truth there was little to cheer about here either. The Air Minister was to memo Hugh Molson that: 'It is quite true, as Geoffrey Mander told you, that the long delay in the delivery of these dive bombers is due to failures in production in America. So inefficient indeed was one of the companies concerned that the United States Government had to take over the plant.'

Nor were things any better six months later. Stafford at the MAP wrote to Sinclair:

> We have been doing all we can to get ahead with this but it is the most appalling production! We hope to get the first one to Boscombe Down this week. It had been awaiting flying weather only. If everything went perfectly and there were no accidents or unexpected difficulties (which is most unlikely) we might get the modifications finished and on the first plane in six weeks time and thereafter go ahead with the others. It is, however, far more likely that you will not get any of them under three months from now, and even that date may be postponed.

Meantime the dive bomber refused to lie down as an opponent, as well as a self-inflicted headache. With the Italian surrender in September 1943, a vacuum was left in the Balkans and Aegean areas which the Germans quickly filled, disarming the Italians there and moving in strong air and ground forces of their own to protect the south-east flank of Europe. Included in these reinforcements were the Ju87s of StG3 and StG151, as well as the long-range Ju88 dive bombers, all these latter coming from the Eastern Front. At the same time that the Germans were thus increasing their grip on this vital area, the Allies were involved in a dispute over the need to beat them to it, the Americans refusing to become involved and the British lacking the forces to do so effectively. Churchill insisted on sending troops into the islands, with little or no air cover and then sent the Royal Navy in to support them. The result was a repeat of the Crete fiasco of two years earlier, the British leader having apparently learnt nothing of the power of dive bombers.

With the Balkans in the balance the stakes were high, but the Germans were the quickest to react. The Stukas, based initially on Croatian and Greek airfields, struck hard. On 21 September 1943, they subjected the island fortress of Cephallonia in the Gulf of Corinth to heavy dive bombing attacks and when this key position quickly fell, they switched their assault to Corfu on the 24th, crushing all resistance quickly. The following day the dive bombers directed their attentions to Split in Yugoslavia and by the end of the week all these three vital places were firmly in German hands. Their flank thus safe StG3 was shuttled via Crete to Rhodes and turned on the small British garrisons on Leros, Cos and Samos to the north of them, and also started to operate against the British and Greek warships which were these troops only links with Middle East Command in Egypt.

Continuous attacks by Ju88s resulted in the elimination of the only Spitfire squadrons available for local defence at Cos Island and the sinking by LG1 of the destroyer *Queen Olga* (Greek) and *Intrepid* off Leros on 26 September was but a portent of what was to come. The only opposition the Ju87s now faced in the air was from long-range Beaufighters operating from Cyprus and, for a short period only, until they were withdrawn on orders from Eisenhower, USAAF Lightnings from North African bases.

Rhodes had been secured by the Germans from the numerically superior

Italian forces on 12 September and the whole of SG3, with about sixty Ju87Ds was quickly established there. On 3 and 4 October the Germans invaded and took Cos, over half the Luftwaffe sorties flown in support of this invasion were by the Stukas, which yet again proved the decisive factor in breaking all resistance.

SG3 now concentrated on the Royal Navy ships attempting to supply and reinforce the surviving garrisons. On 7 October Ju87s scored direct hits on the cruiser *Penelope,* and, although one of the 1,100lb SAP bombs failed to explode correctly, the others damaged her very severely. Two days later the Ju87s again penetrated a gap in the fighter cover and hit the cruiser *Carlisle* with a heavy bomb aft. Although she struggled back to Alexandria she was a write-off. In the same attack the destroyer *Panther* took a heavy bomb amidships, broke in half and sank with heavy casualties. When the USAAF Lightnings finally arrived they chased the smaller dive bombers back to Rhodes and subsequently claimed to have destroyed no less than fifteen of them, with another three claimed shot down by ship's gunfire. These figures are still repeated in books today, but German records clearly show at the time that only half that number failed to return. These losses also failed to prevent SG3 meting out similar punishment to subsequent naval squadrons that believed such figures.

On 17 October for example the cruiser *Sirius* was hit by a heavy bomb in an attack by the Ju88s of LG1 and limped back to port. The Ju87s sank the motor launches *ML563* and *ML835* in Leros harbour on 17 October and the supply ship *Taganrog* at Samos on 24th. On 28 October they caught the landing ship *LCT115* carrying guns and troops off Castelrosso and sank her, while the same Stukas dive bombed the cruiser *Aurora* on the last day of October and put a heavy bomb into her which killed forty-six of her crew, wounded twenty more and wrecked her AA guns, directors and radars. They also scored a hit on the destroyer *Belvoir* which badly damaged her.

Preparations were then made to take the last remaining Allied held island, Samos. But before the Germans landed the bulk of the British garrison was evacuated through 'neutral' Turkey and, after a heavy dive bombing attack by II/SG3 on Tigani on 22 November, Samos fell, leaving the whole of the Balkans firmly in German hands.

Table 37: Basic Details of the Six Main Dive Bombers in Combat Service 1942-5						
Aircraft	SB2C-1 Helldiver	D4Y 'Judy'	Vengeance II	Ju87D	Pe-2	Barracuda
Country	USA	Japan	USA	Germany	USSR	Britain
Engine (hp)	1 x 1,700	1 x 1,010	1 x 1,700	1 x 1,415	2 x 1,100	1 x 1,640
Span (ft/in)	49'8¾"	37'8¾"	48'	49'2"	56'3"	49'2"
Length (ft/in)	36'7"	33'6⅜"	40'	37'8"	40'10"	39'9"
Height (ft/in)	14'9"	12'3¼"	15'	12'9"	13'1"	15'1"
Max Speed (mph)	285	343	279	255	361	228
Weight (lb)	10,114	5,379	12,480	8,600	13,119	9,350
Ceiling (ft)	23,000	32,480	24,300	24,200	29,500	16,600
Range (miles)	695	978	700	500	1,100	686
No of Bombs	1	1	4	1	4	1
Bomb Load (lb)	1,000	1,100	2,000	3,960	2,205	1,800
Crew	2	2	2	2	3	3
Designed Base	Carrier	Carrier	Land	Land	Land	Carrier

21 THE SECRET SUCCESS

The Far East: Allied operations and Vengeance missions, 1942-44

At the end of 1942 dive bombers again dominated the scene in all areas of the Far East. USAAF A24s dive bombed Japanese Navy airfields in the Lae and Salamaua area during April 1942, aided by Kittyhawks. In July they were withdrawn following the heavy losses of the 29th. But USAAF P40s from Darwin were flown into airstrips in New Guinea and began dive bombing with two 300lb bombs under either wing. They attacked targets in the Buna area and were joined by RAAF Wirraways using two 250lb bombs for dive bombing, from September onward. A third RAAF Vengeance squadron was formed by the end of 1943 and, based in New Guinea, undertook missions in the Nadzab area, operating in strengths of up to thirty-six aircraft and using standard RAF Vengeance tactics as perfected in Burma. Over the six-week campaign they proved invaluable.

The small Royal New Zealand air force underwent considerable expansion in 1942-3 but the first dive bomber unit was not established until July 1943, when eighteen SBDs were transferred to No 25 Squadron at Seagrove. This unit was brought up to full strength from its SBD3s by the purchase of twenty-seven SBD4s later in the same year, and training commenced in their usage at Santo airstrip in the New Hebrides. In March 1944, No 25 Squadron was modernised by the arrival of twenty-three SBD5s and it then embarked for Bougainville and combat service. The airstrip was under continual shellfire from the Japanese attack when the leading elements flew in, and no sooner had the SBDs landed than they were thrown into action against artillery and other targets.

Later they also operated against targets in New Britain with Australian Boomerang fighters, also equipped as light dive bombers with 500lb and 1,000lb

Trainee pilots from Laverton RAAF base practice the 'peel off' for dive bombing attacks in their Wirraways, February 1943.

bombs, with great success against isolated Japanese garrisons, before finally disbanding in May 1944.

In the RAF following the initial operations by the Vengeance aircraft of 168 Wing in November 1942, and the Arakan operations of March to July 1943, the lessons absorbed, plus the consideration of operating in even larger formations in the future, led to the issuing of a Tactical Memorandum on future employment. It was a valuable document in which to find details of the tactics adopted by the RAF's only dive bombers for the late 1943 offensive, the Japanese counter-blow and the extensive dive bomber operations that continued in Burma up to June 1944.

The RAF equipped with the Vultee A-31 in late 1942 and used it in combat in Burma with great success. Named the Vengeance AN889 is seen here over the English countryside.

Based on earlier operations, plus considerable training programmes and trials, it was anticipated that the four Vengeance Squadrons being employed would have to conduct two types of operations: predetermined operations against known targets and direct support operations with the Army, with the squadrons on call through Air Support Control organisation.

In the first type the operation assumed the form of any normal bomber sortie with the take-off time well known in advance, but in the second the squadrons, or parts of squadrons, adopted various states of readiness after the manner of fighter units. As usual, the main factor in such jungle versions of the 'Cab Rank' system was the rapid take-off times achieved after the receipt of the call through the ASC. It was anticipated that, in the earliest state, the aircraft could be airborne after a briefing in fifteen to twenty minutes. Naturally this time varied according to the local conditions, liason with fighter cover, etc, and about thirty minutes was the time recommended from receipt of call.

Another factor vital to the efficiency of the direct support given was the turn-round factor between sorties, which limited the actual number of sorties per aircraft. About forty-five minutes was the estimated turn-round time for the Vengeance to refuel, re-arm and turn round six aircraft, and two hours for twelve.

For army support operations of this nature the stand-by crews were briefed by the Intelligence Officer and the Army Liaison Officer as the information on his battle zone allocated target came through, so that they were up-to-date on the general situation before a specific mission request came in from the front line, which saved considerable time at the main briefing. Meanwhile their aircraft were standing bombed-up and ready to go near the down-wind end of the   179 airstrip. In the forward areas the aircraft were kept at readiness throughout the hours of daylight, so that they could scramble away in the event of hostile bombing attacks.

There were three types of basic attack: (1) High dive, (2) Shallow dive and (3) Low level. Although it was stated that the Vengeance could obtain considerable accuracy, by method 2, it was also made quite clear that *better* results could be obtained from traditional dive bombing as in 1. Shallow dive bombing was more of a useful alternative should weather conditions over the target consist of low cloud. Method 3 was also rejected as a suitable Vengeance tactic because: 'In level flight the forward visibility is extremely poor owing to the high nose of the aircraft.'

It was necessary to approach the target from a turn off from a shallow dive. This left the Vengeance as an extremely vulnerable target to forward enemy flak positions, to which it could not reply. 'This type of attack can be better carried out by a more suitable type of aircraft, ie a Hurribomber', as it was not true dive bombing.

Method 1 was therefore adopted as the principal Vengeance tactic, as the American, and earlier British reports, had already stated over the years that it should be. 'A high degree of accuracy can be obtained in this type of bombing and this is the aircraft's primary role', the memo was forced to emphasise.

The bomb load continued to be as earlier: two 500lb bombs or four 250lb bombs carried under the wings in external racks. This load could be released in salvo or sticks, but the main bomb load was carried internally. With dive bombing the bombs were released in salvo, so that they fell in a very concentrated cluster. Thus, again, actual combat experience proved that theory and pre-war practice and claims, were false. A reasonable stick could be achieved by releasing in the pull-out from a high diving attack if required, the spacing of the bombs being dependent on the rate of pull-out: 'From a normal pilot a stick of four bombs will cover about 150yd.'

The final verdict was: 'The Vengeance should be used against small and precise targets where accuracy is essential — while stick and spread bombing for area targets should be undertaken by level bombing aircraft.' Quite so!

The Vengeance took over all such duties and operated with fighter cover save when there was sufficient cloud. Take-off and forming-up procedure was that each dive bomber took off singly at 500yd intervals when using a good runway. The leader flew straight after taking off for about forty-five seconds and then started a gentle left-hand turn, as the others joined.

When he was satisfied that he had all his formation together he steepened his turn and set course straight away for the target zone. From first take off to setting the course by the formation was about seven minutes. Meanwhile the fighter escort took off after the bombers under their own arrangements and it was left to the fighter leader to locate and take station on the bombers, which was easy enough when operating from the same airfield as indicated in the diagram. Rendezvous over a particular landmark was effected otherwise.

The Vengeance leader climbed at 140mph to between 6,000 and 7,000ft and, thereafter at 135mph to 10,000ft or up to a normal ceiling of 15,000ft. For the flight to the target the cruising speed was 155-160mph. The formation adopted depended as always on the number of aircraft employed, but the 'box in line astern' was the most favoured. For six aircraft two vics in 'line astern stepped down' was used. For eight aircraft the formation was two boxes of four and for nine aircraft three vics in 'line astern stepped down'. With increasing numbers of dive bombers being deployed for the new offensive even larger formations were considered, but these were thought unwieldy.

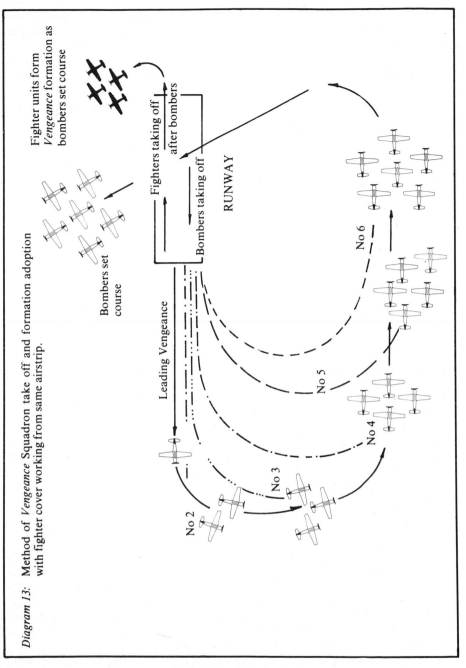

Diagram 13: Method of *Vengeance* Squadron take off and formation adoption with fighter cover working from same airstrip.

Instead it was deemed advantageous to split the formation up into two sub-formations. With twelve aircraft two boxes of six were used, the second flying *en echelon* to the first and stepped down. Trials were conducted with more spread out formations, such as squadron vic but it was rejected as little supporting fire could be given and it was thought that: '. . . the concentration of fire power provided in the box type of formation is considered more desirable.'

In the recommended schemes for operations against naval targets (which in the event did not materialise), navigation duties were laid down in some detail.

The navigator was to fly in the leader's aircraft and it was recommended that he should also be trained in fire control — if not a separate fire controller was to be carried in the deputy leader's aircraft in the second vic or four of the leading sub-formation.

For land operations the same principle applied, but it was felt at that time that the introduction of VHF and the limited range of the Vengeance meant that such sorties would only involve pilot navigation and that therefore squadrons would use a gunnery leader, flying the leading aircraft as fire controller. Some squadrons preferred this method anyway and it was duly noted that: 'This is considered a domestic problem and is left to the individual tastes of each squadron with Wing standing aside.'

It was freely admitted that evasive action was not easily affected against determined fighter attack. The usual methods of evasion, turning, undulation, corkscrewing etc, were to be employed and so was the old Stuka tactic.

> Shallow diving had been found effective against Hurricanes in tests. When diving at an angle of 25^0, indicated air speeds of about 260mph can be held. At this speed the Hurricane has a relatively higher speed of only about 20mph over the Vengeance formation. This enables the bomber to make good ground towards the target and may well enable them to carry out their attack before being engaged by fighters. The approach to the target is made at a height considerably above the bombing height (10,000ft), to enable this form of evasion to be used. Ample warning of an impending attack is desirable for the success of this manoeuvre.

This of course was just whistling on the wind, for the sort of opposition a hotted up 'Zero' and 'Tojo' fighter could offer was hardly to be compared with a Hurricane, and it is left to the imagination as to what degree of early warning the obliging Japanese fighter pilots would give. It was just as well perhaps that this was never put to the test. Indeed it was readily admitted that:

> In the event of the formation being seriously jumped and it is found necessary to abandon the operation, the formation should dive to ground level, if necessary jettisoning bombs, relying for evasion on their low altitude and concentration of fire power. Little is to be gained by opening dive brakes as large formations cannot dive steeply and it is almost impossible for aircraft in formation to extend brakes in unison.

However it was further noted that *individual* aircraft diving away from an enemy interceptor could employ their dive brakes in the old Stuka manner to cause their pursuer to overshoot. A note of warning was added for this was an old trick now: 'It is however the opinion of fighter pilots who have experienced these tactics, that the wary pursuer will anticipate this action and will rather wait to catch the Vengeance after he had pulled out of the dive.'

When the formation approached the target zone it lost height down to around 10,000ft at the point of the attack. About a minute (or less) before the dive position was reached, the leader gave a pre-arranged signal, usually by opening the bomb doors. The pilot's procedure was then to open bomb doors, fuse and select bombs, put all petrol switches on, engage low blower, rich mixture and put rudder trim in neutral.

Sections then took up echelon formation in line astern, open formation. In order to keep position within the optimum diving cone it was laid down that not more than four aircraft were to be in echelon. The rear sub-formation followed in line astern of the leader, who approached the target in a wide sweep to one target and then turned in towards it. This manoeuver enabled each pilot to keep the objective in view to one side of the aircraft's nose and, incidently, give a little throw-off to the flak predictors.

The leader allowed the target to disappear under the leading edge of the wing and, after about ten seconds, did a wing-over and dived 'at an angle of 80° *or more steeply',* and opened his dive brakes as he commenced the dive. The others followed him down at intervals of about 500ft in succession. No straffing was done on the way down, as 'front guns are not effective in the dive and are dangerous to the aircraft in front.'

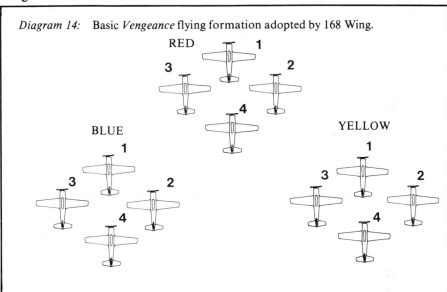

Diagram 14: Basic *Vengeance* flying formation adopted by 168 Wing.

Diagram 15: Showing Sequence and Direction of Vengeance attack

Planes attack from sun if possible

The bombs were released at about 3,000ft and the pull-out was effected below 1,000ft. While the Vengeance aircraft were carrying out the actual bombing their own fighter cover maintained visual contact. For the getaway and to form up for the return flight the Vengeance depended on its speed and turning to avoid the worst areas of AA fire. In order to reform quickly the following aircraft had to close their dive brakes earlier in the last part of the dive than did the leader, so that he did not have to throttle back for them to catch up, thereby exposing his own aircraft to unnecessary damage. As each aircraft came out of its dive in a different direction a distant rendezvous spot was selected, in the same general area well away from the target, and in the case of the Vengeance this had to be pre-determined.

Once assembled the Vengeance aircraft formed up in vics of three (or boxes of four if there were only eight aircraft) to enable them to concentrate their defences in the recognised way, and at low level. This return was taken at 190mph with the nose well down, giving a good vantage point in which to take stock of the land contours to give natural cover, as per the textbook.

For shallow dive bombing attacks, if needed, the formation took advantage of the cloud cover to the target area and the attack was carried out from the cloud base to 1,500ft or lower. With light defences working against them this type of attack could be well pressed home down to bomb fragmentation height. On sighting the target the leader would put the whole formation into echelon and approach the target well to one side, as in high bombing. A turn of 45⁰ would be made to the target and the dive commenced at up to 60⁰ with getaway at ground level.

Much of the outstanding success achieved by 168 Wing in 1942-4 was due to the enthusiasm and completeness with which the new tactics were worked out in the period before the campaign opened. Despite the fact that they were a unique formation in the RAF's line of battle, and an embarrassment to their senior leaders because of their successfulness and fighting on a front the press always ignored, or perhaps *because* of these handicaps, 168 made every effort to

Dianne, *a Vengeance of No 12 Squadron, RAAF, piloted by Flt/Lt C.J. McPherson over Merauke, Dutch New Guinea, on 23 December 1943.*

produce plans, almost from scratch, that covered every aspect of their operations. In the event, these worked out in combat with only slight modifications *and* with *zero* losses. This was such a contrast to the gloomy forecasts of the preceeding twenty years that they are worthy of examination before they are completely forgotten.

No 110 Squadron was the main workhorse for these trials and tests, which translated theory into trial, and trial into combat results in the space of six months. By the end of that period the six most experienced pilots were attaining an average error of about 40yd (sometimes from single dives and sometimes from vic dives), after an average flying time in the Vengeance aircraft of 50 hours.

It was found that the ideal dive was from approximately 10,000ft to around 4,000ft as this allowed the pilot to go into a sufficiently steep dive, and to remain in it for a long enough time to get an accurate sight, release his bombs and pull out with a reasonable margin of safety. It was thought that this could be extended down to 2,000ft in some cases, but if the pull-out was left later than this the crew were likely to experience 'rather a high "G" '.

The terminal velocity with the dive brakes extended and one-third throttle was approximately 320mph at 90^0 and 290mph at 75^0. As the mainplanes on the Vengeance had no incidence the angle between the datum line of the aircraft and the actual line of flight was nil at 90^0 and negligible at 75^0. Pilots, as always, had to judge the trial angle of the bomb, which varied with the steepness of the dive, as explained earlier.

The suggestion that the German method of painting lines on the cockpit cover to represent the angles was rejected *without trial*. The reason given for this was that: 'The pilot must concentrate on looking at the target and the nose of the aircraft, and when his head is in a correct position for this, lines of 60^0 and 75^0 on the cockpit are outside his vision. To raise the head to look at them during the dive would interfere with the sighting and would also be physically difficult. The angle of 45^0 is not sufficiently steep and would merely confuse the pilot.'

It was found that heights of bomb release could be read from altimeters as the instrument lag was negligible compared with the speed of descent, or in other words, 'pilots do not worry about 100ft or so when approaching the ground at more than 400ft per second.'.

The report ended uncompromisingly: 'With regard to the Memorandum of the Role of the Vengeance, this is an attempt to establish the policy that the use of this aircraft should be confined as far as possible to the role for which it was designed, and in which it is effective, viz: dive bombing, *and not frittered away on odd jobs for which it is unsuitable.*'

It is doubtful whether this had any effect on Whitehall however, still bedazzled as they were by the 'thousand bomber' raids against civilian targets, for precision was not an argument to win over such men. It is significant that the words used by the young RAF dive bomber pilots in 1943 were almost exactly the same as the epitaph written for the Navy's Blackburn Skua three years earlier, another fine dive bomber which had been 'frittered away' pretending to be a fighter!

The Solomon Islands were still the hot-bed of the Pacific War at the beginning of 1943, for although the Japanese had pulled out of Guadalcanal in defeat they had no intentions of giving up the whole area and from their base at Rabaul they continued to sustain other island garrisons in the face of increasing American pressure. Again it was 'Val' and Dauntless aircraft that were used. The gradual introduction in the Marine Wings of the fighter dive bombers followed developments elsewhere, especially in regard to the powerful Chance-Vought Corsair. Japanese dive bombers found it increasingly impossible to infiltrate the huge AA screens surrounding the US Task Forces and more and more were reduced to suicide attacks. The final battles saw the Helldiver come into its own and the remnants of the Japanese fleet were destroyed in a whole series of battles and attacks. Finally the Royal Navy made a brief re-appearance in Far Eastern waters, but still without a satisfactory dive bomber of its own, it was forced to use an American torpedo bomber in the dive bombing role, and later used fighter adaptations.

The destroyers of the 'Tokyo Express' continued to suffer at the hands of the SBDs in early 1943 in the Solomons. On 2 January Marine Dauntless dive bombers damaged the *Suzukaze* in the 'Slot' and on the 15th fifteen SBDs were destroyed in return by the Japanese destroyers *Arashi, Hamakaze, Tanikaze* and *Urakaze* which escaped unscathed.

On 23 January *Saratoga* launched twenty-four SBDs in a attack on Vila airstrip on Kolombangara Island. Twenty Japanese destroyers conducted an evacuation run to Guadalcanal. They were attacked by seventeen Marine SBDs at 1820 on 1 February, which damaged the *Makinami*. A return strike by 'Vals' from Rabaul damaged the American destroyers *De Haven* and *Nicholas*. A night attack by the Henderson Field Dauntless team failed to score any further hits, nor did another attack the day after.

On 7 April 1943, Yamamato launched operation I-Go, a series of heavy attacks against US airfields in the region in an attempt to pre-empt further attacks. Many 'Vals' were employed including many landed from carriers and operational from land strips. Despite the size of the effort the Japanese lost twice as many aircraft as they themselves destroyed and many precious D3A1s and their highly-trained crews were thrown away. The empty carriers had to withdraw to replenish with new aircraft and fresh aircrews and the 'Val' almost vanished from the south-west Pacific for a time.

In the New Georgia campaign Marine Air Groups developed close support techniques to a high degree, with Air Liaison Parties under Maj Wilfred Stiles. On 1 August 1943 and again on 25 August, heavy dive bombing attacks by SBDs and Avengers swung the battle against the Japanese. When fresh waves of 'Vals' were again sent in from the ships of Adm Koga's fleet in November against Bouganville, they again suffered a bloody nose, some 75 per cent being destroyed and they again had to be pulled out for further replenishment.

By December Marine Air Wing Four was operating from Tarawa in the Gilbert Islands and in March 1944 moved on to Kwajalin. Their targets were Japanese positions and guns in place on the islands of Jauluit, Manoelap, Mili and Wotje as well as airfields. The units employed included VMSB151, VMSB241, VMSB331 and VMSB341, and these were joined by the famous 'Ace of Spades' squadron, VMSB231, which was commanded by a real dive bomber ace, Marine pilot Elmer Glidden. They were all equipped with SBDs, but during 1944 many changed over to the Corsair which proved itself a formidable dive bomber.

It was first used in this role on 18 March 1944, by VMF111 who dive bombed AA guns on Mille with 1,000lb bombs. Earlier VF17, a US Navy unit, had experimented with the same aircraft, both Navy and Marine pilots using improvised bomb racks. Subsequent experiments revealed that the Chance Vought F4U Corsair could be safely and efficiently employed as a dive bomber in dives of up to 85⁰. The plane's six .5in calibre guns were used for straffing in the latter stages of the dive. In fact the incredible Corsair could eventually be employed to lift *twice* the bomb load of the specially-designed Dauntless.

Back to base. These SBD's have deposited their bomb loads on Japanese positions around Rabaul and are homeward bound for their bases after a strike made on 13 April, 1944

At sea the carrier-based dive bombers were still roaming across the Pacific. On 5 November 1943, the SBDs from *Saratoga* and *Princeton* decimated a Japanese cruiser squadron at anchor at Rabaul. Twenty-two SBDs were included in that strike mission, and several were lost, but the carnage they inflicted was enormous. The heavy cruiser *Maya* was hit in the engine room, the *Mogami* was seriously damaged, *Atago* was near missed by bombs, as was *Takao* and was taking water. The light cruisers *Agano* and *Noshiro* were both hit by bombs and the destroyer *Wakatsuki* also badly damaged. The crippled squadron limped back to Truk in the Caroline Islands to repair and when the new Helldivers of VB17 made their debut over Rabaul on 11 November, they found few targets. The SB2Cs of VB17 were led by Lt Cdr J.E. 'Moe' Vose who had flown SBDs at Midway and Santa Cruz. Now he led the first strike of its replacement. Twenty-three Helldivers took part in this raid from the carrier *Bunker Hill,* along with those from the light carrier *Independence* and SBDs of VB9 from the *Essex.* They sank the destroyer *Suzunami.*

If the Japanese ships had gone their aircraft had not, for on the airfields were   187 some 270 aircraft, 100 of which had been flown in from the fleet's carriers. With these the Japanese launched counter-attacks against the US Task Force and caught them with their decks full. Twenty-seven 'Vals' were included in this formation, but they were annihilated by defending fighters and AA fire and not a single hit was scored by the Japanese dive bombers on this target. Again battered and depleted the 'Vals' withdrew.

On 25 December VB17 attacked the Japanese base at Kavieng in New Ireland, sinking a freighter and two minesweepers, and on 1 January 1944 the same unit dive bombed a Japanese cruiser squadron in the same area, damaging the *Oyodo, Noshiro* again, and the destroyer *Yamagumo*. Aircraft from the carrier *Monterey* also participated in this action.

The next major action was a heavy dive bomber strike on the main Japanese base of Truk in the Carolines which took place on 17 and 18 February 1944. Dauntless dive bombers flew from the *Essex* and *Yorktown* in this raid, but they were now in a minority and Helldivers operated from the *Enterprise, Intrepid, Belleau Wood, Cabot, Bunker Hill, Cowpens* and *Monterey*. In the two-day period US Navy aircraft from the nine carriers flew a total of 1,250 sorties and the Japanese lost the cruiser *Naka*, destroyers *Fumitsuka* and *Oite*, four auxillaries, six tankers and seventeen freighters as well as 250 aircraft, mainly fighters.

Among the few Japanese dive bombers operational against this mighty array were some Seusei's making their operational debut as a dive bomber, but they could achieve nothing. On 30 March twelve SBDs from *Enterprise* dive bombed the old destroyer *Wakatake* at Palau, sinking her with two direct hits, at the cost of two aircraft. *Satatoga's* SBDs helped patrol the Marshall Islands but saw no action.

A graphic account of one of the Helldiver attacks on Truk was given by Robert Olds in his book *Helldiver Squadron*, written with typical American style:

> Just west of Uman Island, the formation broke up. Helldivers, their wing guns flaming, dive on the merchant ship anchorage. Jeff picked out an 8,000-ton

The trim, pleasing lines of the Judy, the Yokosuka, D4Y, a dive bomber of great promise that never fulfilled its expectations because it arrived too late.

cargo ship. Three others followed. Jeff or Cliff made the hit which went through the forward deck and exploded below. A few miles further north Gus DeVoe and Tee-Square Thomas picked out a merchant ship of 4,000 tons. Their high explosives touched off a rumbling explosion. Fire broke out all over the AK. A large 500ft merchantman of about 10,000 tons rode at anchor south-west of the island. The Gedunker brought his section screaming down as a fan of Avengers approached across the water. When his Helldiver reached 800ft, Bob squeezed the bomb release and pulled out of his dive. Uman Island was dead ahead. Bob felt the dull 'crump' that followed a hit. 'Bullseye!' sang out Gene O'Brien. 'It burst on the bridge, Mister Friesz.'

The Battle of the Philippine Sea in June 1944, was the largest carrier-to-carrier duel in history. Re-building their shattered air arm the Japanese assembled a fleet under Adm Jizaburo Ozawa with no less than nine aircraft carriers, six of which had dive bombers embarked: *Shokaku, Taiho* and *Zuikaku* with a total of eighty-one 'Judys' plus nine reconnaissance version, and *Hiyo, Junyo* and *Ryuho* which had a total of twenty-seven 'Vals' aboard, plus nine 'Judy' reconnaissance aircraft. The remaining three Japanese carriers did not have dive bombers among their aircraft complements due to the high losses sustained earlier.

They were opposed by Adm Marc Mitscher who had no less than fifteen fleet and light fleet carriers. Of these the faithful old SBD equipped but two units, VB10 aboard *Enterprise* and VB16 aboard the new *Lexington,* with totals of twenty-three and thirty-four aircraft respectively. Helldivers now predominated, equipping the dive bomber units of the new *Hornet, Yorktown, Wasp, Essex,* and *Bunker Hill.*

Four waves of attackers were sent off the Japanese carriers at 0830 on 20 June, out of range of the Americans. Included in the total of 372 planes were most of the dive bombers. They were intercepted far from the American fleet by no less than 450 American fighters and completely wiped out. Only a few aircraft managed to break through this mass of interceptors to make attacks on the Task Forces, and here an enormous AA barrage (larger than for the whole of the United Kingdom), awaited them. Only one hit was made, while the battleship *Indiana* and the carrier *Bunker Hill* were both near-missed. At a cost of only twenty-nine fighters the Americans destroyed 242 of the Japanese aircraft and this carnage was given the appropriate title of 'The Great Marianas Turkey Shoot'.

On the evening of the 20th the return American strike was sent off at extreme range in the gathering darkness. They caught the Japanese fleet refuelling and with only twenty-five fighters and twenty bombers left on their decks. 216 US aircraft attacked, twenty being shot down. *Lexington* launched fifteen SBDs and *Enterprise* twelve, led by Lt Cdr Ralph Weymouth and Cdr James D. Ramage. Despite being almost unopposed the only Japanese ships sunk were the carrier *Hiyo* and two refuelling tankers, although the carriers *Zuikaku* and *Chiyoda,* the battleship *Haruna* and the heavy cruiser *Maya* took bomb hits and were damaged. US submarines sank other ships.

This battle marked the end of the dive bombing era at sea for the Japanese, for almost all their aircraft of this type were wiped out and they only reappeared in small numbers as true dive bombers as distinct from *kamikazes.* On the American side the last SBDs were phased out after this action, although the Marine Corps flyers were still using them with good effect in the coming campaigns ashore. More and more though, at sea in the Pacific as well as ashore in Africa, the merging of the fighter bomber type and the true dive bomber was coming about. Conversely the dive bombing technique itself was becoming even more accepted and widespread in its application.

In the Fleet Air Arm the Grumman TBF torpedo bomber had made considerable impact, its spacious weapons bay being capable of lifting internally a 1,000lb bomb with no difficulty. As suitable torpedo bomber targets dwindled in numbers, it was employed increasingly as a shallow dive bomber, by the US Marines in the Pacific, but more spectacularly by the Royal Navy in the latter stages of the Pacific War.

Over 1,000 of these were taken over by the Royal Navy, the first joining No 832 Squadron on 1 January 1943. By the war's end some fifteen FAA squadrons were flying Avengers. The most outstanding of its operations were the attacks made by the British Pacific Fleet carriers *Illustrious, Indefatigable, Indomitable* and *Victorious* against the oil refineries of Pladjoe and Songei Gerng near Palembang in Sumatra on 24 and 29 January 1945. For the loss of four Avengers the plants were heavily hit, the planes dive bombing through a balloon barrage and in the face of strong fighter opposition, and inflicting grave damage on both plants.

After the Japanese Naval Air Arm had been decimated in the Battle of the Philippine Sea in June 1944, the next American target was the Philippines themselves. The Japanese were prepared to throw in all their remaining fleet to stop this objective being taken, as they would be cut off from their oil supplies. But this meant that their own carriers, with no planes to embark, had only one role, that of an elaborate decoy force to draw away the American carriers and battleships and thus allow the Japanese battleships to slip through and annihilate the American invasion convoy, and the thousands of troops on the beach-head.

Accordingly the plan was put into effect and while three separate, but powerful, surface fleets made their way to the attack, Vice Adm Ozawa sortied with the carriers *Chitose, Chiyoda, Zuiho* and *Zuikaku,* the hybrid battleship/ carriers *Hyuga* and *Ise* and light forces. On 24 October these ships launched a pitiful air striking force of twenty-three bombers and thirty fighters, followed

Loading drop tanks on SB2C Helldivers aboard the USS Lexington (II) *before a search mission during the Battle of Leyte Gulf, 25 October 1944.*

later by a second, smaller force, from *Zuikaku* only, and waited for the Americans to take the bait.

The fate of the aircraft from these decoy carriers was predictable, for they failed to penetrate the enormous fighter and AA defences of the three US Task Forces off Leyte, which consisted of twelve carriers, six battleships, nine cruisers and forty-three destroyers. So the carrier strikes and the land-based Japanese air attacks which co-ordinated their efforts, caused little or no damage. Only twenty-five Japanese aircraft survived from the seventy-six launched from the carriers and these, which included only eight D4Y 'Judy' dive bombers, landed on Luzon afterwards.

Meanwhile the American carriers had been launching massive air strikes at the oncoming Japanese battleship forces. The first wave, which included twelve Helldivers, scored one bomb and one torpedo hit on the giant battleship *Musashi* in the Sibuyan Sea on the 24th. These Helldivers came from *Intrepid* and *Cabot* who were closest to the enemy, and a second force was sent off from the same two ships which again included twelve Helldivers, and they scored four more bomb and torpedo hits on the same ship. A third wave, from the *Essex* and *Lexington*, with twenty SB2Cs, scored a further four bomb hits on *Musashi* and two on *Yamato*, as well as further torpedo hits on the former. A further thirty-three Helldivers from *Enterprise*, *Cabot*, *Franklin* and *Intrepid*, hit the *Musashi* again and again until she finally rolled over and sank and taking six torpedoes and ten bombs.

Despite the great surface battle that night, when six old US battleships pulverised two of the other Japanese forces, this main Japanese fleet, mistakenly thought to have been turned back after the loss of *Mushashi*, had in fact pressed on without further hindrance and at dawn fell in with a small escort carrier force which had been supporting the troops ashore. Fortunately for the Americans of this group the Japanese Admiral, Kurita, mistook at long range the little 'jeep' carriers for fleet carriers. He only attacked half-heartedly before calling off the

Covering the Philippines invasion a SB2C Helldiver is launched from the USS Hancock on 25 November 1944, for a strike on Manila Bay.

operation and withdrawing, even though he was almost in gun range of his main objective, the helpless armada of transports and landing ships which he could easily have annihilated. He thus missed a great chance of a smashing victory.

Meanwhile the main US fleet had fallen for Ozawa's decoy trap and had sped off to the north to engage. Heavy air strikes were sent in against Ozawa's empty carriers off Cape Engano on 25 October, a total of 326 Helldiver and Avenger sorties being made escorted by 201 Hellcat fighter sorties, in six massive waves.

They hit and sank all four carriers and a destroyer, the two battleships and the other escorts having done their job of sacrifice escaped. But it was all in vain and the American conquest of the Philippines continued.

The small force of 'Judy' and 'Val' dive bombers on hand to the Japanese in the Philippines when the Americans invaded in October 1944, were soon annihilated on the ground or in the air in near-suicidal missions. One of the most notable Japanese dive bomber sorties was by thirteen 'Judys' from Nichols Field, led by Rear Adm Masafumi Arima of the 26th Air Flotilla. They attacked the huge US Task Force on 15 October and were set upon and destroyed by the CAP of Hellcats before they could reach the ships. Arima, seeing the useless sacrifice of all his young dive bomber pilots, decided to sell his own life more dearly. He put his machine into a screaming dive against the aircraft carrier *Franklin,* appearing suddenly out of thick cloud. The heavy AA fire from the target and the massed escorts caught him in a cone of fire on the way down, hitting him hard enough to deflect his aircraft off course. The dive bomber plunged into the sea hard alongside the carrier, one wing landing on the ship's flight deck. From then on true dive bomber missions became more rare and the *kamikaze* attack took over, utilising not just dive bomber types but any kind of aircraft which could fly and carry high explosives to the US warships on one-way missions.

Once the American troops were firmly established ashore the US Marine Air Groups quickly followed into the newly liberated airfields to provide close support, many still flying the faithful SBD. With their ground-attack methods perfected from their many previous campaigns these units gave the Army invaluable assistance in the protracted period of surface fighting in the islands and the mopping-up operations which continued until the very end of the war.

The reason that the Marines were called upon to support the Army in this manner was that, despite all the experiments and combat experience, the USAAF was still not fully convinced of the value of tactical air support. Typical of their attitude to the subject was this judgement, given in July 1943: 'In the zone of contact, missions against hostile units are most difficult to control, are most expensive, and are, in general, least effective. Targets are small, well-dispersed and difficult to locate. In addition, there is always a considerable chance of striking friendly forces . . . .'

The US Marines however had worked hard at overcoming these problems and thus when, on 10 October 1944, Col H. Meyer, informed MAG24 that they had been given the job of army support in the Philippines, the Marine flyers, then at Bougainville, quickly and enthusiastically organised an intensive course under the direction of Lt Col Keith B. McCutcheon, their Operations Officer. All the doctrines and procedures of this type of operation were assembled and closely studied. A course of forty lectures was given, after being researched, printed and organised in three days. With MAG32 joining MAG42 for this operation, some 500 officers and gunners of the dive bomber squadrons were put through this detailed resume.

The basic guidelines for the subsequent operations were laid out by Lt Col McCutcheon in his personal monograph, which laid down that it was always to be a system to be used at the discretion of the ground commander, '. . . against targets that cannot be reached by his weapons or in conjunction with the ground weapons in a co-ordinated attack. Close support should be immediately available and should be carried out deliberately, accurately and in co-ordination with other assigned units.' This monograph, *Close Support Aviation,* was to become their textbook in the subsequent perfection of that technique.

During the Lingayen landings in January 1945, the Marine SBD squadrons cut their teeth, flying 255 sorties and dropping 104 tons of bombs for the loss of just one Dauntless and earning themselves an accolade from Maj Gen Mudge. During the capture of San Jose, north of Manila, the 1st Infantry had been badly smashed up by straffing from 'friendly' USAAF fighters, and took casualties which made them very reluctant to call on such 'help' again. But on 28 February they asked the Marine dive bombers to help in a particular tricky operation. The nine Dauntless aircraft made accurate attacks, the most inaccurate of the twenty-seven bombs dropped being only 30yd from the target spot! This impressed the soldiers so much that from then on nine flights of nine SBDs each were always on standby at the request of the regiment for operations. The Marine dive bombers had made their point.

While the SBD was thus flying its last highly-successful missions of the war the Helldivers with the fleet moved into the South China Sea and conducted a series of heavy strikes against targets at Saigon and Formosa, which wiped out the bulk of the Japanese aircraft based there as well as vital installations. During the dive bombing of Saigon on 12 January 1945, Helldivers from eleven US carriers sank four cargo ships, two oilers and the Vichy cruiser *Lamotte-Picquet,* as well as destroying the oil-storage tanks of the Caltex and Shell depots along the river front. The 300 tons of bombs used by the Helldivers to wipe out these targets in precision attacks contrasted well with the 3,000 tons dropped by B24s and B29s of the USAAF which followed. These hit a hospital, the British consulate and killed hundreds of civilians, a butcher's bill common enough to the heavy bomber in World War II, but one that did not subsequently endear the Americans to the French in the post-war period in that part of the world!

The landings on Okinawa that followed, provoked the Japanese Navy into launching one last surface ship sortie in a gigantic *kamikaze* operation against the US beach-head. The giant battleship *Yamato* (78,000 tons) with her nine 18.1in guns, was despatched, with her fuel tanks holding only enough oil to make a one-way trip, together with the light cruiser *Yahagi* and eight screening destroyers.

This force sailed from the Inland Sea on 6 April 1945 and next day was located and set upon by waves of carrier aircraft from the American fleet, some 386 sorties being flown, and ten aircraft lost. The Helldivers involved in the last great dive bombing battle at sea came from Bombing Squadrons 9, 10, 83 and 84.

VB83 approached the target from 6,000ft and circled the Japanese force at a range of six to ten miles, periodically under fire from the battleship's main armament. VB83 finally attacked the battleship at 1250 in conjunction with Avenger torpedo bombers from *Essex* and scored four hits.

VB84 attacked a destroyer of the screen and scored several hits, leaving their target dead in the water. Explosions followed which were witnessed by circling planes and shortly afterwards the destroyer, the *Hamakaze,* sank by the stern.

VB9 took the light cruiser *Yahagi* as their target and Lt Wolsey was shot down. The remaining Helldivers scored numerous hits and the cruiser blew up and sank at 1425.

The final dive bomber attacks were made by VB10 and again the battleship was the alloted target. They approached her from the east and although four

Table 39: US Marine SBD Communication Nets in the Philippines Operations 1944-5			
No	Title	Abbreviation	Description
1	Support Aircraft Direction	SAD	A channel linking ALP with the Support Aircraft Commander (SAC) and the airborne air co-ordinator
2	Support Aircraft Control	SAC	A channel linking the SAC, air co-ordinator and supporting aircraft by two-way channel
3	Support Aircraft Direction Emergency	SADE	An emergency channel linking ALPs with the supporting aircraft
4	Support Aircraft Observation	SAO	A two-way channel linking SAO with the airborne observers

aircraft were hit by AA fire most of their bombs were direct hits or near misses on the already crippled vessel. In total the *Yamato* was hit by four bombs in the first attack. The first two hit amidships on the starboard side, blowing two holes about twenty feet in diameter in the weather deck and destroying a heavy AA turret and several small AA mountings. Two other bombs hit aft of the secondary armament rear mounting, wiping it out with its entire crew, wrecking the directors and penetrating the upper armour deck. A fire was started that was never subsequently brought under control.

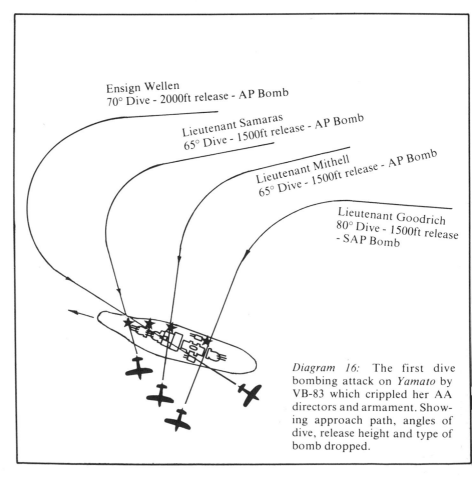

Ensign Wellen
70° Dive - 2000ft release - AP Bomb

Lieutenant Samaras
65° Dive - 1500ft release - AP Bomb

Lieutenant Mithell
65° Dive - 1500ft release - AP Bomb

Lieutenant Goodrich
80° Dive - 1500ft release
- SAP Bomb

Diagram 16: The first dive bombing attack on *Yamato* by VB-83 which crippled her AA directors and armament. Showing approach path, angles of dive, release height and type of bomb dropped.

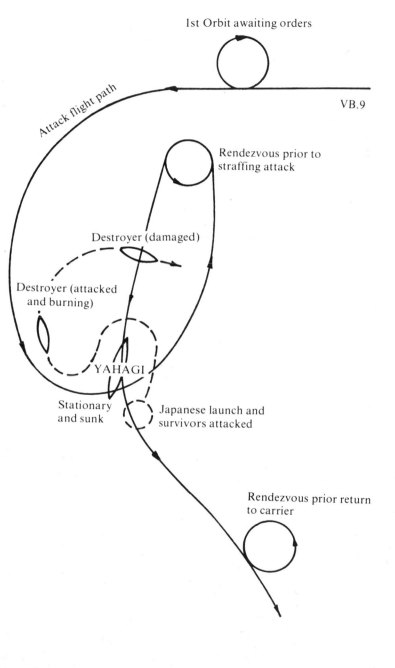

Diagram 17: VB-9's attack on the light cruiser *Yahagi* showing the flight path for all the stages of the attacks made

1st Orbit awaiting orders

Attack flight path

VB.9

Rendezvous prior to straffing attack

Destroyer (damaged)

Destroyer (attacked and burning)

YAHAGI

Stationary and sunk

Japanese launch and survivors attacked

Rendezvous prior return to carrier

Diagram 18: The attack by VB-9 on the *Yahagi* showing estimated number and the positions of bomb hits

★ = Direct Hits (Coded to Crews)   • = Near Misses (Coded to Crews)

Code to Pilots:
1 - Lt H.W. Worley
2 - Ensg J.J. Bell
3 - Ensg W.W. Bowers
4 - Lt T.F. Schneider
5 - Lt R.S. Ploss
6 - Lt J.W. Shreffier

7 - Lt L. Frewin
8 - Lt R.L. Verrall
9 - Ensg J. Greenwell
10 - Lt J.H. Durio
11 - Ensg W.H. Hanawalt
12 - Lt Martin
13 - Ensg W.H. Sigman

No bombs were admitted from the last attack, but there must have been many despite this for she was a sitting duck. Nonetheless only torpedo hits are credited in Japanese reports, the great ship taking eleven and possibly thirteen of these, a tally no ship could withstand, and she finally sank.

The battle resulted in the destruction of the *Yamato, Yahagi* and destroyers *Hamakaze, Isokaze, Asashimo* and *Kasumi,* leaving only four destroyers, three of them badly damaged, to return to Japan. It had cost the Japanese Navy 3,665 officers and men and the Americans just ten aircraft. Never again did the Japanese fleet venture out of its harbours — not that it had fuel enough to do so anyway.

The tasks remaining for the vast dive bomber forces of the US fleet, and those Avengers of the BPF that joined forces with them during the closing months, was the pounding of Japanese air bases, destruction of all merchant shipping at large and the wiping out of what remained of the Imperial Fleet as it lay at anchor impotent. In all this activity the dive bomber played a major role.

The carrier task forces roamed at will in Japanese home waters and the dive bombers and fighter bombers ranged up and down the coast in search of targets. Only a small handful of the once-powerful Japanese fleet remained afloat at the end of this period. Meanwhile the British Pacific Fleet had been blooded in its own actions against shore targets. The Avengers of the BPF earned further laurels during the Okinawa campaign when they pounded Japanese airfields and installations on the Sakishimi Gunto group of islands to prevent the Japanese flying in aerial reinforcements from Formosa.

Through the months of March and April 1945, the Avengers continued to crater runways and bomb AA positions, wearisome work with little reward. In

June Avengers from *Implacable* dive bombed Truk in the Carolines, but there was little left of value as targets — the tide of war had long since passed this fortress by. In July the British bombers took their place alongside the US Task Force 38 off mainland Japan and here more worthwhile targets were plentiful. Hellcats and Corsairs joined in the dive bombing with 500lb bombs. On 24 July the four British carriers mounted 416 sorties over the Inland Sea, twelve Avengers, each from both *Formidable* and *Implacable* being the first British bombers to hit Japan proper in World War II, when they attacked Yokushima airfield. Meanwhile No 849 Squadron attacked the Japanese escort carrier *Kaiyo* and left her burning and with a broken back, fitting revenge for the *Hermes* three years earlier.

Avengers flew the last combat missions of British forces in the war with strikes against Honsu and Shikoku on 28 July and the following day hit Nagoya Bay and Maizuri, sinking a freighter and the destroyer *Okinawa*. On 9 August Avengers dive bombed and sank two auxillaries in Onegawa harbour, while Lt R.H. Gray dive bombed another Japanese destroyer and earned a posthumous VC in Corsairs. On 10 August targets were found on the Sandai plain.

The last Avenger mission of the war was flown by *Indefatigable's* bombers on 15 August 1945, against targets around Tokyo itself. Just about the last Japanese dive bomber attack was made against this same ship later that morning. A 'Judy' was detected at 1120 over the fleet and immediately went into a vertical dive against *Indefatigable*. It dropped two bombs which were near misses before being shot down by the fleet's AA fire.

Thus the Japanese dive bombers ended the war as they had begun it, in spectacular fashion.

The final strikes go in. SB2C Helldivers from Task Force 38 making low-level bombing runs against a Japanese coaster off Nokkaido, Japan, 24 July, 1945

23 ON TO BERLIN !
The final European Campaigns-West and East, 1944-45

By late quarter of 1943 in Italy the Axis fighter defences were on the wane, and soon became almost non-existent. The German army however soon proved itself more than a match for the Allies, even without this support and the Allies were soon using their strength in the air more and more as a ground support system. The favoured method was the use of the fighter bomber with fighter cover overhead in the traditional manner. But once the fighting on land moved up the coast and stabilised, with the Germans well dug-in with strongly entrenched positions, then innumerable targets in these regions offered themselves as ideal for dive bombing proper for the area was mountainous, and top cover was found unnecessary. And so, gradually, the Spitfire pilots were coverted to ground support operations using the well-known 'cab rank' system as before. But gradually the purely dive bombing side of these missions developed special systems of their own.

Typical of the units involved in this thankless work was No 43 Squadron flying Spitfires in 324 Wing Desert Air Force and operating from a strip on the beach near the Italian town of Riccione during the winter of 1943-4. Their targets were railways, strong points, and even, later in the war, lone snipers. The most common were the 'rail cut' missions and the efficient German flak organisation proved a tough opponent.

'Somewhere in Italy' - 1944. A Mk9 Spitfire with a 500-lb bomb in place and its pilot, 'Ginger' Hollis. Despite not being in any way stressed for dive bombing the Spitfire performed notably in that role during the closing stages of the war in Europe

At first the Spitfires carried 250lb bombs but these soon proved inadequate and inaccurate in use and they switched to carrying a single 500lb bomb under the fuselage on a medium service bomb rack with two adjustable arms, with electrical release. No special bomb sight was employed, the graduated lines on the windscreen being tried and rejected by the pilots. Instead a small dot was marked on the hood to give the correct angle to the horizon.

The most common formation adopted was known as the 'fluid four' — four Spitfires flying in box formation 200yd apart with the two leading aircraft flying straight and true at a height of 18,000 to 20,000ft while the rear two weaved on their flanks and varied their height.

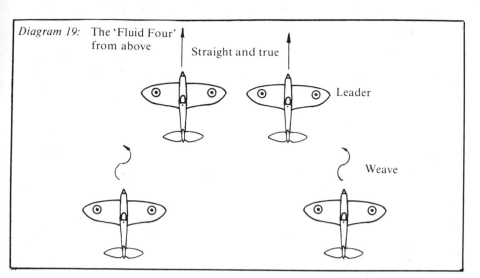

Diagram 19: The 'Fluid Four' from above

Straight and true

Leader

Weave

Diagram 20: From the side

Back pair

Front pair

Straight and true

Height alteration

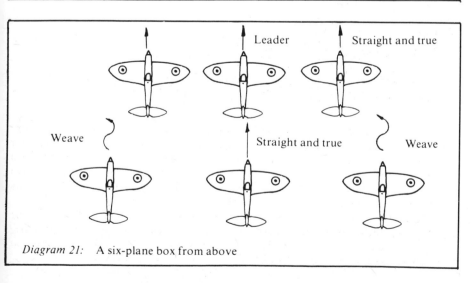

Leader

Straight and true

Weave

Straight and true

Weave

Diagram 21: A six-plane box from above

An alternative formation was the six-plane box with the front three and mid-after plane flying straight and level, with the two rear flankers weaving.

Once the leader had found the target the whole box circumnavigated the target, retaining its formation to assess it and weigh up the flak position and weaknesses. Once a decision had been reached they would adopt a line ahead formation ready for the attack dive. When parallel to the target the leader would bank hard to port and go in out of the sun if possible, at an angle of around 80^0 using the propeller-boss to line up the target. Once the target vanished under the nose the bomb was released from a height normally between 2,000 and 4,000ft. At a few seconds intervals the rest would follow the leader in at slightly varying converging angles.

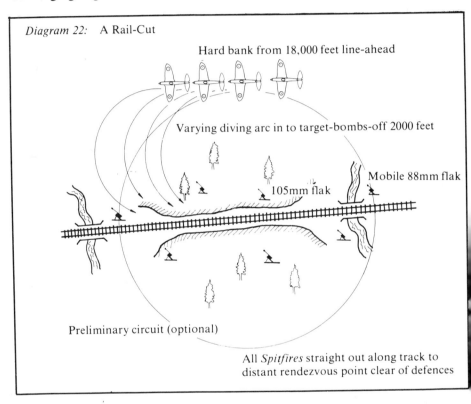

Diagram 22: A Rail-Cut

Hard bank from 18,000 feet line-ahead

Varying diving arc in to target-bombs-off 2000 feet

Mobile 88mm flak

105mm flak

Preliminary circuit (optional)

All *Spitfires* straight out along track to distant rendezvous point clear of defences

At such angles speed could build up rapidly, going off the clock to around 600mph, and a certain amoung of wing root stress was encountered. Buckling was quite common in No 43's Mk VIII Spitfires at such speeds during dive bombing and the aircraft were not given any special bracing in their new role. This was a far cry from the desert for these Spitfire dive bomber pilots and a far cry too from the first dive bomber missions carried out by aircraft of that famous force. This had been conducted in December 1940, by the ancient Gloster Gauntlet aircraft of No 3 Squadron RAAF, armed with 40lb bombs! They operated as the Allies' only 'Answer to the Stuka' in North Africa for a month without loss, and so the Spitfires of 1944 were heirs to a dive bomber tradition had they known it.

Also heirs to a dive bomber tradition of more potency was the Fleet Air Arm, but after the destruction and retiring of the Skuas in mid-1941 almost two years of war were to pass before they again embarked aircraft capable of dive bombing! This strange period was one of the most intense periods of dive bomber activity of all time and the Royal Navy missed it. When it did resume operations of this nature it was once again saddled with a strange hybrid, the Fairey Barracuda.

The TBF Avenger proved suitable for dive bombing later in the war, and the Barracuda was designed and built with dive bombing as one of its major roles, although it was classified for the main part as a torpedo bomber. But its most famous exploits were those associated with dive bombing. It was a three-seat high-wing monoplane of typical British construction, ungainly and bulky, heir to several changes of specification, unworkmanlike and unpopular. It was soon replaced aboard the fleet's carriers, but during the brief period it served afloat it conducted one of the most famous and precise dive bombing attacks of all.

The design dated back to 1937 as a replacement for the Albacore, which itself had carried out dive bombing in the Western Desert in 1941-2 with some success, and the first two prototypes flew in 1940. Its original power plant was the Rolls Royce Exe but this was dropped and the Merlin adopted. This was needed for fighters during the aftermath of the Battle of Britain, which yet further delayed the Barracuda and it was not until 1942 that the first production model flew. Twenty-five Mk1 Barracudas were built before being replaced by the Mk2, which featured the more powerful Merlin 23 engine and a four-bladed instead of a three-bladed airscrew. This version first flew on 17 August 1942 and entered squadron service with No 827 Squadron in January 1943.

By January 1944 it had equipped twelve squadrons then it was phased out quickly in favour of the more modern and efficient Avenger. The Barracuda had a top speed of 228mph and a ceiling of 16,600ft and could be dived at 280mph with a load of four 500lb bombs. Its range was a modest 524 miles. One of its most noticeable features were the Fairey-Youngman diving flaps which were mounted underneath the trailing edge of both wings. They could be inclined to 30^0 to act as dive brakes and were very effective.

On 3 April Barracudas from four Squadrons, Nos 827, 829, 830 and 831, were embarked on carriers *Furious* and *Victorious* of the Home Fleet ready to conduct

Tirpitz here we come! Heavy formations of Barracuda dive bombers from Home Fleet carriers wing their way across the Norwegian coast on their way to deliver their stunning attack on the German battleship. They scored a record number of hits and near misses on the giant vessel and caused heavy casualties.

a mass dive bombing attack on the huge German battleship *Tirpitz* which was anchored in Kaa Fiord, northern Norway, where it exercised enormous influence over the convoys to Russia. Torpedo bombing was impossible owing to the ship's position and the nets that surrounded her but dive bombing over the mountains was possible, in much the same manner as the attack on *Scharnhorst* many years before. Again, although the dive bomber force to be employed was much greater, so was the target and there was obviously no question of sinking her, but it was hoped to immobilise her for a long period by demolishing her upperworks.

Two waves of Barracuda were sent in, the first carrying 500lb Mk2 bombs with instantaneous fuses and with .07 second intervals on the distributor, with the aim of obtaining air bursts from the second and third bombs of the stick which would devastate the ship's upperworks and neutralise her AA armament. The second wave carried 500lb SAP Mk V bombs with .14 second delay fuses, which would be dropped en masse to ensure many hits and the smashing up of her upper decks above her main armour decks. Others carried 600lb A/S Mk1 bombs which were

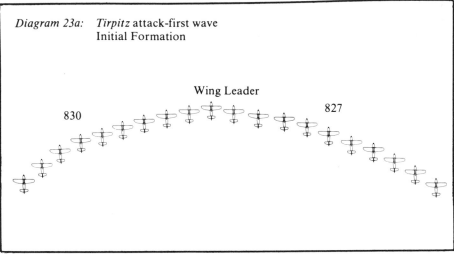

Diagram 23a: *Tirpitz* attack-first wave
Initial Formation

Diagram 23b: Formation 2

Diagram 23c: Final attack

Wing Leader

827

830

hydrostatic, and, as with the SAP, had a stick spacing of 65ft and were designed to burst alongside the ship's hull and open her up underwater. Finally the third wave carried the 1,600lb AP Mk1 bomb with .08 second delay. It was hoped that this weapon, if released from above 3,500ft, would penetrate the deck armour.

Intensive preliminary work had been done, utilising a mock-up target at Loch Eribill in which live bombs were employed. The aircraft were flown off from 0405 onward and, escorted by Corsairs, Wildcats and Hellcats from accompanying escort carriers, the whole force took departure at 0438 and crossed the coast at 7,000ft. The approach was made at 8,500ft and a synchronised wing attack was made.

Twenty-one Barracuda formed the first wave and completed their bombing runs on the *Tirpitz* within the space of one minute, the first bombs dropping at 0529 from 1,200ft height after 50-60° angle dives. The second wave struck half an hour later, diving from 10,000ft at angles of 45-55° and releasing higher with their heavier bombs. By this time the *Tirpitz* was utilising smoke to hide her, but nonetheless good practice was made. It was estimated that no less than five AP and four HE bombs hit the *Tirpitz* in first wave and she took five more hits in the second wave, for the loss of one Barracuda.

The battleship suffered considerable damaged to her exposed upperworks, and many compartments above her main armour were also smashed open. Some 122 of her crew were killed and 316 wounded and she was out of action for three months. It was a remarkable attack, both in terms of surprise and accuracy. Only the size of their bomb loads prevented the dive bombers from achieving more than they did. Unfortunately follow-up raids conducted on 15 May, 14 July, 22 August and 24 August 1944 were not carried out in such force and achieved much less, as only one further bomb hit was achieved.

The Barracuda went out to the East Indies with Nos 810 and 847 Squadrons aboard the *Illustrious* and they made dive bombing attacks on the oil storage depots and refineries at Sabang between 16 and 21 April 1944 in conjunction with SBDs from the American carrier *Saratoga*. Similar raids were made by Barracudas of Nos 815 and 817 Squadrons from *Indomitable* and Nos 822 and 831 Squadrons from *Victorious* before these ungainly and little loved aircraft were dumped ashore and replaced by the Grumman Avengers as related earlier, and these took the Royal Navy's dive bombing teams to Japan as we have seen.

Back in Europe in 1944 the western allies were preparing to finally implement

HITS OBTAINED ON TIRPITZ IN ATTACK BY F.A.A. AIRCRAFT
OPERATION 'TUNGSTEN' 3RD APRIL 1944

HIT	SIZE OF BOMB (Probable)	POSITION OF HIT
1	1600 lb. A.P.	Upper deck stbd side. (Failed to detonate)
2	500 lb. M.C.	Upper deck port side.
3	500 lb. M.C.	Superstructure stbd side.
4	500 lb. S.A.P.	Upper deck port side.
5	500 lb. M.C.	Upper deck port side.
6	1600 lb. A.P.	Upper deck stbd side.
7	500 lb. S.A.P.	Upper deck stbd side.

HIT	SIZE OF BOMB (Probable)	POSITION OF HIT
8	500 lb. M.C.	Funnel
9	1600 lb. A.P.	Armour deck port side.
10	500 lb. M.C.	Upper deck stbd side
11	500 lb. S.A.P.	Superstructure & upper deck on the centre line.
12	1600 lb. A.P.	Stbd side armour plate.
13	500 lb. S.A.P.	Upper deck stbd side.
14	500 lb. S.A.P.	Armour deck stbd side.

NEAR MISS   500lb M.C. or S.A.P.   Close against stbd side.

A.P. = Armour Piercing   S.A.P. = Semi – Armour Piercing   M.C. = Medium Case their own version of close-support by bomb dropping and rocket-firing fighter bombers and the Tactical Air Force was set up in November 1943. Hurricanes and Typhoons, and later Spitfire Vs and Xs, were employed by the RAF, as were Mustang IIIs. From March 1944 these aircraft trained in their role in readiness for the invasion of France, but suffered heavy casualties, as forecast, from German flak. Dive bombing still formed but a minor part of these operations, which explains their vulnerability. They were still using the same basic approach as the old Battles of 1940 at low level and had to re-learn the same lessons afresh.

The American equivalent, the 9th Air Force, employed their aircraft in a similar manner, using P51 Mustangs and P47 Thunderbolts. Their first operational missions however showed they were more willing to take advantage of the dive bombing approach to lessen losses, perhaps adopting it more readily because their aircraft were more robust in construction, only the Typhoon matching them on the British side. On 5 March 1944, for example, Thunderbolts of the 366th Fighter Group carried out a dive bombing attack on the airfield at St Valery, but with a bomb load consisting only of 250lb bombs. Similarly small bombs were also used by the early Mustang dive bombing missions over France, but gradually their pay-load was increased, first to 500lb weapons and then to 1,000lb.

Although the rocket attack gained the greater publicity during the battles in Normandy after the invasion of June 1944, the RAF and USAAF fighter bombers frequently carried out dive bombing missions, similar in nature to those described by the DAF in Italy. Spitfires dive bombed gun emplacements in the Calais area and also used this method against pin-point targets like the V1 launching sites throughout 1944. American Thunderbolts were usefully employed as dive bombers against vital rail links, bridges, troop concentrations and strongpoints. The fighter bombers were joined in this period by traditional dive bomber forces with the re-formation of the French Air Force, both Army and Navy. Thus the SBD Dauntless finally made its combat debut over Western Europe.

Although the famous Dauntless had been replaced in the US Navy by the last year of the war it soldiered on with the US Marine Corps, and it also saw employment on the battlefields of Europe, thus confounding its critics in Britain which had rejected it in 1942. Two French Navy and two French Army units were formed with the SBD and took part in numerous successful actions in Normandy in 1944-5 with minimal losses. Here is a French Navy SBD of the Vendée *squadron with sixteen mission markers painted up.*

Bombing-up Pe-2 at a forward air base during the great Soviet offensives of 1944. The Russian dive bombers played a major role in the classic manner in this grand 'Blitzkrieg' in reverse, which carried the Soviet Armies to the borders of the Reich.

In November 1944, two *Flotilles* (3B and 4B) were formed at Agadir, Morocco by the Free French with thirty-nine SBD5s supplied by the Americans. After a brief period of training thirty-two of these aircraft, forming the GAN2 group, flew to Cognac and gave dive bombing support to Free French ground forces engaged in mopping-up operations against the German-held Atlantic ports, seeing action at Rajan, Le Verden, La Coubre, Grave and the Ile d'Oléron. They flew a total of 1,500 sorties between December 1944 and May 1945 and dropped 500 tons of bombs for the loss of only five aircraft.

The A24B was also taken by the French at this period, some forty-five being handed over. The French formed two dive bomber groups with these, the GBI/17 *Picardie* and the GCBI/18 *Vendée*. The formed was based at Rayack in Syria for the re-pacification of that area after Vichy rule, but *Vendée* was based at Toulouse from September 1944 and attacked German forces in south France. It then transferred to Brittany and was based at Vannes with a strength of sixteen A24Bs. From here it conducted dive bombing missions until the war's end against German troops in the Lorient and St Nazaire areas, during which time they lost only four aircraft. This proved an effective reply to words of warning uttered by the RAF in 1942, that the SBD could not operate in Europe!

But by far the biggest operator of traditional dive bombers and dive bombing methods during the period 1943-5 continued to be the Soviet Union. After the Kursk debacle and with the Luftwaffe heavily tied down in the Balkans in late 1943, the Soviet Air Force dominated the Eastern Front. The effectiveness of the Pe2 was increased as its numbers grew and expertise improved. A new engine, the VK-105RF, was fitted in 1943 and some modifications to the fuselage helped increase its top speed yet further. More important was the improvement of technique.

Col A.G. Fedorov carried out tests of the 'Dipping Wheel' method in combat conditions at Roslav to develop the idea further. From this came the use of sections, each one of three aircraft, which broke away from the 'Vertushka' to dive at 60⁰ on flak positions, while the others circled continually. After one attack by a section another section would break from another angle and so on, continually confusing the gunners and leaving the armoured columns exposed.

While this became the standard Pe2 technique, selected pilots who were considered to be extra proficient at dive bombing were used in specialised attacks on pinpoint targets. Known as 'snipers' they saw action throughout the summer of 1944 when retreating German forces in the Bobruisk Cauldron sought to break out across the Beresina River in June. Repeated attacks by Pe2 snipers succeeded in destroying the solitary bridge which trapped the bulk of the German forces.

On the Ukraine front in July 1944, a massive Soviet offensive was spearheaded by the Il2s and Pe2s of the 2nd Air Army, and contributed vastly to breaking up the dangerous German counter-attack on the 15th of that month. One feature unique to the Soviet Union was the front-line employment of women pilots; at Borisov in June 1944, the 125th Guards Bomber units under Col V.V. Markov included several such resolute females, surely the only women dive bomber pilots to ever see action, although the Germans had several female test pilots, who had tested the Junkers Ju87 pre-war.

As the Soviet colossus crashed through Eastern Europe in 1944 the allies of Germany hastily made plans to change sides as the tide of war altered. This led to the situation in these battle areas where the Ju87 was actually used against German forces, who for so long had looked to it for succour when hard pressed. On 23 August 1944, the Rumanians capitulated and on the following day opened hostilities against Germany. This led them to hastily re-mark their Ju87 *Doras* with the pre-war red, yellow and blue roundels and all operational Stukas were formed into the *Escadrila* 74. In a like manner the small batches of *Doras* belonging to the Bulgarian Air Force engaged in anti-partisan operations on the Eastern Front, switched allegiance in September 1944.

More loyal to the Axis were the Stuka crews of 102/1 *Zuhanóbombázó Század* of the Hungarian Air Force, which were also heavily engaged on the Eastern Front. In steadily decreasing numbers they fought on to the end. Another ally, the Croatian Air Force Legion was established with a few Doras as the tide of war crept towards the Balkans in 1944. Again they were mainly employed in anti-partisan operations in Yugoslavia, in conjunction with those Italian dive bomber forces that had remained loyal to Mussolini.

By the start of 1945 the Soviets were ready to launch the final offensive against the borders of Germany. Their dive bomber forces suffered a heavy loss on 14 February 1945, when Maj-Gen Polbin was killed, but within a month the Russians had reached the banks of the Oder River, within forty miles of Berlin itself and soon they threw strong bridgeheads across it. Heavy Pe2 attacks were mounted against the fortress of Küstrin in March 1945 by the 24th Bomber Air Regiment, which helped contribute to its fall, and on 16 April the final all-out drive on the German capital commenced.

On the German side the steady replacement of the Junkers Ju87 in the SG units by the Fw190F8 was almost complete by June 1944. A few Stukas remained, mainly with Rudel's famed Immelmann squadron in the east, and a few others in the Balkans. But the Ju87 had not completely passed from the scene. As they left the SG units they were refurbished as Night Attack Bombers, the *Nachtschlachtflieger* units (NSGr). Some 300 D3 and D5s were thus fitted with flame-dampened exhausts which led back over the wing-root. Seven NSGr Wings were then equipped, each with between forty to sixty aircraft and used operationally on the Eastern Front, in north Italy, over France, Belgium and Holland, as well as in the final German offensive in the Ardennes, in December 1944.

With the Allied advance to the Rhine, repeated attacks were made by the NSGr Stukas on vital bridges, but with little result and heavy losses from both

Red Star over Berlin. May 1945 and the Soviet armies, spearheaded by the Pe-2 dive bombers, crash into the final defences of the German capital and crush the final resistance amid the rubble.

the night fighters of the allies and the normal hazards of such missions. Perhaps their most famous action on the Western Front was the attack on the Remagen bridge mounted on the night of 19-20 March 1945, by just five Stukas that remained to I/NSGr2, led by Maj Rohn.

In April 1945, I/NSGr9 was still conducting operations over Bologna from Villafranca di Verona airfield and later from Ghedi and Thiene. In the east the handful of Ju87s still operational tried to hold back the Soviet tide along the Oder with some isolated success, but they were eventually overwhelmed by the general collapse in April and May. A large number of the remaining NSGr units were destroyed on the ground in these final days by Allied fighter and bomber sweeps which ranged unchecked over the last scraps of German air-space between the two fronts.

In the final days the Soviet Pe2s were flung into the Battle of Berlin *en masse* and regardless of losses with complete air mastery assured, attacking houses and blocks map in hand as the German had done at Stalingrad. But on 8 May the last Stukas took off from their base in the east and headed towards the American lines in a final defiant gesture. With three Ju87s and four Fw190s they flew to the airfield at Kitzingen and crashed their aircraft in front of the astonished Americans. The Stuka was finally dead, five years *after* the RAF had bragged it was finished!

The final actions for the Soviet Pe2 dive bomber forces lay thousands of miles from this scene, for on the fall of Berlin many units were hastily shipped eastward to take part in the new war against Japan that Stalin had finally seen fit to declare. However most of the fighting was over before more than a handful of the Pe2s could contribute, although during the July offensive in Manchuria they were employed to good effect.

These were, with the Helldiver and Avenger missions over Japan described earlier, the last dive bomber operations of World War II.

24 THE FINAL VINDICATION
Post-war developments, and combat in Indo-China, Korea and Vietnam

With the end of World War II and the advent of the Atomic Bomb and jet propulsion it seemed that the era of the dive bomber had passed away. With such developments the need for accuracy and precision was overshadowed with the new idols of ever increasing speed and mass destruction. It was forgotten already that there was little point in an aircraft going 200mph faster to the target if, when it got there, its payload missed, nor that with weapons like the A-Bomb the destruction would be so great as to make the great powers think carefully before using them and so allow conventional warfare to wage unabated between 1945 and the 1980s in all parts of the globe. The Communist plan of world subversion depended for a large part on the undermining of nations from within, either politically, as in Western Europe, or by guerrilla warfare, as in Asia, Africa and South America. The policy had met with continued success since 1945 with more and more nations passing under Soviet domination, but initially, before their own will was eroded, the western nations tried to stand up to the threat. Thus conventional or guerrilla wars were fought against Red armies in Indo-China by the French, in Malaya by the British and open full-scale Communist invasion was combated by the United Nations, but with only the western powers providing the hardware and main manpower, in Korea. All these battlefields gave scope for precision bombing. Later the United States attempted to save the small nations of the former French Indo-China region from Communist take-over, but her allies turned their backs. She also found that there was still, in the 1960s and 1970s, a need for an aircraft which could deliver precision bomb loads into small targets and linger to provide support. Jet aircraft of the day could not

Among the advanced designs under development towards the end of the war which featured dive bombing as one of their principal roles was the Commonwealth CA-11 Woomera, a twin-engined aircraft of great potential. With the end of hostilities in sight, development ceased after prototype stage.

do the latter, nor, until the development of the 'smart' bomb could they do the former. And so, against all predictions, the dive bomber soldiered on until the late 1970s in a combat role.

Let us first examine some of the ideas in the planning or prototype stage which developed very little further once peace arrived in 1945.

Commonwealth CA-11 Woomera

This aircraft was under development in Australia at the end of the war and was another attempt to combine the functions of dive and torpedo bombers with those of light attack bombers. With a length of 39ft 7in, a span of 59ft ½in and a gross weight of 22,287lb the Woomera was powered by two 1,200hp Pratt & Whitney Wasp engines which gave it a maximum speed of 282mph. The crew of three and armament of two 20mm cannon and five .303 in machine-guns, were coupled with a ceiling of 23,500ft and a range of 2,225 miles. The maximum bomb-load was 3,000lb. Although not outstanding this aircraft featured a novel remote control barbette behind each of the engine nacelles. It arrived for too late for the war and never went into service.

Fairey Spearfish

This aircraft was also designed as a combination of dive bomber and torpedo, bomber under specification 0.5/43 as a replacement for the Barracuda, but with a very much improved appearance and performance. It was of course too late to see combat in World War II and the only production order, which was for forty Spearfish to be built at Stockport, was subsequently concelled when the new Government slashed defence spending in the usual manner in 1946.

The Spearfish was a single-engined mid-wing monoplane powered by a 2,320hp Bristol Centaurus 58, 59 or 60 engine and had a maximum speed of 292mph at 14,000ft, with a range of 1,036 miles. It had a length of 44ft 7in and a span of 60ft 3in. Only the second and third prototypes (RA360 and RA363), along with a solitary production model (RN241) ever flew, although one was serving with the Carrier Trials Unit at Lee-on-Solent and Ford as late as 1952.

Blackburn Firebrand

Originally designed as a fleet fighter to replace the Fulmar, this powerful aircraft had its specification changed several times between 1940 and its eventual appearance in September 1945. The first prototype flew in February 1942, while a second, with 20mm cannon, followed in July of the same year. The adoption of the Seafire meant that fighter coverage was adequate and the Firebrand was therefore further developed as a torpedo bomber/strike aircraft, as the Firebrand II. The original power plant was the Napier Sabre II engine but production shortages meant that the Centaurus radial was adopted and this became the Firebrand III, which first flew in December 1943.

The two dozen production models of this aircraft had followed by the next year but they suffered from inadequate direction control at take-off. This fault was rectified by the adoption of a larger fin and rudder and this became the Firebrand IV. Some 140 of this version were built, the first flying in May 1945.

The Firebrand IV had a length of 38ft 11in, a span of 51ft 3½in and a height of 14ft 11in. It was a single-seater and its maximum speed was 350mph. Although dive bombing was not a main feature of this aircraft, it was fitted with dive brakes on the wings and could carry a bombload of two 1,000lb bombs. The first squadron was formed in September 1945 (No 813 at Ford) and further modifications in design resulted in the MkV and MkVa between then and the end of 1947, when about 150 had been built and production ceased.

Saab-17

In Sweden development of dive bombers continued during the war and the final result was the SAAB-17, a low-wing monoplane, powered by the Bristol/SFA MkXXIV engine, but of Swedish manufacture. Bearing a strong resemblance to the ill-fated Brewster Bermuda in appearance, this dive bomber had a 980hp aircooled radial engine with a top speed of 435kmph (270mph), improved ceiling and range. The B17 formed the mainstay of the Swedish dive bomber units during the war years, but in 1945-6, with the introduction of the SAAB twin-engined B18B, this type performed both functions, light bomber and dive bomber and the specialised types were phased out.

The B18 was not strictly a dive bomber, being a high wing monoplane with twin tail fins, but bearing some resemblance to the Junkers Ju88 or Dornier Do217 in cockpit layout with all the crew concentrated forward. Two SFA/DB engines, DB605s, gave it a maximum speed of 570kmph (355mph) and a range of 2,200km (1,370 miles). It had a bomb load of 1,200kg (2,650lb).

Ilyushin Il20

In the Soviet Union the main dive bomber development towards the end of the war was in improvements to the already well-proven Tupolev Tu2, and mainly after the war through the Tu2D series which featured an increased wing-span and redesigned nose, coupled with increased range. The -D series had a top speed of 321mph and a bomb load of 2,204lb over 1,864 miles. The Petlyakov Pe2 continued to be the most favoured aircraft of this type. In all some 11,427 'Peshkas' were built, in particular the Pe21 produced from 1943 onward which featured the 1,650hp VK107A direct fuel injection engines, solid nose and deeper fuselage. It could carry a payload of 2,204lb and had a top speed of 408mph at 18,800ft. The first prototype flew in 1944 but this aircraft crashed the following year and with the end of the war further development was stopped.

The Ilyushin Il20 was not a dive bomber, but an attack plane designed to act as an anti-shipping as well as ground attack role and was a development of the shturmovik type. Nicknamed the Hunchback because of its appearance, the object of which was to give the diving pilot the maximum view, the pilot was seated above the 2,700hp engine. The gunner operated a barbette containing two NS23 cannon, while further cannon and rockets could be carried as well as a maximum bomb load of 2,204lb. The whole aircraft was armoured in the ground attack tradition. It has a span of 45ft 11in, length of 37ft 5¼in and a maximum speed of 320mph, with a range of 1,044 miles. Although a diving attack must have been essential to attain the accuracy to attack ships, little is known of any special features to facilitate this. In the event the end of the war brought about the ceasation of further experimentation on this unique model.

Douglas SB2D1, 'Destroyer'

The Douglas team under Ed Heinemann had plans ready in 1942 for a similar monster dive bomber to replace the SBD. This was the XS2D-1, a two-seater dive bomber double the weight of the Dauntless. It featured an internal bomb-bay, a range of 1,490 miles and mounted two 20mm wing cannon and a remote-controlled rear turret carrying twin .5in machine guns. It had a tricycle landing gear and was powered by the Wright R3350-15 engine rated at 2,300hp for take-off. It had an all-up weight of no less than 19,000lb.

The Douglas Destroyer, as it then stood, would have been one of the most powerful Navy attack planes built, but already the US Navy was seeking to combine the functions of dive- and torpedo-bombers, as in the Royal Navy, and the design of the Destroyer was therefore modified to suit this requirement. The result was the single-seater XBTD. By dropping the second crew member and

Mighty Maulers en echelon. *TBM aircraft of VA9A commanded by Lt Cdr Lawrence G. Traynor, on exercises from the USS* Philippine Sea, *14 June, 1948*

the rear turret the bomb-bay was increased in capacity to 3,200lb. Dive flaps were fitted operating from the fuselage sides. Top speed was 340mph in this configuration and some 358 BTD1s were ordered in April 1942. By 1944 all had been cancelled.

Martin AM-1, 'Mauler'
This formidable aircraft was Martin's last venture into the dive bomber field and they went as far as they could in producing a powerful all-round aircraft capable of lifting a very heavy payload with maximum effect. The result was the XTBM, a low-engined monoplane that could carry 7 tons of weaponry into battle. But by the time it appeared the US Navy was turning away from this concept. Some 750 Maulers were ordered in January 1945, but final production after severe post-war cuts in budgets reduced this to only 149 actually built. These were delivered to the fleet between 1947 and 1949.

Although fitted with slotted dive flaps and capable of employment in torpedo bomber or rocket-firing roles as well as dive bombing, the Mauler was just *too* big for the carriers then available. It had a top speed of 367mph, a range of 1,300 miles, was fitted with 20mm cannon and could land, despite its great bulk, at 88mph. It was a perfect vehicle for the three new *Midway*-class carriers then entering service, but too late for its time.

The Hawker Sea Fury was a piston-engined fighter of high performance which was utilised with great success as a dive bomber by the Royal Navy in Korea. Here a light fleet carrier off the coast with United Nations forces prepares for a mass strike

As well as the last generation of true dive bombers, most powers continued to operate fighters in this role, continuing the tradition of the US Corsair, the RAF Spitfire, the USAAF Mustang and the German Fw190. It was mainly the air arms of the two premier navies that adopted this method however. In the US Navy light dive bombing was done by Grumman Bearcat, a powerful and versatile fighter-bomber, a descendant of the same company's Hellcat. In the Royal Navy two types predominated, the Fairey Firefly, MkV and the Hawker Sea Fury, the latter being particularly suitable and effective in the dive bombing role.

The French Navy post-war was a hotch-potch of types, a mixture of the best of the few surviving French ships, mainly destroyed in Vichy service, ex-British and ex-American warships purchased from their overlarge peacetime fleets, and ex-German war prizes. The two carriers, *Arromanches* and *Dixmude* reflected this, being the ex-Royal Navy *Colossus* and *Biter* respectively. The aircraft they carried post-war were a similar mixture and the dive bombers were old friends.

At first they were the SBDs, the bulk of which formed 3F and 4F (*Flotilles*) respectively post-war. With the Soviet-backed Viet-Minh operations in Indo-

The Fairey Firefly saw war service in 1944-5 with the British Pacific Fleet in the final drive on Japan as a fighter-bomber making rocket attacks. Later marks emerged post-war and during the Korean conflict these were used by the Fleet Air Arm in shallow dive bombing missions.

China they went out in the carriers and conducted numerous missions. During the years 1946-8 the value of such piston-engined precision attacks against elusive targets was proven, and the SBDs were not retired until 1949.

The A24Bs were incorporated into the French Air Force and were mainly employed on training duties from bases at Meknés in Morocco and Cazaux in France at this time, although they were from time to time utilised on survey and patrol duties in North Africa. These old faithfuls were finally grounded in 1953.

The Helldiver was phased out of the US Navy service in 1949 but the famous dive bomber had not finished combat duties even then. In 1950 the French Navy took delivery of four dozen and equipped two operational units. They embarked on the carrier Arromanches *and left France for the Far East in 1952.*

As late as 1950 the French Navy took delivery of Helldivers from the USA and two fresh Flotilles were created, 3F and 9F, with these aircraft. Forty-eight Helldivers were taken over in the initial batch, two dozen equipped 3F in 1951 and a similar number went to 9F later. All these similarly went to Indo-China, where once more they were very valuable in containing the growing Communist armies. 9F left France aboard *Arromanches* at the end of 1952 and carried out a total of 824 war missions. Their duties included true dive bombing, straffing and rocket attacks and their targets were AA guns, troop concentrations, bridges and the endless supply convoys wending their way down from China. 9F returned to France in 1953 and converted to Avenger aircraft. After 1954 the remaining Helldivers in French service were utilised as trainers.

When Communist North Korea invaded South Korean territory in a blatant act of aggression the United Nations, for the first and last time in its history, stood up to the Red aggression. Both US and Royal Navy carriers were used in the four years of combat which followed to provide the troops ashore with close-support of the precision types, which meant dive bombing. The British used the Firefly and the Sea Fury with great success. Many of the pilots were veterans of the final stages of the Pacific War and improvised tactics based on those methods.

Targets, more often than not, proved to be bridges and the communist forces were adept at using slave labour to re-build these time and time again. They also employed heavy AA batteries to defend these vital targets and the continued smashing of them proved a wearying and endless task, and also a thankless one. In two periods, for example, the Air Group working from HMS *Glory* in 1951-2, flew almost 5,000 sorties, for the loss of twenty-seven aircraft and nine crews.

While the FAA used fighters to dive bomb, the US Navy was more fortunately placed for it had a brand-new dive bomber with which to pound the enemy. Brand-new that is to combat, but, in reality, itself already a rather elderly warrior, an aircraft that was to soldier on for longer than any other combat plane in the front line, an aircraft that was to become a legend — the Skyraider.

The unforgetable SBD, the Dauntless, shown here in US Marine Corps livery

With the aborting of the 'Destroyer' concept Heinemann and his crew set to work with a will and after some time introduced radical design changes to the XBT2D and came up with a real champion. The original flared cockpit was replaced by a bubble canopy, and the original faired tailplane was smoothed into a gentle curve into the fuselage. The inverted gull-wing of the Destroyer became instead a graceful mid-wing straight design. This provided the extra-lift to get the Dauntless II, as it was termed, off the carriers' decks. It weighed about one ton less than the Destroyer which made it more acceptable in the fleet.

At the same time as this reduction in weight was achieved its bomb load was increased to a remarkable 5,000lb and its top speed went up to 375mph. After the initial trial flight in March 1945, the US Navy placed a contract for 548 but with the end of hostilities this was reduced to only 277. Given the designation AD, then named Skyraider and designated A-1, the new aircraft found itself unique in a very short period. Only four squadrons had equipped with the Mauler, while the Kaiser Fleetwing project, the XBTK, had been aborted. The Skyraider thus soon became the only heavy hauler in the fleet and it soon expanded through numerous varients between 1946 and 1948, to the AD2 and AD3 and by the early 1950s continued production had resulted in the AD4 and AD5 types. With the outbreak of hostilities the planned termination of the design was hastily shelved.

With the US 7th Fleet in position off the Korean coast Skyraiders were soon in action, VA55 from the carrier *Valley Forge,* led by Lt Cdr D.E. English, being the first into battle with a strike on the aircraft at Pyongyang on July 1950. From then on ADs were rarely out of the headlines and new order for the old 'Able-Dogs' began to pour in as their merits were seen to be numerous in the new jet-age. Just how vast was their contribution to this conflict can be seen by the fact that no less than twenty-two different squadrons utilised this aircraft between 1950 and 1953.

Not only did the front-line and reserve Navy aircrew enshrine the name of this dive bomber in the Korean skies, ashore the US Marines resumed their close-support mantle with the same aircraft. In October 1951, VMA121 equipped with AD3s moved into Korea. Nicknamed the 'Heavy Hauler' and led by Lt Col P.B. May, they soon won fresh acclaim, taking heavier and heavier loads into combat and dropping them precisely on target against the swarming Red hordes.

Much the same story followed the cease-fire. A period of run-down and then, with the renewal of Communist aggression against another Asian country the US, on her own this time, had to go to its aid. Again the Skyraider remained the only aircraft able to both deliver and 'linger' in the target area to give the sort of cover the troops on the ground really wanted, the sort provided by the Ju87 to the Germans and SBD to the US Army in the Philippines. And so as the bitter Vietnam War dragged on its every more weary course it was the old Douglas A-1H that continued to be the mainstay of the rescue and support missions.

Thus passed the last of the dive bombers and with them a whole era of air warfare in which the individual skill of the pilot counted for more than all the technology in the world and, right up to the end, proved far more adept at doing what all bombers were supposed to do — hit the target!

Select Bibliography

1- Published Books

Berry, W.H, *Aircraft in War and Commerce,* New York, 1918

Bishop, Edward, *The Battle of Britain,* London, 1960

Borelli, G., Borgiotti, A., Caruana, R., Pini, G., Gori, C., *Junkers Ju87 Stuka,* Modena, 1975

Borgiotti, A. & Gori, C., *Gli Stuka Della Regia Aeronautica 1940-5,* Modena, 1977

Brütting, Georg, *Das waren die Deutschen Stuka Asse 1939-45,* Stuttgart, 1976

Casey, Louis J., *Naval Aircraft 1938-45,* London, 1975

Cathcart-Jone, Lt Owen, *Aviation Memoirs,* London, 1934

Douglas, Sholto, *Years of Command,* London, 1963

Gould Lee, Arthur, *No Parachute,* Norwich, 1968

Green, William, *Warplanes of the Third Reich,* London, 1970

Herlin, Hans, *Udet: A Mans Life,* London 1960

Higham, Robin, *Air Power: A Concise History,* London 1972

Hinkle, Stacy C., *Wings over the Border,* El Paso, 1970

King, H.F., *Armament of British Aircraft 1909-39,* London, 1965

Lawrence, T.E., *Revolt in the Desert,* London, 1925

Levine, Isaac D., *Mitchell: Pioneer of Air Power,* New York, 1943

Macleod, Col Roderick, *The Ironside Diaries 1937-40,* London, 1962

Masatake, Okumiya & Horikoshi, Jiro, *Zero! The story of the Japanese Navy Air Force 1937-45,* London, 1957

Melhorn, Charles M., *Two Block Fox: The rise of the aircraft carrier 1911-29,* Annapolis, 1974

Mizrahi J.V., *Dive- and Torpedo-Bombers: US Navy,* Los Angeles, 1971

Olds, Robert, *Helldiver Squadron,* Washington, 1980

Passingham, Malcolm & Waclaw, Kelpacki, *Petlyakov Pe2 and Variants,* Windsor, 1975

Pearson, Lee M., *Dive Bombers-The Pre-War years,* Washington, 1949

Popham, Hugh, *Into Wind,* London, 1969

Price, Alfred, *The Bomber in World War II,* London, 1976

Roskill, Stephen, *British Naval Policy between the Wars,* London, 1968-76

Schliephake, Hanfried, *The Birth of the Luftwaffe,* London, 1971

Sherrod, Robert, *History of Marine Corps Aviation in World War II,* Washington, 1952

Simmonds, Ralph, *All About Aircraft,* London, 1915

Sims, Edward H., *Fighter Tactics and Strategy 1914-79,* London, 1970

Shores, Christopher, *Ground Attack Aircraft,* London, 1977

Slessor, Wg Cdr J.C., *Air Power and Armies,* Oxford, 1936

Stewart, Maj Oliver, *The Clouds Remember,* Aldershot, 1936

Stewart, Maj Oliver, *The Strategy and Tactics of Air Fighting,* London, 1925

Smith, Peter C., *Impact! : The Dive Bomber Pilots Speak,* London, 1981

Smith, Peter C., *Stuka at War,* London, 1980

Tillman, Barrett, *The Dauntless Dive Bomber of World War II,* Annapolis, 1976

Turbill, Capt A.D. & Lord Lt Cdr C.L., *The History of United States Naval Aviation,* Yale, 1949

Winston, Robert Alexander, *Dive Bomber: Learning to Fly the Navys Attack Planes,* London, 1941

Wilkenson, Erik A., *Dive Bombing: A Theoretical Study,* Aktiebolag, 1947

2- Original Documents and Pamphlets

Air Ministry, *Notes on Dive Bombing for the Information of Designers of Aeroplanes for the RAF,* London, 1936

Air Ministry, *The Theory of Dive Bombing,* London, 1938

Air Ministry, *Dive Bombing,* London, 1940

Air Ministry, *Notes on Dive Bombing and the German Ju88 Bombing Aircraft,* London, 1940

Bellinger, Cdr P.L., *Aviation,* Naval War College Lecture, 1 August 1924

Jones, Maj Ernest L., *Information Pertaining to the Development of Dive Bombing 1910-30,* USAF Historical Division, Research Studies Institute, Maxwell AFB, Alabama, May 1956

Jones, Maj Ernest L., *Bomb Dropping with Carranza,* 'Aeronautics', London, 1 December 1915

Larkins, William T., *The Evolution of Naval Dive Bombing,* 'Flight', London 1943

Leighton, Lt Cdr B.G., *The relation between Air and Surface activities in the Navy,* Lecture to Naval War College, 23 March 1928

McGee, Capt Vernon E., *Dive Bombing,* Washington, 1937

Overfield, Lt David B., *Dive Bombing compared with bombing from Level Flight,* Washington, 1939

Royal Aircraft Establishment, Farnborough, *Dive Bombing as practiced by the German Air Force and a comparison with proposed British system, London, 1940*

Wilson, Eugene E., *The Navy's First Carrier Task Force,* USNI Proceedings, February 1950

3- Specific Sources

'Bomb dropping from Aircraft', *Aeronautics, London, October 1914*

'Bomb dropping from Aeroplanes', *Flight, December 1914*

Scientific American, supplement No 2103, April 1916

'The Elements of Bomb dropping', *Flying, October, 1917*

Aerospace Historian, 'The Heritage of Flight', Vol 16, No 2, Summer 1969

Low Height Bombing from Scouts, 18 May 1918, AIR 1/1200/04632

Bombing from Sopwith Camel using Aldis sight, 27 May 1918, AIR1/1200/04632

Maritime Aeronautics, 1 January 1923

USAS Bulletin, No 304, 16 November 1918

Interview by Maj Gen Ross Erastus Rowell, USMC, Aviation History Unit, 24 October 1916

Statement by Maj Norbert Carolin to Maj Jones, AC/AS Intel, 1943

Aviation and Aircraft Journal, Vol II, No 14, dated 25 July 1921

VF Squadron Two-Individual Battle Practice (light bombs)-Report of scores, 28 December 1926

Report of Board to consider and recommend upon present Aeronautical Policy, 11 May 1927

Experimental Light Bombing practice, 27 May 1927

XT5M-1, Dive test of, Memo of Conference Plans Division, 16 October 1929

Diving tests on Martin XT5M airplane, 3 April 1930, William H. McAvoy

Report of acceptance trials of Model BM-1 airplane, 21 September 1931

Bombing, Dangerous incident to and methods of minimizing, 5 December 1929

Bomb and Bomb Fuzes-Investigation of in connection with dive bombing, 18 July 1930

Bomb Displacing gear, 12 February 1931

Bomb Displacing gear for 1,000lb Bomb, 15 January 1932

Policy of procurement of experimental dive bombers, 25 August 1931

Experimental dive bomber airplane (Class VB), 14 August 1931

Report of production inspection trials on XBF2C-1 No 9269 and BF2C.1 (Experimental and production models), 29 May 1933

Board to consider Naval Aeronautic Policy, 3 May 1927

Isle of Ely and Wisbech Advertiser, 28 September 1932

Outline of Naval Armament and Preparations for War, Part 1 (1922-34), Japanese Study Monograph No 145, US Navy Historical Centre, Washington

Contract Nos 27648 schedule 900-5854 XF120-1, Airplane, conversion to Scout airplane change 311, 12 December 1933

Experiments and production aircraft procurement for Fiscal years, 1934, 1935 and 1936, 19 January 1934

VB Airplanes-Request for Informal Quotations, 15 March 1934

VSB Airplanes-Request for Informal Quotations, 19 March 1934

VSB and VB Airplanes-proposals, 25 April 1934

Contract 27648 Navy Contractors Proposals (in view of crash of XSBC-1), 6 July 1934

Contract 7648-Model XSBC-2 Airplane, 26 June 1935

Experimental Funds 1935, 24 July 1934

Dive flaps on SB2U-1 Airplane, 30 January 1939

Model SB2U-1 and SB2U-2 airplanes-conversion to permit dive bombing ops, 16 November 1939

Flying the Vought SB2U, Boone T. Guyton

Model BT-1 and SBD-1 airplanes-Improvements in stalling characteristics, devices for, 22 January 1940

Hart K-2466 Diving Bombing Trials, February 1934. AIR2/655/831592

Hart K-2967 Diving Bombing Trials, March 1934, *ibid*

Note on dive bombing for information of designers, March 1936, (Air Ministry Confidential Scientific and Technical memoranda)

Dive Bombing technique with high speed aircraft of clean Aerodynamic design, 2 April 1936. AIR2/1655/5/36709

Minutes of 9th meeting of the Bombing Committee 27 April 1936. AIR14/288/IIH/241/4/104

Use of Aldis sight when carrying out dive bombing, 26 February 1937, AIR14/29-04362

1st meeting Bombing Policy Sub-Committee, 22 March 1938. AIR2/1787/04811

Meeting to consider dive bombing, 19 September 1938. AIR2/1787/04811

Comparison of British and US Naval Air Services, ADM116 3473

Bombing developments, 11 May 1933. AIR116 3473

12th Meeting of Advisory committee on aircraft for Fleet Air Arm, 15 November 1934. AIR2/607/359533/34

Specification No 0.27/34-Dive Bomber Fighter, 12 December 1934. AIR2 *ibid*

Discussion on Armstrong-Whitworth Fighter Dive Bomber, 10 April 1936. AIR2 *ibid*

Report of CO HMS Glorious, dive bombing tests, 1939. AIR2/3176/04811

Report of No 100 (T.B.) Squadron, dive bombing tests, 8 October 1938. AIR2/1787/04811

Report on the German Air Force, 1936. AIR5/1137004811

Air Intelligence Report, 31 October 1936 AIR5/1137/04811

China Incident-Naval Air Operations (July-November 1937). Japanese Monograph No 166, US Navy Archives, Washington

Japanese Navy Air Force-Air Ministry Intelligence Memorandum. AIR/1021647/04811

Aviation, Paris, 14 August 1972 (No 591)

Outline of the history of dive bombing in Sweden, Col Nils Kindberg, Flygvapnet, 1978

Notes by Director of Naval Air Division on Report, 25 April 1940. ADM199 478/X/LO4326

Operational Order No 1, 9 April 1940. ADM 199 *ibid*

Naval Air Division Forms by Surviving crews, 23 November 1939 (729/39) ADM199 *ibid*

Letter from Maj Alan E. Marsh, R.M., *Globe & Laurel,* Vol LXXXIII, No 6, December 1974

'Skua'd Prisoners for Breakfast', *Globe & Laurel,* Vol LXXXIII No 5, October 1974

Dive Bombing-A review of Policy, 9 May 1940. AIR2/3176/S4583

Loss Report of HMS Wessex, 19 June 1940. AIR2/4221/04811

Summary of Air Intelligence Report No 302. AIR22/9/04811

'Could Sealion have succeeded?', by Alfred Price. Contained in *The Battle of Britain,* New English Library, 1977

Secret report on damage in action to HMS Boadicea and Bulldog, 11, 7, 12 June 1940. AIR2/4221

Confidential report of interview with Master of SS Aeneas, 5 July 1940. AIR2/4221

Report of Air attacks on HMS Illustrious on 10 January 1941, operation MC4, 26 January 1941, *Notes on Air Tactics, Air Ministry Memorandum 1941.* AIR23/5287

AA Defence, Tobruk, IG Report No 712. AIR20/2970

Report of No 5 Group-High diving bombing trials, 27 March 1941. AIR14/672/IIH/241/3/38

Use of bombers in close-support of the Army, 6 May 1941. AIR20/2970

Rise and Fall of the German Air Force, Air Ministry, Pamphlet 248, 1948

'The Dive Bomber does it again', by Ronald Walker, *News Chronicle,* 11 April 1942

'Dive Bombers — Why this awful delay?', by Gen Sir R. Gordon-Finlayson, *Daily Sketch,* 22 April 1942

Betwixt Sea and Sky, Gen Cumbat. Personal account of August 1942 convoy action.

'Can we check Rommel without the dive bomber?', Maj O. Stewart, *Sunday Express,* 31 May

'Dive Bombing', Maj C.S. Pearson, *The Aeroplane,* 1942

'Again we missed the dive bomber', Maj O. Stewart, *Sunday Express,* 28 June 1942

'Dive Bombers, the Army and Navy view', *Daily Sketch, 3 March 1942*

'Our new Dive Bombers', *Daily Sketch,* 20 February 1942

Report on US Dive Bomber supply situation. AIR20/1763

Milwaukee Journal, Lt Louis Olszyk, 23 September 1944

'Still kicking against the Dive Bomber', Maj O. Stewart, *Sunday Express* 5 July 1942

Army requirements of the RAF for Direct Support in battle, 30 November 1942. AIR20/4249

Notes on Tactical qualities of the dive bomber, 9 September 1943. AIR20/4249

Tactical trials on Vengeance dive bomber and *Dive bombing in Vengeance,* 4 October 1943, AIR19/233

Vengeance Operations in Arakan, Tactical Memo No 35, AHQ India. AIR23/3288

Vengeance Operations in Burma, AIR23/5288/06726

Report on Operation 'Tungsten', 5-10 April, ADM199 941

Command and Employment of Air Power, US War Dept, July 1943

Air-Ground Support Training Programme, MAG-24, 8 December 1944

Action Reports and War Diaries and Report on sinking of Yamato, Microfilm NRS.1971-7

Svenskt Flyg och dess Män, KSAK, Stockholm, 1940

Notes on Hawker Hart bought and imported from Britain for Sweden, Flygvapnet, 1977

4- Further general related books

Bryant, Arthur, *The Turn of the Tide 1939-43,* London, 1957

Churchill, Winston S., *The Second World War, Vols 1-4,* London, 1948

Crimp, R.L., *Diary of a Desert Rat,* London, 1971

Cynk, Jerzy B., *The History of the Polish Air Force 1918-68,* London, 1972

d'Astier de la Vigerie, Gen, *Le Ciel n'etait pas vide,* Paris, 1957

Goutard, Col A., *The Battle of France,* London, 1958

Guderian, Gen Heinz, *Panzer Leader,* London, 1958

Horsley, T., *Find, Fix and Strike,* London, 1943

Irving, David, *Hitler's War,* London, 1977

Jackson, B.R., *Douglas Skyraider,* California, 1969

Lapraik, Sqdn Ldr, 'Pe2 twin engined dive bomber', 11 September 1941, AIR40/29

Macleod, Col R., *The Ironside Diaries* 1939-40, London, 1956

Marder, Arthur J., *Operation Menace*, Oxford, 1976

Maugham, Barton, *Tobruk and El Alamein*, Canberra, 1956

McKee, Alexander, *The Coal-Scuttle Brigade*, London, 1957

Neave, Airey, *The Flames of Calais: A Soldier's Battle*, London, 1972

O'Ballance, Edgar, *The Indo-China War 1945-54*, London 1964

Roskill, Capt S.W., *The War at Sea*, 4 Vols, London, 1954, 1966

Ruby, Gen Edmond, *Sedan: terre d'epreuve*, Paris, 1956

Rudel, Hans-Ulrich, *Stuka Pilot*, Dublin, 1953

Schmidt, Capt H.W., *With Rommel in the Desert*, London, 1968

Seive, Gen, *L'Aviation d'Assault dans la Campagne de 1940*, Paris, 1949

Smith, Peter C., *Task Force 57*, London, 1969

Smith, Peter C., *The Battle of Midway*, London, 1976

Taylor, A.J.P., *Beaverbrook*, London, 1972

Taylor, Telford, *The Breaking Wave*, London, 1967

Tedder, Lord, *With Prejudice*, London, 1966

Tomlinson, Michael, *The Most Dangerous Moment*, London, 1976

Select Index

DAR10F, 132
Dark, Wg Cdr A.E., 113
Davis, R/Adm A.C., 24
De Havilland DH4B, 20, 22, 27-8
Diaz, President, 27
Dillon, Lt Wallace M., 25
Dinort, Maj Oskar, 112, 153
Dipping Wheel tactic, 206
Dixon, Lt Cdr Bob, 162
Doolittle, Gen, 72
Dornier Do17, 197
Dorsetshire, 159
Douglas SBD, Dauntless et al, 7, 45, 91, 100, 106-9, 144, 158, 170, 178-85, 187-9, 192-3, 205-6, 213-14
Douglas XS2D-1 later AB2D, Destroyer, 211, 213, 215
Dowding, Air V/Mshl, 33
Dunkirk, evacuation from, 116

Egusa, Lt Cdr Takashige, 157, 160
Ennerccerus, Maj, 132, 138
Enterprise, 158, 162-7, 188-9
Ercolani, Capt, 94-6, 131
Essex, 188-9, 191

Fairey Albacore, 66-7, 201
Fairey Barracuda, 201-3
Fairey Battle, 7, 54-5, 57-61
Fairey Firefly, 213, 215
Fairey Flycatcher, 18, 32-3, 66
Fairey Fulmar, 160
Fairey PV4, 53
Fairey Spearfish, 210
Fairey Swordfish, 66-8
Fairbairn, Capt, C.E., 13
Fedorov, A.G., 156, 206
Feland, Brg Gen, 27
Felt, Cdr Eric A., 165
Fenton, F/O I.O., 112
Fiat CR42, Falco, 907
Fieseler, Gerhard, 70
Fieseler Fi98, 101
Fink, Kanalkampführer Johanne, 117
Focke-Wulf Fw56, Stösser, 73
Focke-Wulf Fw190, Jabo, 156, 173, 207
Fokker D-X111, 18
Formidable, 138, 197
Fujite, Capt Y, 86

Galasso, G, 96
Gallaher, Lt Wilmer E., 163
Gardner, P/O J.A., 124-5
Glidden, Maj Gen Elmer, 187
Glory, 215
Gloster Gauntlet, 200
Goake, Tokukishio, 82
Goering, Hermann, 70, 72, 104
Gould Lee, Arthur, 12
Gourdou-Leseurre GL430B1, 37, 89
Graham, Flt Lt R.R., 32
Gourdou-Leseurre GL432, 89
Gourdou-Leseurre GL521, 89
Gray, Lt R.H., 197
Great Lakes XGB-1, 30, 40

Grenzel, Gerhard, 114
Grinnell-Milne, 11
Grumman Avenger, 186-7, 190, 196-7, 201, 208
Grumman Hellcat, 203, 213
Grumman Wildcat, 203, 213
Guderian, Gen Heinz, 116
Guilfoye, Grp Capt, 55
Günther, Siegfried, 76
Günther, Walther, 76
Guyton, Boone T., 91

Handley Page Hampden, 7
Hawker Audax, 18, 32, 50, 56
Hawker Demon, 64
Hawker Fury, 98
Hawker Hardy, 50-1
Hawker Hart, 34, 49-50, 53, 55-6, 64, 98-9, 145
Hawker Hector, 130
Hawker Henley, 51, 61, 76
Hawker Hind, 57-8
Hawker Nimrod, 55, 66-8
Hawker Osprey, 63, 66-7, 98
Hawker PV4, 50
Hawker Sea Fury, 213, 215
Heinemann, Ed, 40-1, 45, 215
Heinkel HD17, 18
Heinkel HD27, 18
Heinkel He50aW, 35-7, 70, 78, 81, 98
Heinkel He66aCH, 35-6, 98
Heinkel He70 Blitz, 82-4
Heinkel He118, 74, 76-8, 84
Heinrichs, Flugkapitan, 77
Henderson, Maj Lofton R., 163-4
Henschel Hs123 Angelito, 70-1, 78-9, 98, 104, 115
Hermes, 160-1
Hiryu, 157, 159
Hitler, Adolf, 70
Hitschold, Hpt, 138
Hozzel, Hpt Paul-Werner, 114, 132

IAR80, 132
Ilyushin IL-2, 206-7
Ilyushin IL-20, 211
Illustrious, 132, 135, 189, 203
IMAM Ro41, 96
IMAM Ro57bis, 96, 175
Implacable, 196
Indefatigable, 189, 197
Indomitable, 149, 189, 203
Ironside, Gen, 141
Irvine, Eng. Charles, 167
Irwin, Earl, 91

Johnstone, Sgt A., 33
Jones, Maj B.M., 13
Junkers, Prof Hugo, 315
Junkers J-1, 34
Junkers J-10, 34
Junkers K-47, 34-5, 73, 99
Junkers Ju-87, Stuka, 35, 73-4, 76-80, 96, 100-1, 104, 112-20, 126-7, 131-40, 143, 147, 148-56, 171-4, 176-7, 207-8
Junkers Ju-88, 97, 100, 104, 112-3, 114, 116-20, 137-9, 146-9, 153-4, 176-7
Junyo, 166

221